The Kluane National Park Hiking Guide

*For Tony &
Sandra.
I hope to
see you on a
trail one day!
V. Lougheed.*

The **K l u a n e**
National Park
HIKING GUIDE
2nd Edition

V I V I E N   L O U G H E E D

New Star Books
Vancouver
1997

New Star Books Ltd.
2504 York Avenue
Vancouver, B.C.
V6K 1E3

Editing by Carolyn Stewart
Design, production and maps by Carol Fairhurst
Photographs by Vivien Lougheed unless otherwise credited

Printed and bound in Canada by Webcom
1 2 3 4 5   01 00 99 98 97

Canadian Cataloguing in Publication Data

Lougheed, Vivien.
  Kluane National Park hiking guide

  Includes bibliographical references and index.
  ISBN 0-921586-60-4

    1. Hiking—Yukon Territory—Kluane National Park—Guidebooks.
2. Trails—Yukon Territory—Kluane National Park—Guidebooks.
3. Kluane National Park (Yukon)—Guidebooks. I. Title.
GV199.44.C22K52 1997   796.51'09719'1   C97-910705-9

This book is for Levi, who promised to chase away the bears as soon as he is old enough to hike with me.

Contents

ROUTES AND TRAILS 33

Ⓝ North Section   161

Acknowledgements

Wilderness travel has fascinated me since my youth. However, it was not until I entered my late twenties that I discovered back-country travelling need not consist of sleeping on willow bows, eating dry bannock, drinking only water, and walking for days in wet and ill-fitting boots. My friend K. O. Kamstra taught me that one could purchase Therma-rest mattresses, down sleeping bags, lightweight tents, comfortable boots that could be waterproofed and backpacks that fit comfortably. She showed me my first trails – and I became addicted.

I, in turn, converted Joanne Armstrong and she became my constant travelling and hiking companion. She has an easily-mended memory. I have often heard her say at the end of a trip, that this would be the last time she would be in a canoe or a pair of boots, or on a chickenbus. But after a glass of wine and a steak dinner, she is always ready to be talked into another adventure.

My partner, John Harris, is afraid of bears, afraid of heights, and afraid of a wet tent. He is not afraid of books, however, and without his push and technical advice, this guide would have never been written. He did most of the editing and a lot of the historical research; by spending rainy days in the Yukon archives he was able to avoid the wet tent.

Kathy Hughes, a friend and hiking companion, has encouraged me at low times and promoted my writing at all times. If she ever gets tired of teaching, she could become a bookseller.

All Kluane National Park personnel, from the interpreters to the trail crews to the wardens and their supervisors, have contributed to this book. Without their advice it would have taken us far longer to explore the park. The interpreters have spent hours of their own time sharing information, correcting any errors we made, and hiking the recommended routes we suggest in order to give visitors firsthand knowledge. Their dedication has helped to make this a safe and accurate book.

Kim Henkel, who has lived in the area for most of her life, has given us constant support and direction. Her love of the park and its resident bears is infectious. I want to thank all the interpreters working at the information centres, especially Kim Henkel, Allison Wood, Judy Unrau, Pat White (Kluane's best storyteller), Marsha Flumerfelt, Cecile Sias, Ann Marie Jim, Gordon Joe, Michelle Oakley, Mary Jane Johnson, and Josie Sias.

Thanks to Dwayne West, chief warden, and to all the people who have worked with Dwayne, and in turn helped me, over the years. Some of these wardens are Andrew Lawrence, Lloyd Freese, Terry Skjonsberg, Rick Staley, Craig Mackinnon, Ray Breneman, Rhonda Markel, Kevin McLaughlin, Glen Dubian, and Tom Bussel.

I want to give Brian Bakker from the trail crew a special mention for the emotional support and hot coffee after my encounter with a bear. He looked after me until he could safely put me in the hands of warden Andrew Lawrence, who then took me back to my truck at Kathleen Lake.

Thanks also to Henry Henkel who, besides adding beauty to the park with his environmentally-compatible signs, has told me more stories than I can remember. Others who have added beauty or safety to Kluane are Wilf Oakely, Vi Oakely, and Claude Dulac.

Will Jones, trail-crew worker, river guide, and man about town in Haines Junction, has shared hiking information with us over the years, thus saving us a lot of dead-end walks that could never be recommended. Although I must always adjust his estimated hiking times, his route recommendations have been excellent.

Frank and Josie Sias of Kluane Lake are human encyclopedias about Kluane. Josie's father was Louis Jacquot, who started the trading post at Burwash Landing. From him Josie started picking up her knowledge. Not only do Josie and Frank know the history of the area, but they also truly care that the information is presented accurately. Consequently, they have shared stories with us over many pots of tea. Josie was also instrumental in having local people hired as park interpreters, rather than having workers imported from other areas of the country.

Brent and Wenda Liddle of Cabins B&B have told me numerous local stories that have added historical flavour to this edition. They also keep my favourite cabin ready for me whenever I need a dry bed at the south end of the park.

Liz and Boyd Campbell, Mark Ritchie, Val Drummond, Lorn LaRocque, and Todd Heakes have given me accurate information that is pertinent to travel in the area at the present time.

This book is written for everyone that we have met and talked to over the years – not only in Kluane, but on every hiking trail in the world. Fellow hikers have added to my knowledge and have given me the incentive needed to complete the project.

Introduction to
Kluane
NATIONAL
PARK

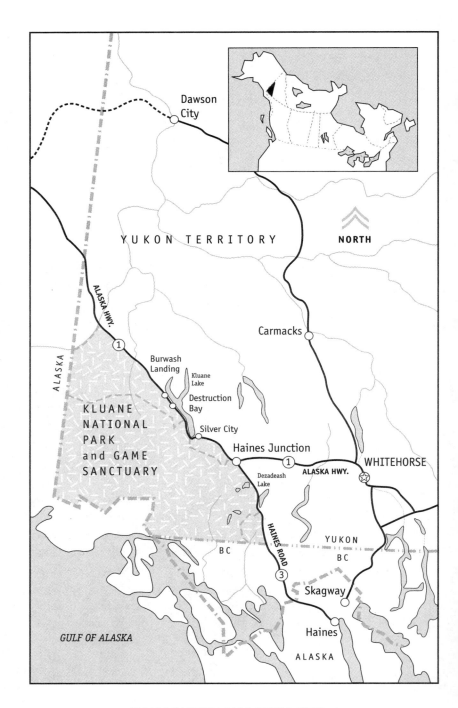

Introduction

Kluane National Park is a wonderful area of land tucked into the south-west corner of the Yukon. It is adjacent to Wrangell-St. Elias National Park and Glacier Bay National Park in Alaska, and the Tatshenshini Provincial Park in British Columbia. Combined, these four parks contain the largest non-polar icefield in the world. Since the formation of the Tatshenshini Park, the area – which falls under the protection of the United Nations – has become the largest land preserve on the planet. Kluane has Canada's highest mountain and an abundance of big game animals, including the largest grizzly bear population in Canada. Kluane National Park is a total area of 22,000 square kilometres (8,500 square miles) of which about 2,600 square kilometres (1,000 square miles) are a green ribbon bordering the icefields. This is the area that beckons the wilderness hiker.

"Kluane," pronounced "Kloo-AHN-ee," is derived from the Tutchone Indian phrase "Lhu' An Mun," meaning "plentiful fish lake." Although the 396 square kilometres (153 square miles) of Kluane Lake is not included in the park, it does border the park and is the largest body of water in the Yukon. On sunny days, this lake is the same dazzling blue as the Caribbean Ocean; on stormy days, the Caribbean blue turns to North Sea grey, becoming a bit foreboding. The lake usually freezes over by the beginning of December and remains frozen until June.

Kluane is a wilderness park, with few trails or established campsites. There are no bridges over most creeks and almost all routes require some bushwhacking. If you are looking for groomed trails, designated campsites with outhouses and bear caches, other hikers to share a campsite, or stacks of cut wood waiting for your fire, you should go to Jasper or Banff, not Kluane. *Because of the special challenges Kluane offers, you are well advised to make safety and health a priority in the park; read the chapter on this before you go.*

For the hiker, Kluane National Park offers over 800 kilometres (497 miles) of charted trails and mapped routes, plus the possibility of another 300 kilometres (186 miles) of uncharted routes. These trails and routes lead to historical sites, spectacular glaciers, alpine lakes, challenging passes, and cold streams. They take the biologist to animal feeding grounds, the botanist to rare plant species, the bird-watcher to great nesting grounds, the geologist to new land formations, the archeologist to 6,000 year-old artifacts (that they must find themselves), the photographer to stunning views and the hiker to pristine areas.

The Canadian Parks and Wilderness Society is currently trying to establish park status for the Kluane Game Sanctuary: when bulldozers roar over this delicate tundra, not only do they chase away the animals, they scar the earth for centuries. Kluane is a new land and any damage to the forming vegetation can be irreparable. If you want to preserve the sanctuary, I strongly suggest you send a financial donation with a letter of support to the society at 401 Richmond Street West, Suite 380, Toronto, Ontario M5V 3A8.

In many ways, Kluane National Park is like nowhere else in the world. In this book, I share my experience, both with Kluane and with hiking in general, so that your trip will be as safe and as pleasurable as possible. You may hike, mountain-bike, canoe, ski, mountain-climb, photograph, or just enjoy the vistas and silence of this wonderful World Heritage Site. Kluane National Park has something for everyone.

ABOUT KLUANE NATIONAL PARK

History: About 20 million years ago, the St. Elias Mountains were just being formed by the glaciation of the earth. This land change is still occurring today. About 100,000 years ago, Kluane Lake had about 2,000 metres (6,500 feet) of ice at its south end.

East flowing glacial floes from the Dusty River Valley moved into the Alsek Valley and then travelled west down to the Kaskawulsh Valley. The eastern lobe of the icefields went to the Dezadeash River area, while the western lobe went the Jarvis River Valley.

The Shakwak Valley, through which the present day Alaska Highway runs, was formed by these ice flows and became the divide between ice flowing east and ice flowing northwest. Ice flowing northwest created the Slims, Duke, and Donjek Valleys.

About 6,000 years ago, humans appeared in the area – but left quickly because world temperatures dropped and glaciers began advancing. Later, as the glaciers receded, humans and animals both re-entered and stayed.

On the north, or little arm of Kluane Lake is an archeological site where anthropologists found chipped obsidian set in bone and antler. These tools were once used as knives and chisels, and are believed to be more than 5,000 years old. The theory is that the Little Arm Indians left the area during a temperature change and were replaced by the Tutchone when the climate warmed. Another indication of this human migration was found at the mouth of Gladstone Creek, where stone chips and primitive tools were found on a dry terrace beside the creek.

The Tutchone Indians were a nomadic tribe who have lived in the Kluane region from the time of the climatic warming. They built villages and camps on the lakes and rivers where food was abundant; permanent villages were found along the Alsek and Tatshenshini Rivers. The Tutchone followed the caribou and salmon runs, while trading with the coastal Tlingit Indians living farther south.

The Tutchone hunted, fished, and collected berries in the summer. In winter, they walked from cache to cache, eating the food they had stored. Traditionally, they hunted with bows and arrows or they set babiche (rawhide) snares in tree-branch fences across animal routes.

Besides eating the meat from captured animals, the Tutchone Indians were creative in using the rest of the animal. They made ladles and bowls from sheep horns; made winter clothes from the fleece and hide of the mountain goat; made ceremonial robes, parkas, and hats from the fur of ground squirrels and rabbits; and used lichen to dye their wool. After the mid-1800s, they traded with the Tlingit for European products and oolichan grease for food seasoning.

Today, the Champagne/Aishihik and Kluane First Nations are the two Tutchone groups involved in co-managing Kluane National Park. This agreement was signed in 1993, as part of a land claim settlement.

The Kluane is an area of high geological activity. There are on average three minor tremors a day, and one major tremor every five years. Next to the Queen Charlotte Islands, the Kluane is the second most geologically active area in Canada. There is evidence of two volcanic eruptions in the Kluane area: one occurred about 2,000 years ago and the other about 1,200 years ago. From a small vent in the hill west of the Klutlan Glacier, the eruptions spread tons of volcanic ash as far as the central Yukon. Layers of white ash can be seen along cutbanks beside roads and rivers in the Yukon, including areas of Kluane. The ash from the Klutlan eruptions covers a large portion of the glacier, which has the widest terminus of any glacier in Canada. The ash is about three feet deep on the land surrounding the glacier.

The Lowell and the Kaskawulsh Glaciers started separating from the rest of the icefields about 3,000 years ago. When the Lowell advanced the first time, about 1,200 years ago, it pushed up against Goatherd Mountain and dammed the Alsek River, forming Lake Alsek. It has repeated this performance many times since. The last time was about 200 years ago, when the lake flooded the present area of Haines Junction. After the lake disappeared about 100 years ago, it became known as "Recent Lake Alsek." Stories about Recent Lake Alsek abound in Indian legend, and the Russians appear to have explored the lake. Remains of an old raft have been discovered among the driftwood left on the slopes between the Alsek Trail and the upper end of Quill Creek. Some scientists believe that this glacier will surge again in the near future. The last advance made by the Kaskawulsh and Donjek Glaciers, north of the Lowell Glacier, was about 400 years ago.

The Kluane area was sighted from the sea by the explorers Vitus

Bering, Alejandro Malaspina, James Cook, and George Vancouver. In 1873, trader Arthur Harper, travelling by dog team from Fort McPherson via the Rat River, became the first white man to see the St. Elias Mountains from the east.

Mount Logan was first named by mountaineer and scientist I. C. Russell in 1890, when he was on a National Geographic expedition. He named it after Sir William Logan, the founder of the Geological Survey of Canada and father of Canadian geology. Standing at 5,959 metres (19,545 feet), Mount Logan is the highest mountain in Canada and has more mass than any mountain in the world. It is the second highest mountain in North America. Mount McKinley, in Wrangell-St. Elias Park in Alaska, stands at 6,194 metres (20,320 feet). Mount St. Elias, the first mountain to be named in the park, was named by Vitus Bering on July 16 (St. Elias Day), 1741. This mountain stands just below Mount Logan at 5,489 metres (18,008 feet).

Mount Logan has been the source of intrigue for many mountaineers. In 1887, an Italian expedition led by the Duke of Abruzzi , a world renowned climber, was the first to see its southern exposure. But it was not until 1925 that W. W. Foster, president of the Alpine Club of Canada, and his buddy A. H. McCarthy actually scaled the peak.

The three large peaks seen from the eastern hills of the park, Steel, Walsh, and Wood, were named by J. J. McArthur in 1900.

It was not until the twentieth century that Europeans came into Kluane to explore the land and to hunt the abundant wildlife. The Kluane gold rush was a short-lived offshoot of the Klondike rush, but it brought modern civilization into the area. The early explorers blazed the Dalton Trail, remnants of which are visible at Champagne, on the Alaska Highway between Whitehorse and Haines Junction. In 1898, Alder Creek was mined, and then the prospectors moved to Shorty Creek. In 1903 gold was found at Bullion and Sheep Creeks, and in 1904 at Burwash Creek. There were one to two thousand men at work in the area during the 1904 season, but the take did not exceed $20,000. Freight costs were extremely high: twenty to thirty cents per pound from Whitehorse to Kluane, and then another forty cents per pound up to Burwash. At these rates, the cost of a pound of sugar became prohibitive. By 1906 there were, in the entire area, only twenty men working on private claims.

After 1906, mining companies continued to operate in the area, but productivity was low. One company spent $300,000 trying to get gold which at the time sold for $17 per ounce. They managed to earn only $1,000 in revenue.

The gold miners were followed by the copper miners, who operated until the 1960s, when the Johobo Mining Company mined near Sockeye Lake on the Cottonwood Trail. Most recently, Imperial Oil conducted an exploration of the Tatamagouche Creek area in 1971. However, in 1970 the Territorial Lands Act and the Yukon Placer Mining Act were amended, and today there is no mining in the park, though there is mining in the sanctuary.

The Alaska Highway was built during the Second World War, and public access to the area raised awareness of its splendour. Then, in 1942, Americans working on the Shakwak Trench section of the Alaska Highway brought the Kluane area to the attention of Canada's park administrators. In 1943, the area was designated the Kluane Game Sanctuary, but the government still allowed prospecting, claim staking, and the granting of mineral rights to both mining companies and private individuals. Only hunting and trapping were restricted. It was not until 1972 that a formal park was established, and in 1976 the area actually fell under the National Parks Act. However, even today there are no controls over mining in the area that has remained a sanctuary.

In 1980 the park, along with the Wrangell-St. Elias Park in Alaska, became a World Heritage Site and fell under the protection of UNESCO. Now this is one of the last places on Earth where one can immerse oneself in the wilderness – with a feeling of being the first person to have left a footprint on that piece of ground.

Climate: Located north of the 60th parallel, Kluane has nineteen-hour days in summer. This allows the earth to warm quickly, though frost and snow are possible at any time of year. Hiking is best between late May and the middle of September, when average temperatures are 12°C (54°F) in the valleys. Hiking in January can be a bit chilly; the lowest temperature ever recorded was -62°C (-80°F) at Kluane Lake, but this was long before global warming.

There are sharp climatic contrasts between the southern area of the park, which falls under the Pacific rain belt, and the northern area, which falls under a rain shadow. If it is raining in the south, where precipitation averages 150 centimetres (59 inches) a year, change routes and head north of Bear Creek Summit, where the average precipitation is 22 centimetres (9 inches) a year. The icefields catch most of the moisture along the northern section of the Shakwak Valley, while the south end of the park gets many cyclonic storms from the Gulf of Alaska. There are an average of six serious thunderstorms per year in the southern section of the park.

Temperatures decrease proportionally with increased elevation. Permafrost will not be found below 1,200 metres (4,000 feet) in the southern section of the park. However, permafrost is more prevalent in the northern section where the slumping ground leads to pooling water, which creates thermokarsts and bogs. The most noticeable feature of slumping ground above permafrost is the spindly tree that bends in all directions, giving the forest a ghost-like appearance.

Winds blow down valleys and are stronger on passes. Glacier winds are strongest during mid day. Slims River Valley has an average wind velocity of 27.5 kilometres (17.1 miles) per hour during the day, dropping to 7 kilometres (4.3 miles) per hour during the night.

HIKING IN KLUANE

Kluane National Park is one of the last true wilderness areas left on the planet; the park's management plan is to keep it that way. This means there are few trails and almost no bridges, outhouses, or trail markers. You must be able to pick and follow a route by your own abilities, not by the markings of those who have gone before you. The exception is the Cottonwood Trail, the park's Cadillac show-piece which has a visible trail and some signposts. However, it does not have bridges over Goat or Victoria Creeks, and finding a camp fire ring or an outhouse will be rare. Routes like the Lowell Glacier Overland or the Donjek Glacier Trails have nothing to guide or assist you, which puts you on the same footing as Alexander MacKenzie and other European explorers. You must be prepared for physical and psychological challenges not present in more developed parks.

On the other hand, if you are skilled in back-country hiking,

Kluane is the most spectacular area in the world (in my humble opinion). Because the landscape is so vast, landmarks are easily spotted and often remain in your view during two days of hiking. This means that getting lost is the least of your considerations, as long as you are skilled in map reading.

There is an overnight park fee of $5 per night, which must be paid at registration time. Visitors may also purchase a $50 season's pass. **Everyone hiking in Kluane overnight must register at the Kluane Park Visitor Information Centre. Failing to do so may result in a fine.**

Low-Impact Camping: Low-impact camping is mandatory in Kluane National Park. Low-impact camping means leaving no marks behind. You will not leave markers in the bush or cairns along the creeks. You will spread out when walking in the alpine or attempt to stay on rocks in creek beds. You will cover your excretions with natural products such as moss or leaves and you will burn your toilet paper. You will use a stove instead of a campfire and, if using a campfire, you will remove the ring and ashes before leaving. In fact, you will cover campfire scars completely. One man I met cut a spot for his campfire in the turf, removed the turf and then made his fire on the bare ground. When he was finished, he made certain the fire was out, returned the piece of turf to the campfire spot and then watered it before heading down the trail. He certainly left no mark. If you must make a campfire in a grassy area, use the above method or find a gravel or sand bed.

Never cut vegetation to make room for your tent and never cut vegetation to make shelters. Place a tent on sand or gravel whenever possible. Wash water should be dumped at least 30 metres (100 feet) away from water sources. If possible, filter dish water through gravel and stones instead of pouring it onto vegetation.

Spread out while walking in the alpines thus preventing a trail becoming visible in the delicate ground. Do not plan on going in British India's fashion, with 300 porters and helpers. Keep your groups small. Less than five people are recommended. If there are more than five in your party, break into two groups, using different routes.

Although most of Kluane National Park is open to public access, some delicate areas have been designated as Zone 1, a classification which means public access might be restricted at certain times. Check with the park warden to make sure you aren't planning a hike through a restricted area.

The face of Sheep Mountain is *always* off limits to hikers.

Laws of the Land

The following laws are recommended everywhere in Canada, not just Kluane. In this book, I suggest places to camp or vantage points from where to get photos but if you notice a spot being overused, move on for a few hundred feet. Try to keep the area pristine.

- Carry out all garbage – "Leave only your tracks, take only your snaps." I was appalled by the garbage left along the Yukon River, another high-use area in the Territory. I carried out other people's junk. Do the same. If you see a tiny piece of anything belonging to man, unless it is an artifact of course, carry it out. Become fastidious.

- Do not pick, move, remove or change anything natural that is in the environment. This includes flowers, rocks, horns or berries. Adding berries to your food supply is hard on the environment and against park regulations. Over-picking of any wild plant anywhere could result in extinction of the species.

- When breaking camp, make certain all traces of your presence are gone. That plastic bag will not disappear from under a rock nor will the toilet paper. Carry the bag. Burn or carry the paper.

- Take food that does not smell. If using tinned food, burn the tin after emptying it in order to burn out the smell. Flatten the tin and carry it out with you in your bear-resistant food canister.

- Never leave garbage buried in the ground or dumped in the rivers or streams. The fish do not eat our garbage! Animals will eat plastic bags but their digestive systems have not evolved enough to benefit.

- Always take wash water away from the creeks. Wash and then dump your water in a rocky spot when you are finished. This helps filter the water before it goes back into the stream. When I had my bear encounter, I was going to throw my porridge down the creek but I instinctively stopped myself and put the porridge (still in the cooking pot) into my backpack. That way, I left no

N T R O D U C T I O N

pollution and the bear did not get any food from me.

- Human waste should be buried at least 30 metres (100 feet) from any water and all toilet paper should be burned or carried out. You may feel that low-use areas can take some garbage without it making any difference to the environment, but that's not true. Don't be the first to leave a mark.
- Make certain that the fire is out after burning toilet paper. When moss is dry, it does not take much fuel to start a fire. 7.5 cm (3 inches) of peat land takes a hundred years to form. Moss also burns and smoulders for years, thus causing a tremendous amount of air pollution.
- Unnecessary use of firewood will end in shortage, as has happened in other Canadian and American parks. Making a fire outside a designated fire pit (if there is one) will leave a scar in the environment. Build small fires on gravel or sand and stand close to them. Do not make fires on moss or peat as peat fires can burn underground and are almost impossible to extinguish. Do not make rock cairns or leave fire pits in the park. Fire pits should be dismantled and the ashes from the fire should be scattered.
- Use the bear canisters offered by the park wardens, as they prevent all animals from associating humans with food. Do not feed any of the animals, including the pesky ground squirrels.
- Use a camp stove instead of a fire as often as possible.
- Using hiking boots with good grip but shallow treads, and light runners or sport sandals while in camp will minimize the impact in a highly-used area.
- Always camp on sand or gravel beds if possible. Move to an unused spot if signs of camping are present, especially in delicate areas. Tramp on as little vegetation as possible while walking or camping. The more often a piece of vegetation is ground by a boot, the more permanent the resulting scar.
- On the trails, hike single file in order to keep the trails narrow. In the alpine, spread out or stay in the rocky creek beds. Avoid loose or steep terrain as it will slide.
- View wildlife from a distance only. Never follow animals as you may be separating a mother from her young. It is against the law

KLUANE NATIONAL PARK HIKING GUIDE *12*

to harass or harm wildlife and if an offender is caught fines can be up to $150,000.

- A Parks Canada fishing permit is required for those fishing within park boundaries and a separate permit is required for fishing outside the park. For an example, fishing in Kluane Lake would require a Yukon government permit, while fishing in Mush Lake would require a park permit. A Parks Canada fishing permit is good in any other national park in Canada for that calendar year.
- Firearms are illegal in all Canadian Parks. Anyway, anything light enough to carry would be useful only for shooting yourself.

Equipment: Equipment can make or break a person when on a trip of any duration. Cheap gear is not safe and is usually heavy. As a rule, the better the equipment, the lighter the weight.

The better thought-out the trip, the more pleasurable the experience. Before you purchase an item, make certain that it is needed. The more important an item is relative to your personal safety, the better the quality should be. For example, boots must be excellent whereas you can get away with an okay dish or set of pots. Rain gear must keep you dry and sleeping bags must be warm but it really does not matter if you have climbing rope or binder twine for a clothesline. Tents must be waterproof but you can wear cheap t-shirts or shorts. Personally, I tend to make sacrifices in the luxury section of my pack so that I can take along my deluxe sleeping bag, which will keep me warm even if it gets wet. Get to know your body, your limitations and your needs. Then decide what you really need and why.

Before going, fill your pack with everything needed for your planned hike and carry it on a full, strenuous overnighter close to home. If the pack is too heavy, take out the luxuries or change your plans to a shorter hike. Never compromise with food.

Maps: Topographical maps are essential for back-country travel in Kluane. There are few marked trails so a map and compass are needed for orienteering. It was not until 1961 that the first topographical maps of the St. Elias Mountains, made possible by the advent of the airplane, appeared for public use. Every trail and route in this book has map recommendations.

You can purchase the maps from the following places:

Canada Map Office
615 Booth Street
Ottawa, Ontario
K1A OE9

Exploration and Geological Service Division
200 Range Road
Whitehorse, Yukon
Y1A 3V1

Kluane Park Adventure Centre
Haines Junction, Yukon
(see Appendix C for contact information)

Maps used in Kluane Park

These maps are all produced by the Surveys and Mapping Branch of the Department of Energy, Mines and Resources. Following map names are their catalogue numbers.

1:250,000
Kluane Lake 115G & 115F
Dezadeash Range 115A
Mt. St. Elias 115B & 115C

1:50,000
Silver Creek 115A/3
Bates River 115A/4
Cottonwood Lake 115A/5
Mush Lake 115A/6
Kathleen Lakes 115A/11
Auriol Range 115A/12
Kloo Lake 115A/13
Slims River 115B/15
Jarvis River 115B/16

Congdon Creek 115G/2
Bighorn Creek 115G/3
Donjek Glacier 115G/4
Steel Creek 115G/5
Duke River 115G/6
Burwash Landing 115G/7

I recommend obtaining all necessary maps before travelling to Kluane. Once there, if your hiking plans change because trails are closed, additional maps will be available in Haines Junction. However, if you've had a chance to study your maps before coming to the park, you will already have some idea of what your alternatives could be. The Geological Service in Whitehorse will have needed maps but they will not have up-to-date information about open and closed trails.

When ordering maps, remember that the larger the fraction, the smaller the area covered, and therefore the greater the detail. For example, 1:50,000 map shows far more detail (1 kilometre per square inch) than a 1:250,000 (10 kilometres per square inch). Purchase the 1:50,000 maps for hiking.

Coloured maps cost $8.45 plus taxes. There are still some black and white maps around, which cost $7.05 plus tax. The Canadian government is in the process of updating and metricizing map information, so some of the maps are only available in black and white at present.

The terrain is constantly changing in Kluane, so maps do not always correspond exactly with the landscape. Rivers and creeks reroute, glaciers recede, and rocks are shaken about during earthquakes. There are about four hundred quakes a year in Kluane. Most of these are mere shudders that can't be felt, but occasionally you will notice the earth shaking a bit. A recent quake actually caused one of the hanging glaciers on Nines Creek (North) to shake loose and slide into the valley.

If possible, waterproof your maps by laminating them, or painting them with liquid plastic. A permanent marking pen can be used on the protected maps to mark trails or spots of interest .

Kluane's information centres are excellent places for copying trail routes because the centres always have the latest trail information. Besides, registration with parks for any overnight trip is mandatory. The cost is now $5 per person per night or $50 for a year's pass.

UTM Grid References: Trail descriptions in this book have grid references because so many places in Kluane are unnamed. Universal Transverse Mercator (UTM) is the map grid system used worldwide, and the one I have used in the trail descriptions in this book. Grid references are four-digit numbers read from the map "right-up." This means the first two-digit number is the one read from left to right (across) and the second two-digit number is read from bottom to top. The bottom right-hand corner where the two lines intersect is the reference point. For example, if a lake is at 83-73, find "83" along the bottom of the map and follow that line up to the line beside number "73" along the side of the map. The lake is in the square above and to the left of the intersect. Some directions use a decimal point, indicating a tenth of a kilometre. However, for this book, I do not use decimals because the area is so vast and landmarks so distinct that mistakes are unlikely. On a 1:50,000 scale map each square is one square kilometre.

Orienteering: If taking back-country routes, it is essential to be able to read a map and use a compass. Kluane National Park's degree of declination is 27°E of true north. This information is available on all government maps.

Because the degree of declination is so wide in Kluane, it is important to adjust your compass before starting. If you do not, each incorrect degree used will result in an error of 1/60 of the distance travelled. In other words, if you are going 30 kilometres (18.6 miles) you will be 1/60 x 30 x 27° = 13.5 kilometres (8.4 miles) to one side of your destination! In difficult country, that could be two days travel.

Because Kluane's degree of declination is 27° E of true north, you must *subtract* 27 degrees from your compass reading to get your true bearing. Thus, if your map tells you to head 150° to reach a certain pass, subtract 27 from 150 to get 123°, the heading you must aim for to reach your destination. Remember the rhyme, "declination east, compass least."

Even if you are not proficient in orienteering, travelling in Kluane is still possible. There are definite landmarks throughout the park that correspond with markings on the maps, which all have detailed legends on the back. Mark your trail on the map before leaving the information centre and notice the landmarks while walking. Large landmarks such as lakes, rivers, and rock glaciers are easy to spot. Many places are appropriately named, such as Red Castle Ridge along Sheep-Bullion Plateau or Landmark Glacier on the Donjek Trail, which makes identifying them easy.

Even a rough idea of map-reading expands your range. By studying the map before starting a hike, you may notice areas that are of particular interest to you. If comfortable with map reading, this makes exploration to these areas possible and makes the hike more exciting. Except for short day trips, do not hike in Kluane without a map and compass.

Transportation: Transportation may be needed to get to the trailhead and back to Haines Junction or back to your car. This can be arranged at Kluane Park Adventure Centre in Haines Junction. The cost is $1 per mile for the van which holds up to eight people. The more people sharing the van the cheaper it is per person. Arrangements must be made one day in advance. If planning on a pick-up at the end of a hike, give yourself plenty of time to get out – the van will wait for a while but not all day. I highly recommend using this shuttle service for rides along the park's rim if you do not have your own transportation. Hitchhiking is difficult along the highway. I picked up a couple of young women one day who had spent almost forty hours trying to get a ride.

There is a Greyhound bus that goes from the north and south ends of the Alaska Highway back to Whitehorse. You must check in Whitehorse or with the information centre for the current schedule as it changes every year. I understand however, that the bus driver often forgets to stop if he is behind schedule. Inform the bus depot at Whitehorse where and when you would like to be picked up.

SAFETY AND HEALTH

It is not my intention to provide all the information you will need regarding safety and health in Kluane. Anyone hiking in this, or any other, region is responsible for preventing, recognizing, and treating the emergency situations they might encounter in back-country travel – this of course includes having the knowledge and supplies to administer first aid. I do, however, want to share what I know about some of the more likely hazards you'll face in the park. Before undertaking any wilderness trip, I urge all hikers to learn how to avoid emergencies in the first place, and how to react to them if necessary.

Bears: In Kluane National Park, there are both black and grizzly bears. They have been there since before the coming of people and hopefully will be there for as long as people are visiting this park. The grizzly is a beautiful animal (when observed from a distance) but can be more dangerous than any other animal in the wilderness, especially if it associates humans with food.

The differences between grizzlies and black bears extend far beyond their size: they have different habits and, when encountered, they must be treated differently. Because Kluane National Park is pristine wilderness, the bears have not yet become accustomed to humans and do not seem to connect them with food. However, this is beginning to change. Some people are so intent on getting photos of the bears that they are baiting them. Not only is this extremely dangerous, it is highly illegal and you should report any incidents of this nature to the authorities.

Due to the high profits involved, poaching is a serious problem in Canada. According to the Canadian Wildlife Federation, bear gallbladders may sell for as much as $18,000 in Asia. If you see anything suspicious that could indicate the poaching of wild animals, call the authorities. Convicted offenders can face fines of up to $150,000. Refusing to purchase products made from animal parts will also help eliminate the practice. I encourage those interested in preserving our wildlife to financially support the Canadian Wildlife Federation, 2740 Queensview Drive, Ottawa, Ontario K2B 1A2.

The Tutchone Indians believe bears deserve respect. The natives never walk over bear scat, as this is considered disrespectful and likely to result in an unpleasant bear encounter. The natives also speak gently when they see a bear and they never look directly at it. Native people traditionally did not hunt bear and they killed bears only in self-defence.

Park management encourages the use of a round, plastic canister for the safe packing of food. The canister weighs a bit, but also makes an excellent seat. Carrying a canister is mandatory on the Slims River Trail. If you are caught without a canister on this trail, you can and will be fined up to $2,000.

At present, a bear has caused only one fatality in Kluane. In 1992, due to abundant food, a bumper crop of grizzlies was born. By 1994, when their moms kicked them out, there were a lot of young ones looking for places to live. Since it was a hot year, the bears were irritable and this resulted in many minor encounters but nothing that was life threatening. Meanwhile, the bear population continued to increase.

In July of 1996, Paul and Chris Courtney, world travellers and experienced outdoors people, were returning from an overnighter on Sheep-Bullion Plateau. The couple were approached by an adolescent grizzly, which attacked and killed Chris. Although they did not have a pepper spray, the couple had a food canister. They were fastidious with their gear and themselves. They did not panic when approached. They moved off the trail hoping the bear would pass but the bear followed. They dropped their backpacks but the bear took no notice. They played dead and the bear attacked, killing Chris.

A year after the tragedy, Paul Courtney said, "Even though Chris and I knew more about bears than most people, I think it would have helped if we knew more. In particular, knowing what signs to look for in determining the 'mood' of the bear to determine what action to take to minimize the consequences. Having said that, even if you know all there is to know, you just don't know how you are going to react until confronted."

Although your chances of being hit by lightning are greater than those of being attacked by a bear, an attack is so violent that it seems worse than other deaths. I hope this tragedy is the only one ever to occur in Kluane.

Use all possible caution when you are in the bush – not only for your own sake, but for the sake of Kluane's bears. Once bears learn that humans mean food (food and sleep is all they are really interested in once mating is finished) then naturally they will want some. If a bear harasses a human, the bear is usually the one that pays – often with his life. This is not fair.

Being able to identify grizzlies and black bears, knowing their habits, and understanding ways you can avoid running into them is essential to your safety and survival in Kluane. Read the following guidelines thoroughly.

Report all bear sightings to the interpreters at the information centre when you return to civilization.

Identification

- Mature grizzlies may be anywhere from 90 to 360 kilograms (200 to 800 pounds). Generally they are larger than black bears. In northern Canada, the bears are usually smaller than those living farther south. However, bears inhabiting the Pacific moisture rim in the south of the park are generally bigger than those in other parts of Canada. If the vegetation is thick and lush, the bears will be the same. Males of both species are larger than females, but up close even the adolescent bear looks big.

- Grizzlies have a hump on the back of the neck, where black bears do not. This is not always easy to spot, especially in a young grizzly. The species have different noses as well: the grizzly's is concave (a pug nose), where the black bear's is straighter and more Roman.

- Grizzly prints have toes close together and almost straight across; they are not arched. The claws may be 10 centimetres (4 inches) long. The black bear's toes are farther apart and arched; their claws are proportionally shorter, in relation to foot size, than the grizzly's are.

- Grizzly and black bears come in many shades and colours, from albino white to sandy brown to black. Grizzlies sometimes have light-tipped hair with darker fur on the inside, but I hope you never get close enough to check this out. Either species can have a white blaze on its chest. Grizzlies have grizzled fur, thus the name; whereas black bears have smooth, shiny coats.

- Grizzly scat is usually in large piles and black bear scat is usually smaller pieces spread along the trail. If the scat is fresh, the animal may be near. Natives believe that if you step over bear scat, the act is disrespectful and an unhappy bear will visit your camp. If you see people rolling in scat you can be certain they are intent on getting a photo.

Habits

- Grizzlies seldom attack on sight. However, if the ears are erect and the hair is standing up on the back of the neck, assume a charge is coming. If the bear is snorting, woofing, and growling, this also means an attack is possible. Woofing is a sign that the bear knows you are there. A bear standing sideways, showing his size with his head down and his jaws chomping, is a threatening sign. Bears standing on their hind legs are sniffing the air, trying to get your scent.

- Any bear near a carcass or carrion is dangerous. He will protect his food supply from anything threatening. Hovering ravens are an indication that garbage or carrion may be present. Circle away from this sign, or back off.

- Grizzlies usually hunt at night, while black bears usually hunt during the day. However, I have often seen grazing grizzlies during the day.

- Bears accustomed to garbage are a nuisance and are dangerous. Do not feed bears. Use a canister.

- Bears do not stumble when running downhill nor do they run on their hind legs. These are myths; most bears can outrun an Olympic sprinter. Never run from a bear, as it may be interpreted as a sign of aggression.

- Some grizzlies can climb trees and all black bears can.

- Bears, especially adolescents, are curious. They may come into your camp just to see what it is. There was a bear on Hoge Pass one year who found a sleeping bag hanging on a tent. The bear played with the tent and chewed the sleeping bag for hours before he got bored and moved on. For four days before returning to civilization, the owner had to sleep in the bag scented with bear breath.

- Bears turn over rocks, claw deadfall, and dig up plants when they're looking for insects. Watch for these signs. A "bear stomp" is where bears leave tracks going to and from a favourite tree that they rub against. A bear stomp is a good sign that a bear is living in the area. Bears like dense bush for cover, but they also like to wander in the alpines.

- June and July is mating season for bears, but the embryo does not develop until November – and then only if the female is fat and healthy. If she is too thin or sickly to sustain the development of a healthy embryo, she aborts. The natural rule is "If you can't support, abort." With a healthy female, the young are born during the winter and live off the female's fat-rich milk (25-30% fat) until spring. A litter usually consists of one or two cubs, but a sow may have up to four cubs in one year.

- In July, bears hang around hillsides where fresh green shoots grow, moving up as the snow melts. By August they move down to ripe berry patches, or streams where there are fish. Bears like moist areas because there is more young vegetation. Bears eat cow parsnip and horsetail, and they love soap berries or buffalo berries. They also like bearberries (hence the name), low bush cranberries and crow berries. Bears nip the flowers off some plants. This is often evident in the fireweed patches so abundant in Kluane National Park. If the flowers have been recently nipped, be wary.

- September is their most aggressive month, when their daily food intake increases from 8,000 kilocalories to 15,000 or 20,000 kilocalories. By October, grizzlies den on mountain slopes at about 4,000 feet and black bears usually den on forest floors. During winter, their heart rate falls from fifty beats per minute to eight. They keep their body temperatures close to summer levels. They lose 35% of their body weight. Although they sleep most of the time, they have been known to come out for a romp in the snow on a sunny day.

- Black bears do not usually inflict the same degree of injury as grizzlies, but they can do just as much damage to gear or cabins.

Preventing an Encounter on the Trail

Always use the bear canisters offered for free by the parks service!

- Before going on a hike, learn from the interpreters if there are any bears in the area which are recognizable and known to have certain habits. Find out what the habits are and avoid attracting that particular animal.

- Travel in a group; the more of you there are, the safer you will be. Bears, like people, will approach a single person before a group. More than half of the recorded injuries inflicted by bears happen to lone hikers.

- Every member of your party should carry pepper or mace spray and it should be where it can be reached in a second, never inside your backpack. Keep it in the tent at night. If a bear is sprayed once, he will not be able to attack for five minutes. If he is sprayed by three people, there is little chance he will return. However, if he does he will be one angry critter. Be certain to always have a couple of shots left in your sprayer. All used spray containers should be replaced as soon as possible.

- Leave your dog at home. Barking dogs may provoke bears to come into camp. Besides, dogs must be kept on a leash in national parks and this makes hiking less fun for both you and your dog.

- Take binoculars in order to scan an open area before entering.

Food canisters, available from the information centres in Kluane, are recommended for all trails and mandatory for some.

Make noise to let bears know where you are. Also be aware that even if all rules are stringently kept, you still may have bad luck. It is the same as driving down the highway; you could be hit by a drunk driver. You could encounter a curious, angry, or sick bear.

- Always photograph bears from at least 300 metres (1,000 feet) away. Going closer may be considered harassment. If you wish to photograph or observe these magnificent animals, go to the bear blind along the Tatshenshini River near Dalton Post when the salmon are running. You are guaranteed to see a grizzly bear. You may also contact Chuck Hume at Klukshu Village just off the Haines Highway below Dezadeash Camp Site. He is interested in guiding people in bear country. If you're unable to contact Chuck, enquire at Kluane Park Adventure Centre in Haines Junction. Phone (403) 633-5470 and they will set you up to observe these animals.

Preventing an Encounter in Camp

- The natives claim that when a pine needle falls, the deer hears it, the bear smells it, and the eagle sees it. Keeping a clean (odourless) campsite is your best protection from an unwanted bear encounter. This requires fastidiousness, but it could well save your life. Pay particular attention to food and body odours that may draw bears from a long distance away.

- Place everything with an odour into your bear canister. If a bear gets food from you, he may stalk you believing he can get more. Always store food away from camp. Hang it in a tree if the canister is not available. One hiker had her food in a canister and she actually heard a bear knocking it around while she slept (*i.e.,* lay in her tent with her eyes wide open), but the bear was unable to get into the canister so he left. If your food is eaten by a bear on the fourth day of a ten-day trip, it could be a slimming walk back to civilization.

- Camp in open areas, off trails. Like humans, animals prefer trails for walking. If you are in the open, the animal may see and therefore avoid you. If near trees, keep a climbable one in mind. Look for digging signs, claw marks on the trees, uprooted stumps, fresh bear scats, fresh prints and hair rubbed onto trees. If you see fresh signs, make noise and try to leave the area. Do not camp where someone has left garbage. Do take out any garbage you find and report the incident to the information centre.

- Use dehydrated food (it has less scent) and cook only what you need, or overeat. Burning uneaten food may be difficult, especially in the alpine. Besides, food smoke smells.

- Pitch your tent upwind from your camp fire. This will keep the smell of food off the tent. Also, put all sleeping gear in a safe place before making supper, thus preventing food from spilling on the gear. Never borrow gear from someone unless you know it is odour free.

- Do not sleep in clothes in which you have cooked. Carry a pair of long johns only for sleeping. Put your day clothes in your pack and leave the pack 20 or 30 metres (65 or 100 feet) away from the tent or, if available, in a bear cache. Do not leave your pack in the vestibule of your tent. In the case of bad weather, take a plastic bag or pack fly to cover your pack.

- Abstain from having sex in the tent. I believe sex in bear country is dangerous because the resulting bodily fluids have an odour that may be attractive to bears. Steven Herrero, bear biologist and author of *Bear Attacks*, agrees that my hypothesis is reasonable. Until this hypothesis is disproved, I strongly urge hikers to make certain there are no sex odours on their bodies, their sleeping bags, or their tents. If you borrow equipment, make certain it is from someone who is fastidious about keeping his or her gear odour-free.

- Do not use make-up, deodorant, perfumes, aftershave, perfumed soap, or anything else that has scent, especially near or in the tent. Most toothpastes, when spit onto the ground, smell. Dilute the spit with copious amounts of water or swallow it. Some third-world countries sell unscented toothpaste, but I know of none sold in North America. Using baking soda as a tooth powder is an unpleasant alternative.

- Girls and women should use tampons instead of napkins during a menstrual cycle, as there is less odour. Changing these often will also reduce any odour. Burn all used tampons – never bury them.

Dealing with a Confrontation

- If you come around a corner and see a bear, back up slowly, move your hands up and down, and speak in a soft, calm voice. Never run from a bear as this may be interpreted as aggression. If you are retreating and the bear is following, drop an object (not food) to distract him, but do not drop your pack. Your pack may be protection a few feet down the trail when the bear catches up.

- On close confrontation, the accepted wisdom has been to scream, shout, and intimidate a black bear, but never a grizzly. However, there is a theory emerging that you should be aggressive with predatory bears of both types. I think the new term "predatory bear" is simply a euphemism for bears involved in any unexplained attacks, but most bear encounters can be traced to human error. We may not yet know all the parameters of human error. From my own experience, I know that it is almost impossible to remain passive if encountering a bear. During my one encounter, I kept throwing rocks and screaming at a grizzly, and he kept following me. My antics drove him off long enough for me to find a safe place, but he did keep returning.

- If you're suddenly attacked by a grizzly, play dead. Do not fight, yell, or make any aggressive moves. *Play dead!* Cover your neck with your hands and bring your knees up over your stomach into the fetal position.

Creek-Crossings: There are few bridges in Kluane National Park, and most trails have creeks that must be crossed on foot. Some of these are wide, some are deep, most are swift, and all are cold. Proper crossing knowledge is essential, as an improper crossing can cost you your life.

Crossing early in the morning is the first general rule. The icefields do not melt after the sun sets, so the creeks become substantially lower at night. For instance, when we camped by the Duke River one August, we noticed that its volume in the morning was half of what it was in the afternoon, and there was a lot less silt. However, if you happen to have a bad night of rain, the water level may rise substantially.

Wearing special shoes to cross creeks is highly recommended. Neoprene canoe booties are warmer than runners, weigh very little, and have sturdy bottoms. They do, however, take longer to dry than runners. I prefer to wear neoprene socks under sport sandals; the socks keep your feet warm and can be wrung almost dry, making them lightweight for carrying, and the sandals can double as evening slippers. Use bonzo rings on the Velcro straps of the sandals to prevent them from coming undone in the current. Invest in good sport sandals, as the cheaper ones do not have a stiff enough sole to keep them from bending in swift water. Remove long pants before crossing a creek because the extra material will create resistance in the current.

ALWAYS undo the waist and chest buckle on your pack before crossing a creek. If you fall, you must be able to get out of your pack — otherwise you'll be immobilized like a turtle on its back. Many people have died unnecessarily because they did not undo their pack buckles

Elsebeth Vingborg keeps two points on the ground while fighting the current of a swift creek.

before crossing a stream. One of the wardens told me about a hiker who lost her footing while strapped into her pack and drowned in about eight inches of water. Tie an empty water bottle to a rope and then secure the rope to the outside of your pack. This will give you a buoy to grab in the event that your pack does go under water.

Before crossing, walk up and down the creek a bit to find the best spot. Choose the widest (shallowest) spot on the creek, which is usually near the mouth. Look for a flat area where the drop is not significant as this will result in a slower current. Once you have chosen a spot, move upstream a metre or so. When crossing, do not move directly across or up the stream. Allow the current to move your foot slightly backward while you move it to the side, using the same physics as a reaction ferry. This method will be quicker and safer than trying to fight the current by going directly across.

Always face upstream while crossing. The current will soon whip your feet from under you if you lean downstream. *When approaching the far bank, do not turn sideways until your feet are on dry ground.*

Use a sturdy stick for support. Think of your two feet and the stick as three points of support. When you're in the water, you should have two points on the ground at all times. Move one foot, then move the stick, and then move the second foot. In murky water, use the stick to determine the depth of the water before you move your foot.

If there is a group crossing, you may link arms and cross together. This forms a human chain that allows the stronger members to help the weaker ones. One person should co-ordinate the movement by giving a command and then everyone should move at the same time.

If there are only two people crossing deep water, have the shorter person move behind the taller one. The front person will shield the shorter one from some of the current. Cross in unison with the front person giving commands. The person at the back will not be able to use a stick but can lightly hold onto the front person's pack.

If crossing difficult water, secure the crossing person to a rope while holding the other end. In the event of an accident, the current will force the one in the water toward the bank as long as the person on shore pulls the rope. Note however that if the crossing is wide, a long rope will eventually drag in the water and force the crosser off balance.

Hypothermia: Hypothermia is one of the greatest hazards to your health (aside from bears) that you will encounter in Kluane, and it should be treated seriously. Because of sudden winds, rain, snow, and sleet, and because of the glacial-fed streams, the high mountain passes, and the possibility of exhaustion, hypothermia is a constant danger – even in July or August. It usually occurs at fairly mild temperatures, when the person is wet and exposed to the wind. If someone falls into a creek or lake in Kluane, they have very little time to get out and get dry and warm before hypothermia sets in.

Severe hypothermia is a condition that occurs when the temperature of the body's core drops below 32°-33°C (90°F). By the time the body core reaches 30°C (90°F), the victim will be unconscious and heart failure is likely. Preventing hypothermia should be always be priority, but you must also understand it well enough to recognize the symptoms and administer treatment if it should become necessary.

Prevention

- Wear waterproof clothing during wet weather, and a toque in cold weather (40% of all body heat is lost through the head).
- To prevent fatigue, eat high-calorie and high-fat foods, avoid eating snow or drinking icy water if you are chilled, and know when to stop hiking for the day. If you are tired and conditions become difficult, you are far more susceptible to hypothermia. Know your limits, and encourage others to know theirs.
- Even when you're on an easy day hike, always carry some type of shelter (such as a bivy-sack, a piece of tarp, or a survival blanket) and have waterproof clothing with you. Carry extra clothing in a plastic bag, as most packs will leak under extreme conditions.
- Be aware that some people are more predisposed towards hypothermia, especially children and adults with a low percentage of body fat.
- Recognize the initial stages of hypothermia and never be blind to the possibility of this condition, either in someone else or yourself. If any member of your party is shivering, don't pretend nothing is wrong. He is not a wimp. You must help your mate before he or she becomes unreasonable. This is even more

important if everyone is afflicted; once anyone passes to the second stage of hypothermia, where reasoning becomes difficult, getting someone into a safe place may not be possible, especially if that person is bigger than you.

Symptoms

- Uncontrolled shivering
- Blurred vision and lack of co-ordination
- Slurred speech and confusion
- Collapse, weak breathing and pulse – death can occur at this stage.

Treatment

Severe hypothermia must be treated by warming the victim using blankets and other passive means rather than applying direct heat. The increase in body temperature must not exceed more than 0.5-1°C (1-2°F) per hour, as more rapid warming brings cold blood from the extremities, which might cause the cardiovascular system to collapse. However, do not let anyone get to this stage. If someone is shivering, start making camp, and prepare tea and high-calorie food.

- Remove all wet clothing and get the person out of the wind and cold.
- Insulating the victim in a sleeping bag may not be enough; once hypothermia has set in, that person is unable to generate sufficient body heat to warm himself. One or two people should strip and climb into the sleeping bag with the victim, so as to transfer body heat. In the meantime, a fire should be lit and water heated.
- Place warm compresses on the victim's head, neck, chest and groin. Be sure that the compresses are warm, not hot, by testing them on yourself first. Change them often to speed warming.
- If there is a problem with the victim's breathing, give mouth-to-mouth resuscitation, which will transfer some of your hot air into the victim's body.
- Never give the person alcohol, as it will decrease sensitivity and lower the body's ability to produce heat. Give warm tea with copious amounts of sugar to the victim with mild hypothermia.

Sunburn: Be certain to use sunscreen while in Kluane. Longer days in the Yukon result in greater exposure to the sun. Higher elevations also increase the amount of exposure being endured. In addition to this, being on or near snow will double the amount of rays you receive. If you do get sunburned, cover the afflicted area, place cool water or cool wet cloths on the skin, drink lots of cool liquid, and rest. Heat exhaustion may seem unlikely in Kluane, but don't be fooled. Both extremes, hypothermia and heat exhaustion, are possible.

Giardiasis: Commonly known as "beaver fever," the giardiasis flagellate is present in the park. Beaver fever is caused by consuming water that has been contaminated with human or animal excretion containing the bug. I have always drunk the water straight from the creeks and eaten the glacial ice without ill effects, but the park does have official warnings about giardiasis. The closer the water is to a glacier, the safer it is to drink.

Symptoms of giardiasis infection appear anywhere from one to three weeks after ingestion. Common symptoms are explosive diarrhea, flatulence, cramps, bloating, fatigue, and weight loss. Sometimes the condition cures itself, but if not you may need drugs. If you think you have contracted giariasis, see a doctor; if you think that you got it in Kluane, let the park personnel know.

You can prevent coming into contact with the giardias parasite by doing one of three things to purify water in the wilderness. The first way is to boil the water for ten minutes. The second is to use a heavy-metal tablet that contains iodine or silver; chlorine tablets are not strong enough to rid the water of some parasites. Heavy-metal tablets must be dissolved in the water for ten minutes before it is safe to drink. The third way to purify water is to use a water filter. Lightweight, reliable purifiers are available at most sports shops.

To protect water sources from possible contamination, bury all feces at least 30 metres (100 feet) from the high water level of any body of water and 15 centimetres (6 inches) below the surface. This speeds decomposition and is aesthetically more appealing.

If you become obsessed with personal excretions, a good book to read, for sound information and entertainment, is *How to Shit in the Woods* by Kathleen Meyer.

Undernourishment and Dehydration: I cannot emphasize enough the need for proper nutrition while travelling in Kluane. Every day will be a new and difficult challenge, and your body must be in excellent condition in order to supply the needed energy. This is not the time to diet. You must eat a sufficient quantity of high-quality food. Do not use foods that are 90% chemicals and 10% filler – home-prepared foods high in protein and carbohydrates are the best source of what the body needs. Calcium found in milk and cheese is used by the muscles, joints and nervous system. Potassium is needed to make muscles move. Protein is needed for muscle repair and water is needed to prevent both kidney problems and dehydration. If suffering from a headache in the heat of the day, your body is probably down about one litre of water. When exerting physical strength, the body breaks down stored fat. This produces chemical by-products that require water to flush out. Without water kidney damage may occur. Once stored fat is depleted, the body breaks down muscle. If calcium is not replenished, the body draws the mineral from your bones. Fortunately, drinkable water is easy to find in the park. Supply your body with all other nutritional needs by eating well and help your metabolism by drinking a lot of water.

Foods high in proteins that are easy to carry on the trail include nuts, parmesan cheese and soybean products. Carob is high in potassium, calcium and phosphorus. Wheat germ is high in vitamin B necessary for the nervous system. Vitamin B is also reputed to help keep mosquitoes from biting. Pasta, instant potatoes, rice, and couscous are good sources of carbohydrate needed for energy. There should be one meal a day that is loaded with carbohydrates. Consider dehydrating some favourite meals at home before your trip (read Appendix A for more information about this).

Routes and Trails

South
SECTION

Trail Legend

S1	Wade Lakes to Silver Creek (South)
S2	Onion Lake
S3	St. Elias Lake
S4	Mush Lake to Bates Lake to the Lowell Glacier
S5	Rock Glacier
S6	King's Throne
S7	Cottonwood Trail from Kathleen Lake to Louise and Johobo Lakes
S8	Sockeye Lake Trail (side trip)
S9	Campsite Lake (side trip)
S10	Shorty Creek
S11	Lowell Glacier Overland
S12	Quill Creek (South)
S13	Auriol Trail
S14	Dezadeash Wetlands Trail

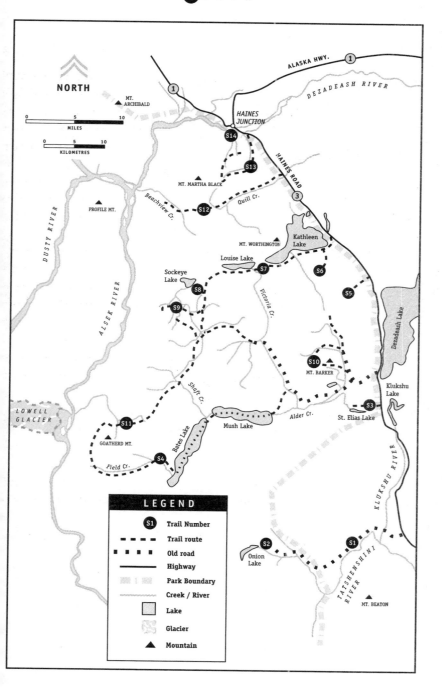

WADE LAKES TO SILVER CREEK (South)

Time: *6 to 8 hours to Wade Lakes, an additional 2 hours to Silver Creek.*

Distance: *12.4 kilometres (7.7 miles) from parking area to Wade Lakes; 16.4 kilometres (10.2 miles) to Silver Creek: Return same route. 9.5 kilometres (5.9 miles) from highway to parking area.*

Difficulty: *Easy to moderate*

Change in elevation: *244 metres (800 feet)*

Maximum elevation: *846 metres (2,775 feet)*

Topographical maps: *Silver Creek 115 A/3. A map is needed for interest's sake only. Otherwise, the trail is clear.*

Equipment needed: *Light hiking boots are sufficient to walk to the Wade Lakes and Silver Creek. Overnight gear is needed and a stove is recommended, but not essential. Maximum bear protection must be carried as this is a heavily populated area for grizzlies. Be aware of smells and read the entire section on bears.*

The route: This is an easy and interesting walk. It follows an unmaintained road past historical spots, an Indian village, and the Tatshenshini River. It ends at picturesque lakes abounding with wildlife.

0.0 km	Turnoff from Haines Road
6.0 km	Klukshu Creek and Dalton Post parking area
6.4 km	Dalton Post Meadows
7.4 km	Mud holes and parking area in dry weather
9.0 km	Nesketahin Village turnoff [UTM (85-67) Silver Cr]
10.5 km	Kane Creek
18.8 km	Wade Lakes
20.3 km	Meadows [UTM (76-61) Silver Cr]
22.8 km	Silver Creek

Trail access: Because this trail is such a long way from Haines Junction, it is best to stay at the Million Dollar Campsite and drive to Dalton Post in the morning. Register at the Information Centre in Haines Junction before heading out. Drive 5.4 kilometres (3.4 miles) north from the M.D. Campsite and turn left onto a gravel road. Continue for 6 kilometres (3.7 miles) down the "Drop of Doom" hill to the Tatshenshini River. Do not park or camp at the parking area because bear activity is high and even staying in a vehicle is not recommended. Continue over the bridge, past the fisheries station for another 0.4 kilometres (0.2 miles). You will come to Dalton Post Meadows where old log buildings and a picnic site are located. The original site of Jack Dalton's home, there were once eight buildings standing here.

Park here or, if the weather is dry, drive one more kilometre to an obvious mud hole where passage is not recommended with a two-wheel-drive vehicle. I have been told that four-wheel-drive vehicles can drive farther, but if rains are heavy, even a 4x4 could get stuck.

The trail: This is not a difficult trail and if you are intent on seeing bears, your best chance is along the Tatshenshini. There is a bear viewing platform, owned by Chuck Hume of Klukshu Village, from which you can safely watch bears fishing. The trail also opens up to good views of the adjacent Tatshenshini Provincial Park.

The trail is wide and clear but the sides are thick with willow and alder – so make lots of noise and carry the food canisters offered by the Parks service. This area has the highest concentration of bears in Kluane. Within the first hour of walking, there are three creek crossings, the last one being Kane Creek, which is usually deep but not swift. You will come to a road turning north (right) that leads to Nesketahin Indian Village [UTM (85-67) Silver Cr] where Jack Dalton was the first white man seen by this band of natives. Because of Dalton's colouring, the natives thought he was diseased and tried to avoid him. The following year, he returned with Edward Glave. The natives were then convinced that the white men were not sick. In 1892, the population of the village was near two hundred; by 1898 it had dropped to half that because of disease and trading disputes with tribes living in the Upper White River region.

The road passes close to the Tatshenshini River and then curves around and starts up a hill. Just before the hill is a viewing platform on the north (right). When the Kluane Range rose, the subsequent melt water flowed from the mountains and carved out the Tatshenshini valley. At present, mining companies looking for silver would like to punch through a road above the Tatshenshini River and over two salmon streams from Dalton Post to the park boundary at Silver Creek. They would mine in the subalpine and alpine hills above the river, which mining companies claim would be of no detriment to the Tatshenshini River.

Proceeding uphill, you will plow through the occasional willow grove blocking the trail. The groves are not long stretches. As the trail undulates more up than down you will get a few glances of the Tatshenshini before passing two bouldered slide slopes. Then the trail drops down to a delightful meadow – an excellent place to camp if not you're not continuing on to the Wade Lakes. Continue across the meadow and pick up the road on the opposite side. The Wade Lakes are about ten minutes farther.

At the Wade Lakes [UTM (78-61) Silver Cr], there is a partially decayed plywood picnic table and bench with a back rest. You may camp here or pitch a tent on some of the flat spots in the woods before the picnic table. There is also a cottonwood tree near the shore of the lake just in front of the picnic table, which can be climbed in the event of a passing bear. I sat in that tree for about an hour while a sow and her two cubs crossed over to the alpine hills behind the table. She had woofed at me to let me know that she was coming through.

The hills in front of the lake are low outcroppings that are covered in vegetation, but the mountain behind has jagged rocky peaks that can be climbed for a view of the area. Check the hills with binoculars and always make plenty of noise if bushwhacking. While sitting at the picnic table, facing the lake and looking to the west (right), the sides of a former rock glacier are visible. This is the slope to climb if you're continuing to Silver Creek.

The road deteriorates partway around the lake. Struggle up and over the two rocky slopes and find the road again. It remains clear all the way to Silver Creek. After rejoining the road, you will pass two more lakes; one is little more than a beaver pond. From the beaver pond, start the steep descent to Silver Creek.

There is an inhabitable cabin [UTM (76-60) Silver Cr] at the creek, on an active mining claim, that could give partial shelter during a bad storm. The roof has started to leak heavily, the interior furniture is disintegrating, and animals have moved in and destroyed most of the inside. There is a cute, but persistent, weasel who lets his presence be known soon after you arrive. Set up a camera.

Silver Creek, the park's boundary, is fast and cold. There is a fire pit, a few flat spots for tents, and a fair amount of wood close to the cabin or along the creek. Directly in front of the cabin there is a well-used trail that follows the creek.

On your return (or before leaving) explore Dalton Post Meadows and Nesketahin Village. In 1890, Jack Dalton crossed the Chilkat Pass along the Haines Highway and reached Nesketahin Village, where he was met by a visiting Chilkat chief. The South Tutchone who lived at Nesketahin were on the Alsek River fishing for salmon at the time. Dalton left and returned the following year and this time he met the people of the village.

British explorer Edward Glave returned to the area with Jack Dalton and together they convinced a native guide to take them north. Glave reported that travelling with a native guide was absolutely necessary while finding the route. Those that followed could dispense with guides. The two men proceeded to Sockeye Lake, the Alsek River, and the Jarvis River as they tried to find an easier route to Dawson City.

Dalton returned to Nesketahin in 1896 and started clearing bush for the 491 kilometres (305 miles) of the Dalton Trail between Haines and Fort Selkirk on the Yukon River, part of which is now the Haines Highway. The Chilkat Pass is between the Dalton Post and the Canadian border station towards Haines, Alaska. When Jack's trail was complete, he charged $2.50 per horse to pass and he patrolled the trail personally, carrying a loaded gun in case he needed to convince someone to pay the tariff. Many miners took this route on their way to the Dawson gold fields.

It did not take long for a small settlement to develop at Dalton Post, complete with an RCMP station. However, the lucrative business of Dalton's trail soon petered out as the gold rush declined. Dalton Post was abandoned in September of 1905. There is little left of the original buildings but a small graveyard can still be found.

Long before Jack Dalton arrived at Nesketahin, the South Tutchone lived there. They called the spot T'at Chua, which means "water goes under rocks." The name refers to the stream that runs through the centre of the village. At that time, it was larger and often full of spawning salmon. Coastal Chilkat natives came to Nesketahin to trade their blankets for the much-needed flint the South Tutchone took from the mountains nearby. Flint was used for tools and weapons by both groups.

 ONION LAKE

Time: *8 to 10 hours, one way from Silver Creek*
Distance: *10 kilometres (6.2 miles) to east end of lake*
Difficulty: *Difficult due to bushwhacking*
Change in elevation: *365 metres (1,198 feet)*
Maximum elevation: *1,035 metres (3,396 feet)*
Topographical maps: *Silver Creek 115 A/3. Since some of this route requires bushwhacking, a map and compass are essential.*
Equipment needed: *Bear canisters and spray are recommended. Prevent all smells and read the section on bears. A compass, overnight gear and supplies for five to six days are required. You must carry adequate rain gear, and wear boots with solid grip. The route is difficult.*

OUTH

The route: Follow the Wade Lakes-Silver Creek trail. The route to Onion Lake starts with bushwhacking through thick alder. However, once above tree line the possibilities for exploring are tremendous. The mountains on the north and south side of Onion Lake both have smaller lakes that beckon. You may also continue around Onion Lake and over to Wolverine and Iron Creeks where prospecting was active until the 1950s. This is an adventurer's paradise.

0.0 km	Silver Creek
0.8 km	Top of hill
1.1 km	Road
7.5 km	Unnamed creek flowing into Onion Lake [UTM (70-63) Silver Cr].
10. km	Onion Lake

Trail access: See Wade Lakes-Silver Creek route for a description of the trail to Silver Creek.

The trail: Once at the Silver Creek Cabin, the road follows the creek upstream for about a kilometre past the cabin. Cross the creek where a path branching to the left off the main road meets the creek. The path is directly in front of the cabin. During high water, this is a difficult creek to cross and you may have to go two or three kilometres upstream to find a suitable crossing. Once across, bushwhacking becomes difficult until the vegetation thins at a higher elevation. Before starting, however, pick your route and be certain to put on long pants, as the alders and birch will rip bare legs to shreds.

Looking across the creek, you will see bits and pieces of the road going uphill. Do not follow the road because it is overgrown and criss-crossed with deadfall. Go to the first gully directly south (left), downstream and on the other side of the creek from the cabin. Bushwhack up the gully. The nonvegetated cutbanks look inviting, but they are unstable. It will take at least an hour to get onto the hill by way of the gully. Once on top of the hill, turn north (right) and continue bushwhacking until you come to the road again. The vegetation on the top of the hill is willow and dwarf birch. The road appears and disappears continually all the way to Onion Lake. For the most part, it is not difficult to follow. The one troublesome area is close to the lake where the vegetation gets thick again and the road makes an "S" curve. You may feel that the road is going in the wrong direction, but it isn't. You can bushwhack across the "S" or follow the road.

George Davidson travelled up the Chilkat River, in the summer of 1869, so he could better see an eclipse of the sun. On the way, he met Chief Kohklux of the Chilkat Indians, who befriended Davidson and drew him the first map of the area which included Onion Lake. It took Chief Kohklux three days to include all the lakes, rivers, significant landmarks, and routes between Kluane Lake and Teslin, and Fort Selkirk and Klukwan. Although Davidson did not publish the map for thirty-two years, the information was tested and found accurate to the last detail. A man by the name of Wells, who was sponsored by the *Illustrated Newspaper* in 1890 was the next man to follow Kohklux's map into the interior.

Baneberries grow abundantly in this area. Be familiar with it because all parts of this plant are highly poisonous. As few as six berries can cause vomiting, diarrhea, and respiratory paralysis. The root word "bana" comes from the Anglo-Saxon word meaning "murderous." The red or white berries grow in clumps, from a bush with toothed, segmented leaves. There is an excellent illustration of this plant in *Plants of Northern British Columbia*, by MacKinnon, Pojar, and Coupe.

Onion Lake is one of the park's three landing strips for float planes. There is also a warden's cabin on the west end of the lake, but the vegetation around the lake is horrific for bushwhacking. The lake itself is 29 metres (95 feet) deep and is reputed to contain lake trout. The upper parts of the hills to the south of the lake are interesting and dotted with small lakes. Once above the vegetation, there are excellent views of the surrounding area. Most of the vegetation on the south sides of the hills is dwarf willow.

Onion Lake was a favourite fishing spot for the South Tutchone Indians. After the gold seekers started arriving, they expanded the natives' trails so they could enjoy some of these beautiful spots. The Tutchone traded with the coastal Tlingit for many things but the most valued commodity was oolichan grease. Extracting the oil from this fish, belonging to the smelt family, required ten to fourteen days of ripening. The fish sat in a pot of water and the water was heated with hot stones. As the fish boiled, the fat rose to the top and was scooped off. After the fish stopped releasing oil by this method, they were squeezed through baskets to release any further residue.

Although I did not hike to the lake, I did climb to the top of the hill on the far side of Silver Creek. The bushwhacking was difficult but, once on top, I found the area to be beautiful. There are numerous lakes to explore if branching from the main road to the alpine in the north. There is also a lake at the headwaters of Silver Creek that is not difficult to reach once past the canyon. I recommend passing the canyon along the hills to the west of the creek.

ST. ELIAS LAKE

Time: *1 to 2 hours one way*
Distance: *4 kilometres one way (2.5 miles)*
Difficulty: *Easy*
Change in elevation: *110 metres (361 feet)*
Maximum elevation: *890 metres (2,920 feet)*
Topographical maps: *Mush Lake 115 A/6. This map is needed for interest's sake only as the trail is clear and short.*
Equipment needed: *For a day hike, running shoes and some snacks are sufficient. There is water along the way unless it is a dry summer in which case the creeks can dry up. If staying overnight, you will need camping gear sufficient for a primitive campsite. Because wood is scarce, a stove is needed.*

The route: The maintained trail follows an old road. It goes up and down through a lovely valley to an alpine lake set between high mountains. There is a primitive campsite at the east end of the lake (where the trail meets the lake) complete with benches, a fire pit, toilets, and a bear cache. Tent sites are slightly back from the lake.

While hiking into this lake I was struck by what a wonderful place it would be to take children for their first backpacking experience. The distance is short and the rewards are great plus there is plenty of space for exploration once there. Highly recommended.

0.0 km   Park gate; park map of trail and lake
1.0 km   One of two lodgepole pine trees in the park
1.2 km   Park trail post and "Y" in road
2.0 km   Bridge and second trail post [UTM (85-89) Mush Lake]
4.0 km   Lake and campsite (2.5 miles)
         [UTM (84-88) Mush Lake]

Trail access: Drive south along the Haines Road for 60 kilometres (37 miles) from the Information Centre at Haines Junction. There is a park sign at the side of the road, 2 kilometres (1.2 miles) before the parking area. The trailhead is well marked and the parking area has a bear-proof garbage container. The trailhead has a park gate obstructing the passage of motorized vehicles.

The trail: The maintained trail has signposts for two kilometres. Take the right-hand fork in the road after the first kilometre post. At the second post, there is a bridge crossing a creek [UTM (85-89) Mush Lake]. This is the last spot for drinking water before the lake, but in the event of a hot summer the creek could be dry. From the bridge you will walk along the gently undulating valley floor. At 2.2 kilometres (1.4 miles) there is a viewpoint along a ridge. Looking below and to the right, there is a typical moose feeding ground. The early morning, and dusk are the best times to try to catch them feeding. Male moose can weight up to 815 kilograms (1,800 pounds) and have up to forty wives at one time – quite a harem.

There are numerous trails going each way around the lake and animal trails cross the main trail on their way to the lake. If you like to bushwhack, climbing the slopes around the lake will not present too much trouble. Midway up the south side of the lake is a draw that leads to a pass dropping into Gibbles Gulch. Going up Gibbles Gulch brings you to a rock glacier. This is a recommended day hike.

You may also continue to the west end of the lake about 2 kilometres farther and arrive at the Secret Lakes [UTM (82-88) Mush Lake]. This is a lovely side excursion, though the hillside is thick with willow and dwarf birch. Children should not be allowed to run through these willows alone in case a bear is on the trail.

Dolly Varden are reported to inhabit St. Elias Lake. There is a pebbly beach at the east end of the lake near the campsite, where children can play. Wood is scarce, however, so bring a stove.

Kluane's forests consist mainly of white spruce and white birch, but there are two lodgepole pine trees in the park. One of these is on a rocky outcrop beside the St. Elias Lake Trail. Look for it! It was planted for Canada Day in the 1980s.

Cow parsnip grows abundantly in the area. The young stems have always been eaten as a vegetable, cooked or raw, but care must be taken not to confuse this plant with the water hemlock, which is highly poisonous. Cow parsnip tastes like celery but feels like rhubarb.

MUSH LAKE TO BATES LAKE TO THE LOWELL GLACIER

Time: *8 to 10 days to the Lowell and back*
Distance: *155 kilometres (96 miles) return*
Difficulty: *Very difficult bushwhacking. Canoeing skills are needed if going all the way to the glacier. There is an overland route to the Lowell if you are unable to canoe.*
Change in elevation: *924 metres (3,031 feet)*
Maximum elevation: *1,600 metres (5,250 feet)*
Topographical maps: *Mush Lake 115 A/6, Cottonwood Lakes 115 A/5, and Bates River 115 A/4*
Equipment needed: *You will need a four-wheel-drive vehicle with high clearance to get a canoe to Mush Lake. Cabin Craft in Haines Junction rents canoes. No motors are allowed on the lakes. You will also need a map and compass, tent, rain gear, leather hiking boots, and food for about ten days. If you have your heart set on this trip, bring your own canoe because during a busy summer there may be none available for rent. See "The Lowell Glacier Overland" on p. 78 for a description of an equally challenging overland trip.*

The route: This is a difficult trip. It requires the use of a four-wheel-drive plus a canoe before starting the bushwhacking that is involved in getting to Goatherd Mountain and the glacier. However, once you are out of the willows above Bates Lake, the walk is spectacular. If you are planning to go only to Mush Lake, you may walk from the highway. The trail is described for walking purposes, but the distance is too great to carry a canoe.

There is high bear activity in this area and it is a long trip. Remember to prevent causing odours attractive to bears. *Read the section on bears.*

0.0 km	Dezadeash Lodge; drive
6.6 km	Alder Creek; 4-wheel-drive or walk to campsite [UTM (82-93) Mush Lk]
15.8 km	Dalton Creek; 4-wheel-drive or walk to campsite [UTM (74-90) Mush Lk]
29.0 km	Mush Lake; 4-wheel-drive or walk to campsite [UTM (69-88) Mush Lk]
40.3 km	Mush Lake warden's cabin; campsite [UTM (60-88) Cottonwood Lk]
40.8 km	River; portage
41.7 km	Bates Lake; campsite [UTM (59-87) Cottonwood Lk]
54.5 km	Bates Lake warden's cabin; campsite [UTM (53-76) Bates R]
57.8 km	Alpine above cabin
65.5 km	Lake at end of Field Creek Valley [UTM (40-77) Bates R]
77.5 km	Goatherd Mountain and Lowell Glacier [UTM (42-85) Cottonwood Lk]

Trail access: Drive 54.4 kilometres (33.8 miles) south along the Haines Road to the site of the old Beloud Post. Today, there are still buildings from Dezadeash Lodge but the lodge is closed. The road turns right and follows the Mush Lake Road, an old mining road first blazed by Dave Hume in 1944 and built by Murray in 1945. Drive behind the lodge in a northwesterly direction for about 1 kilometre (0.6 miles), until you pass a gate and a sign designating the park boundary. This is the start of the trail. Driving to Mush Lake with a four-wheel-drive is possible. You may also drive to the Shorty Creek turnoff, but the vehicle must have high clearance. This road may also be cycled with a mountain bike.

The trail: Continue along the road to the forks at the 2.8-kilometre sign. Take either fork as they join again a short distance ahead. At 5.5 kilometres (3.4 miles), there is a junction and a sign indicating the Shorty Creek Trail. Continue ahead.

Alder Creek is at kilometre 9.1, (5.7 miles) [UTM 82-93) Mush Lk] where there is pleasant camping. Crossing the creek is the first challenge of this trail whether on foot or in a truck. There are about 2 kilometres (1.2 miles) of creek bed that must be crossed. If the water is high, this can be difficult. Partway along the creek is a Youth Corps marker carved into a burl. This is where the kids built the first bridge in the park. Needless to say, the bridge has been washed out and only the marker is left. The Youth Corps have done a lot of work in the park including the building of two of the warden's cabins. The one at Bates Lake was built by sixteen girls.

It may be necessary to cross the creek up to three times. This is cold water and often the crossings are long. Once across Alder Creek for the last time, you will meet up with the Mush Lake Road again. There are park marker posts showing where the road joins up again. If crossing by truck, test the water level before crossing. Also, check with the interpreters for recent information on the water levels.

The next 11 kilometres (6.8 miles) can be a boring, mosquito-plagued walk through the forest. If driving, there are a few potholes and mud spots during wet weather. However the Parks branch is planning to upgrade this road in the near future. Camping is possible at any one of the numerous flat spots found close to water between Alder and Dalton Creek [UTM (74-90) Mush Lk]. Dalton Creek water is fresh and clear. There is a walking bridge across Dalton Creek. If driving, crossing Dalton Creek is not a problem unless the water is extremely high. Again, check with the interpreters for recent water levels. Dalton Creek was a popular camping site at one time. However, shepherdia berries are abundant in the area and since bears love these, it is not recommended to camp there during berry season.

From Dalton Creek to Mush Lake, the trail can be a bit difficult for

The Lowell Glacier

a truck. The road goes up a steep incline, hugging the rock face of the mountain while Mush Creek laps at the window on the other side. Walking is less stressful. However you go, Mush Lake soon comes into view [UTM (69-88) Mush Lk].

Mush Creek first produced gold for M. I. Christner in 1902 but the creek and lake were named by Charles Towl and his partner when they were prospecting in the area. While prospecting, meagre food stores often consisted of nothing more than bacon, beans, and porridge. Finally Towl and his buddy were left with only porridge, often referred to as "mush," and hence the name.

The Mush Lake Campsite is excellent. There is a privy, a fire pit, and plenty of room for tents. The site is about 4.5 metres (15 feet) from the lake and photographing sunsets from your tent door is recommended. Mush Lake is 64 metres (204 feet) deep and has lake trout, Dolly Varden, Kokanee, whitefish, and Arctic grayling so if fishing is your desire, you have a good chance casting from shore. A Parks fishing licence must be obtained for fishing in this, or any, lake in Kluane National Park. Mush Lake was originally believed to be part of Bates Lake, but was renamed when it was discovered that they were actually two separate lakes. If continuing to the Lowell Glacier, this is the start of the second phase of your trip.

To canoe Mush and Bates Lakes could take up to two days each way, due to high winds. Be certain to start early in the morning and canoe close to shore. Winds may start suddenly and they are often strong and dangerous. Due to land/water temperature differences, winds blow onto the shore during the day and off shore during the night. Winds from the glacier are strongest during the afternoons when temperature differences are the greatest.

Mush Lake is not as cold as Bates Lake because it is not glacier-fed. The trip up Mush Lake to the warden's cabin [UTM (59-87) Cottonwood Lk] takes about three hours on a calm lake. If you must get off the lake, there are sandy beaches, pebbly shores, and no high cliffs along the right-hand (north) side of the lake. The warden's cabin at the end of the lake is set on a sandy beach tucked into trees in a wind-protected bay. There are outhouses (complete with a mirror) and a bear cache. If you wish, you may stash your packs while portaging to the river's put-in spot.

To get to the portage, continue around the bay, past the warden's cabin to the next bay. Stay close to the right-hand side, along a shallow, weedy shore, until you come to a park marker indicating the portage. It is close to the river's mouth. Do not attempt to canoe the river from the lake as there is a huge boulder in the centre of a narrow passage that prohibits manoeuvring. Even in low water, this is not a good place to canoe. The portage is easy and only about 100 metres (330 feet) along a wide and well maintained trail. Put back into the river below the rapids and enjoy the meander along the river to Bates Lake. If the winds are high, it is warmer to stay near the warden's cabin overnight and proceed down the river in the morning. Finishing the portage during the day and starting across Bates Lake before dawn is also a good option. There is a sheltered spot to pitch tents at the mouth of the river, just before the shores of Bates Lake.

Bates Lake is considered dangerous because of the unpredictable winds but it is truly a beautiful lake to explore when calm. The bottom is flat but packed with glacial silt and sediment. The lake, fed from Mush Lake, drains into Iron Creek (which carries the run-off from an icefield) and Wolverine Creek by way of the Bates River. These waters then flow into the Alsek River. Iron Creek was originally worked by B. Beloud and K. Chambers, who built a cabin on it in the 1950s. With luck, you will see a family of trumpeter swans living the good life around the river or lake. Bates Lake also has many sandy beaches with driftwood for fires.

During the prospecting years, rafts were made from barrels and used to ferry materials over Mush and Bates Lakes. Men by the name of Gibbons and McDougal were responsible for building these rafts. Gibbons, in the 1950s, built a cache on the south end of Bates Lake while he prospected on Iron and Wolverine Creeks. I have never located the cache, but there is a barrel on the shore of Bates Lake at the mouth of the river.

Along the right-hand shore of the lake are sandy beaches but there are also rock cliffs. Do not canoe across the centre of the lake in case a wind starts to blow. The first set of islands are rocky and uninviting for camping. One of the small islands [UTM (57-84) Cottonwood Lk] is overpopulated with seagulls that will certainly come to see what you are doing on their usually deserted lake. Wear a hat.

Bates Lake is named after Robert Bates, one of the first mountaineers to explore the St. Elias range. He is credited with exploring, in 1935, Mount Hubbard and Mount Alverstone, both near the Lowell Glacier. Bates, then under the leadership of Bradford Washburn, made the first air flight into the region. They are also credited with taking the area's first comprehensive aerial photo. During this trip, Bates and Washburn split company and Bates walked out to Whitehorse, while Washburn waited for the plane to return and fly him out.

Bates made his second flight into the region to the Walsh Glacier, so that he could climb Mount Lucania, which stands at 5,226 metres (17,147 feet). A severe thaw prevented the pick-up plane from landing, so the men had to walk out, crossing Mount Steele on the way. Once at the Donjek River they were unable to cross below the glacier due to high water, so they had to walk another twenty miles across the toe to the headwaters of the Donjek. There they managed to find some packhorses to take them out to Burwash. Bates did not return to the area until 1941, when he and six other men had air assistance both ways. This was the beginning of air-assisted mountaineering in Kluane.

Stay on the right-hand (west) side of the lake, while paddling around the corner to the end. The Bates Lake warden's cabin [UTM (53-76) Bates R], a plywood shack in the wilderness, was built by sixteen Youth Corps girls. It sits a little way into the bush. Even though one cannot get into the cabin, the sight of it is comforting. The last time my companion and I went this route, we met the warden at Mush Lake. When we were leaving, he informed us that we were the only people beyond his cabin. We felt like Christopher Columbus sailing off the edge of the world. It was pretty scary and the comfort of the cabin at the end of Bates Lake dispelled some of our insecurity.

The cabin is set in an open field surrounded by trees, which protect the area from the wind. There is a fire pit and both a men's and women's privy. Very necessary when you are the last two people on earth! The picnic table was a great luxury.

To reach Field Creek Valley, I suggest bushwhacking directly above the warden's cabin to the alpine. Set your compass in a northwesterly direction and start climbing. The willows are thicker than the snow in winter, and you will rarely see daylight through the density of the trees. Climbing from the warden's cabin, look for the first canyon past the highest peak. Go to the *north* side of that canyon and keep working upward until you are in the alpine of Field Creek Valley. The steepness decreases when going up the valley. Once in the alpine and out of the trees, there are many places to camp. The bushwhacking will take three to four hours and the walk up the valley will take another twelve to sixteen, depending on your walking speed.

Another choice, if the weather is foggy and visibility is poor, is to follow Field Creek, which flows behind the cabin. Go to the trail in the field beside the warden's cabin. Cross the field and turn right, continuing through a corridor of open meadows and low bush until you reach the creek – in about half an hour. Cross the creek beside a cairn and proceed up the creek. Going along the south side is easier for a short while. When the creek becomes impassable, cross the creek and bushwhack up as high as possible. There are impassable canyons on Field Creek so you must get out of the creek bed. Once past the canyons, near the fork of the creek [UTM (50-79) Bates River], the valley opens and becomes alpine. When you reach the fork in the creek, stay along the south fork (on your left). Follow Field Creek Valley all the way to the Alsek River. Once in the valley past the fork, the walking is easy and getting lost is not likely.

Once at the lakes near the upper end of the valley [UTM (40-77) Bates R], start veering north. Field Creek Valley has creek gullies and scree slopes, bald hills and grass-covered slopes. At the end of the valley the contrast between the lush green valley and the austere dark mountains is the most extreme that I have ever seen. You will stand on the verdant alpine floor and look across the Alsek to the ice and black rock of the icefield ranges. They appear to be just across the street from where you are standing. Camping beside any of the tiny lakes at this end of the valley is recommended. Leave big packs at the lakes and finish the hike with only a day pack.

Another option is to leave packs at a huge rock on the valley floor, about 4 kilometres (2.5 miles) before the last group of lakes. The packs would be safe from the low bush and high bush grizzlies. However, this spot is not close to a lake so camping is not the best. From the rock, it takes about one day to go to the ridge in front of Goatherd Mountain and back again.

Before going to Goatherd Mountain [UTM (42-85) Cottonwood Lk], first catch your breath, take pictures, and enjoy your personal gods. Then stay on the valley floor until you are past the little lakes. Veer north from there but climb from the valley slowly. It is 8 kilometres (5 miles) from the unnamed lakes to the draw between Goatherd Mountain and the ridge in front of the Lowell Glacier. Although the walk is not difficult, it is a long day trip from the lakes and even longer from the rock. The change in elevation is only 245 metres (800 feet) from the lakes to the ridge. There are many campsites between the lakes and the ridge with clear-water creeks trickling past. Once in the alpine, choices are plentiful.

Continuing north for about three to four hours, there is a draw from which to climb the ridge. Pass Goatherd Mountain, the pyramid-shaped peak without vegetation. The ridge past and in front of Goatherd is where you want to go. Once there, climb as high as you wish in order to enjoy the astounding view of the Lowell, a 72-kilometre (45-mile) long valley glacier. Partway up the draw is a creek that must be crossed. It is not difficult. Once between the ridge and

Goatherd, continue in a northeasterly direction, going into the valley on the north side of Goatherd Mountain. When about halfway into the valley, take the steep but possible climb to the top of the ridge. Going up Goatherd is not recommended because the scree mountain is too steep. Shallow soil layers in varying depths and composition, due to mass wasting and frost action, put it at high risk of erosion. Goatherd is also classified as a Zone 1 area, so access is restricted. Even in dry weather, you would not safely be able to go as high as you can on the ridge. The ridge north of Goatherd is 0.75 kilometres (0.5 miles) closer to the glacier and only sixty metres (195 feet) lower than the mountain. The ridge is grassy with a gentle slope until close to the top where there is a six hundred meter climb in half a kilometre.

You will see the glacier, however, long before reaching the ridge. You may also walk toward the Alsek River from the little unnamed lakes [UTM (40-77) Bates R] and enjoy the view from the cliff's edge. Plan on spending time at this end of the valley, as the Lowell Glacier and the Alsek River are spectacular. Also, you worked hard to get here. There are many clear-water creeks around the ridge and Goatherd Mountain, so if you're planning a rest day, this is the place to do it. The scenery and serenity will remain in your memory forever.

The Alsek River has been paddled by Walt Blackader, one of North America's most daring kayakers and the only person known to have paddled the entire river. He says, "I want any kayakers to read my words well: The Alsek gorge is unpaddleable!" The limestone and granite walls, towering a thousand feet above the river, are twelve miles below the glacier. A two-thousand-foot wall rises above the river near its confluence with the Tatshenshini.

Glaciation occurs when snow crystallizes and moves, causing erosion and deposition; this alters the landscape. Kluane's glacial landforms originated between 29,000 to 12,500 years ago, and minor advances have occurred as recently as 2,800 years ago.

The Lowell Glacier was named in 1908 after Abbott Lawrence Lowell, a president of Harvard University. About 150 years ago the Lowell Glacier surged against the face of Goatherd Mountain, blocking the Alsek River. Water backed up and completely flooded the area to Haines Junction. Eventually, the combination of water and pressure wore away the ice dam. When it broke, the lake waters tore through the valleys of Kluane and out towards the Pacific Ocean. It is believed that the flow swept away an Indian village, killing many. Some prospectors were also drowned. The Lowell's recent surges were small: one occurred in 1953 and the last one occurred in 1984. Beach ridges can be seen in many places in the park, but are especially visible on the Alsek Trail.

Bob Randall is given credit for landing the first plane, a Fokker Super Universal (CF-AAM) with skis, on the Lowell Glacier in 1935. Today, the Alsek River at the toe of the Lowell is one of the three landing spots permitted in the park. However, this is not a popular spot for float planes because the icebergs, which break off from the glacier, causing landing hazards. Helicopters are considered safer for this landing.

S5 ROCK GLACIER

Time: *1 hour return*
Distance: *1.5 kilometres (1 mile) return*
Difficulty: *Easy*
Change in elevation: *30 metres (98.5 feet)*
Maximum elevation: *793 metres (2,602 feet)*
Topographical maps: *Mush Lake 115 A/6 [UTM (87-03) Mush Lk]*
Equipment needed: *Flat-soled shoes, a jacket on a cool day, and a camera. Water should be carried on a warm day.*

The route: This easy walk has interpretive signs along the way that explain the physics of rock glaciers, plus some other important aspects of the area. It is a trail for hikers of any age.

0.0 km   Trailhead at highway
0.1 km   Boardwalk
0.8 km   Toe of glacier

Trail access: Drive 44 kilometres (27 miles) south from Haines Junction on the Haines Road. There is a park sign on the highway indicating the trail.

The trail: This is a well maintained trail that requires only runners or flat shoes. However, there are no hot dog stands or water fountains. The South Tutchone Indians called this spot "Azuch an D akwa'yu," which means "different steps." The name is derived from the waves or steps of the glacier.

The boardwalk along this trail was built by the same man, Henry Henkel, who built the Canada Creek Bridge and the log church in Haines Junction. Follow the boardwalk over a creek and some wetlands, and then the sawdust path to the stone steps. These lead to the toe of the glacier. Lichen on the rocks indicate centuries of glacial inactivity. The ridges of the glacier are caused by compression forces of the ice that was underneath. The ridges may be lateral or terminal but are present on all rock glaciers.

Rock glaciers are formed at the base of steep slopes and are cemented by talus and interstitial ice found below the rock. The glacial ice grinds its way down the mountain and rocks accumulate on top. This glacier is dead which means that it is no longer moving even though ice is still melting from underneath. The vegetation visible on the rocks is young but permanent. If you took a picture today and compared it with one taken twenty years from now, there would be a noticeable change.

Once at the top of the glacier, the views are of Dezadeash Lake and the Shakwak Trench, a distinct trench lying on the Denali Fault. The south end of the trench is at Dezadeash Lake.

Look for bear root, or Indian potato, a plant with a pea-like flower and rosy purple vines. These plants like to grow on open gravel patches or beside trails. In the past, natives collected the root in autumn and cooked it like a potato. As the name suggests, the natives were not the only ones who liked the plant.

S6 KING'S THRONE

Time: *4 to 6 hours return*
Distance: *10 kilometres (6.2 miles) return*
Difficulty: *Moderately strenuous*

Change in elevation: *457 metres (1,500 feet) to rock glacier, 1228 metres (4,030 feet) to summit*
Maximum elevation: *1,990 metres (6,529 feet)*
Topographical maps: *Kathleen Lakes 115 A/11*
Equipment needed: *Good runners will suffice if hiking to the bowl but boots are recommended if going to the summit. Carry water, as there is none at the top. Rain gear is also necessary because the weather can change rapidly. The winds near the top can be intimidating.*

The route: The Sierra Club laid over 2 kilometres (1.2 miles) of trail along this route in 1994, making it safer, easier, and less damaging to the environment. The volunteers, mostly Americans, worked for weeks to reconstruct the route to the tongue of the rock glacier, making the walk accessible to more people. The Sierra Club has been in operation for more than forty years, constructing, cleaning, and restoring trails in North America. The King's Throne [UTM (79-15) Kathleen Lk] is a steep climb and should not be done on a windy day, as the intensity of the wind increases near the top. Walking on top would then become difficult and dangerous, especially if carrying a large pack. Even on a good day, bad weather can come over the mountains quickly, obstructing the views. When this happens, the Throne is a dangerous route.

0.0 km   Trailhead at Kathleen Lake; shelter
1.0 km   81-km sign and the King's Throne Trailhead
4.0 km   Tongue of Rock Glacier
5.0 km   Cirque inside the "throat"

Trail access: Drive south from Haines Junction along the Haines Road for 32 kilometres (20 miles) until you get to the Kathleen Lake campsite. There are large signs along the highway indicating the turnoff. Continue along the road toward the covered shelter and public access to the lake. Just before the shelter, there is a small parking area where the trailhead is situated along an old mining road. There is a gate across the road. A sign showing some pictures of the area is beside the gate.

The trail: The mountain is called King's Throne because that's what it looks like from across the highway. Walk from the gate, behind the

Kathleen Lake shelter, and along the mining road to a stream running under the trail. Here water containers may be filled. Walk another few minutes to a log bench with a view of the lake and a trail going to the left. There is a carved wooden post indicating the turnoff for the King's Throne. The other marker indicates the 81-kilometre (50-mile) sign along the Cottonwood Trail. Follow the route up the mountain.

The Parks service maintains this trail, making it easy to follow. The trail is relatively flat for the first fifteen minutes then starts to switchback toward the tongue of the glacier. The views begin within fifteen minutes of climbing. There are a few cairns to follow, but the trail is clear to the alpine meadow on the left-hand side of the tongue. Cross the taste buds of the tongue and enter the cirque area. You must pick your own way once inside the cirque.

The Auriol Range and Kathleen Lake can be seen from the top of the rock glacier. Mount Worthington is the peak on the far side of Kathleen Lake. It sits at 2,170 metres (7,113 feet). The striations on the side of the mountains going west along Kathleen Lake are superb. They are caused by subterranean pressures that move the rocks.

To the east is the Dezadeash Range with Granite Mountain rising above the rest. Native folklore states that a man was murdered on Granite Mountain and the murderer was sentenced to death. However, the person responsible for inflicting the punishment was unable to perform the deed, so the village of Klukshu was given as compensation to the chief of the Crow clan, the group to whom the dead man belonged. To this day, the village belongs to the Crow clan.

To go to the summit, continue up the main ridge along the left side of the mountain. Again, be aware of the winds and oncoming weather as they can be dangerous. It is not unusual to encounter snow on the summit.

The descent, like the ascent, is steep and dangerous in certain areas. Follow the cairns to the Sierra Club trail. If uncertain, go to the centre of the tongue and pick up the trail from there. Remember that this is new ground being formed and damage to vegetation could take up to a hundred years to repair. Walk carefully. Erosion will not be a problem on this mountain as long as hikers remain on the trail.

COTTONWOOD TRAIL FROM KATHLEEN LAKE TO LOUISE AND JOHOBO LAKES

Time: *4 to 5 days with no side trips*
Distance: *75.4 kilometres (46.9 miles); ranger station says 85 kilometres*
Difficulty: *Easy to moderate*
Change in elevation: *512 metres (1,680 feet)*
Maximum elevation: *1,220 metres (4,003 feet)*
Topographical maps: *Kathleen Lakes 115 A/11, Auriol Range 115 A/12, Mush Lake 115 A/6, Cottonwood Lakes 115/A5. The 1:50,000 maps are recommended. However, some people find the 1:250,000 Dezadeash Map sufficient because the Cottonwood is a marked and maintained trail.*
Equipment needed: *Bear canisters and bear spray are recommended as there is an abundance of both black bears and grizzlies along this trail. Light boots are sufficient unless you are planning side trips. Water is available all along the trail. Creek-crossing shoes are advisable. Be certain to have a stove for the alpine areas, a good tent, and rain gear. If a ride from the end of the trail back to your car is needed, make arrangements for pick-up at Kluane Park Adventure Centre. You can also park your vehicle near Alder Creek, at the end of this route. Vehicles with high clearance can drive part way up Mush Lake Road to Alder Creek; four-wheel-drives can make it all the way to Mush Lake. Should you arrive at the end of the trail late in the day, staying at the Dezadeash campsite 1 kilometre (0.6 miles) north along the highway is recommended. This trail may be done in either direction. Due to high bear activity in this area take all precautions to prevent odours that may be attractive to bears. Read the entire section on bears.*

The route: This is the park's Cadillac of trails and one of its most popular. It is a fairly easy, four-day hike along a maintained trail with interesting mining history, and beautiful scenery. The wheelchair-accessible boardwalk skirting the edge of Kathleen Lake is called the Kokanee Trail. If not doing the entire hike, walking around the lake for a few hours or camping at Goat Creek for one night and returning the same way is pleasant. In that case, runners instead of boots are sufficient.

If you do not have a vehicle at the end of the trail, one option is to book the pick-up van from Kluane Park Adventure Centre. They charge a dollar a mile (one way) for as many as eight people. Hitchhiking is difficult along this road, as the traffic consists mainly of Alaska-bound motor homes, the crew of which seem to be afraid of hikers. I don't think that our smell has anything to do with it – they are just paranoid about bush bunnies. Locals will pick up hikers, but locals are not that abundant. We once met a couple at the Dalton Creek Bridge campsite who were hiking in the opposite direction to us. They had a car at the Dezadeash Lodge and we had a car at the Kathleen Lake parking area. Since we were closest to the end of the trail, they gave us their keys and we drove their car to the Kathleen Lake parking area. Then we hid their keys in a prearranged spot and got our car. This made it convenient for both of us.

0.0 km	Kokanee Trail at day-use cabin
0.9 km	Small creek
2.2 km	Small beach on lake
8.2 km	Goat Creek; campsite [UTM (73-14) Kathleen Lk]
9.5 km	Primitive campsite
16.0 km	Victoria Creek and campsite [UTM (67-12) Kathleen Lk]
16.2 km	Louise Lake
27.9 km	Johobo Lake and mine site; campsite [UTM (58-08) Cottonwood Lk]
33.6 km	Cottonwood Flats; campsite [UTM (57-04) Cottonwood Lk]
35.2 km	Unnamed creek and Cottonwood River; good campsite [UTM (58-01) Cottonwood Lk]
44.0 km	Beloud Creek [UTM (65-00) Mush Lk]
45.0 km	Virgin Creek [UTM (65-00) Mush Lk]
47.1 km	Dalton Creek [UTM (67-00) Mush Lk]
59.6 km	Dalton Creek Bridge; campsite [UTM (74-90) Mush Lk]
68.8 km	Alder Creek Flats; campsite [UTM (92-81) Mush Lk]
75.4 km	Dezadeash Lake; campsite

Trail access: Drive south from Haines Junction along the Haines Road for 32 kilometres (20 miles) to the Kathleen Lake campsite. There are park signs along the highway indicating the turnoff. If you are not staying at one of the 41 campsites nestled among the trees, continue along the road toward the covered shelter near the lake. Just before the shelter, there is a parking area beside the trailhead at the beginning of an old mining road. A park gate obstructs the road. A sign showing pictures of the area is beside the gate. The photo of the creek-crossing at Victoria Creek is misleading to say the least.

The trail: Kathleen Lake's steep, trench-like shape was formed by receding glaciers. The southern shore of Kathleen drops quickly to a depth of 111 metres (364 feet). Motorboats are allowed on Kathleen Lake. From the trailhead, walk along the mining road that soon passes over a small creek where water bottles should be filled. However, if you do not wish to carry water for this first section, there is no problem getting water once past Kathleen Lake. You will not go more than one hour without passing a stream, even during dry weather or late in the season when water levels are lower. There are service roads branching off the main trail but ignore them. Continue along the main road. Half an hour past the first creek is a fork with a carved wooden marker indicating the 81-kilometre (50-mile) spot. In fact, it is only 75 kilometres (47 miles) to the other end of the trail, but by the time you have finished the hike it will feel like 81 kilometres. The other trail goes to the King's Throne.

Where the trail joins the lake, there is a pebbly beach with driftwood logs to sit against and red sunsets to photograph. The trail continues beside the lake. There are many species of birds along this stretch. Some places pass close to the lake and beside steep, scree slopes. Due to constant erosion and snow slides, the trail is difficult to maintain along this section. Continue following the lake. After about 7 kilometres (4.3 miles) or two hours, start veering away from the lake and cutting across to the peninsula. This leads to Goat Creek. There is a "No Snowmobiles" marker indicating the trail through the trees.

Goat Creek [UTM (73-14) Kathleen Lk] must be forded and is often quite low. However, during rainy periods the water may be high and the rocks slippery. Don't let the appearance of the creek fool you.

The water is cold and swift. This is where I spent my first hiking day, a few years ago, drying gear. I had turned sideways one step before reaching the creek's far bank. I was swept off my feet and fifty feet down the creek before I could save myself. There is a fire ring on the far side of Goat Creek where you may camp for the night, dry your gear out as I did, or make tea. This was a popular area for miners sluicing for gold but now such activities are not permitted. The miners did not become rich with their finds. One of them, Dick Dickson, with another prospector and chief guide, built a cache on this creek to store food for when they travelled into more remote areas.

The trail returns to Kathleen Lake and soon comes to a primitive campsite tucked into the bushes. Here there are benches, a toilet, a few tent sites, a bear cache, and fire pits. This is a recommended site; those who have only a day to enjoy the lake and would like to be away from people may like to spend the night at the site. The mountains across the lake from Goat Creek have striations showing how the subterranean pressures caused the rock to tilt, bend, and sink.

There are Kokanee salmon found in this chain of lakes. If you choose to fish you must have a Park fishing permit. Fishing in Sockeye Lake farther along is not allowed. The campsite is protected from the winds that are constant in the area.

Between Kathleen Lake and Victoria Creek is an area of aspen parkland, which has stunted balsam poplars. It looks like farmland going back to bush. The reason for their existence is not known, but it is definitely a parkland and different from most of the terrain in the area. Once past the balsam poplar grove you are close to Victoria Creek. There is little water available between Goat and Victoria Creeks, so carry water.

The camping area near Victoria Creek [UTM (67-12) Kathleen Lk] is situated for those who want to cross the creek in the morning, when water levels are lower. This can be a dangerous creek-crossing. At one time there was a cable for people to hold while crossing, but it has been removed by the Parks service. Now it is advisable to cross in the morning and cross near the lake. This creek can be waist-deep, cold, and swift. Reconnoitre and find the widest section of the creek, as this will be the shallowest. Be certain that you are rested, warm, and psychologically ready. Once you're across, the most difficult part of this hike is over.

In 1972, after remains of moose that had been killed by wolves were found along this section of the trail, it was suggested that the trail should be diverted to avoid disturbing the wolves. But this was never done so you may want to watch for signs of these magnificent animals. At one time the natives killed wolf cubs because the wolves were in direct competition for the caribou. This was an early form of wildlife management.

Conditions may permit crossing Victoria Creek late in the day. If so, many suitable campsites may be found farther along the trail. There are creeks running through old wooden culverts under the road between Victoria Creek and Sockeye Lake turnoff. This part of the trail still runs along a mining road that rolls gently up and down hills, through wooded areas, and above Louise Lake. The next watering hole past Victoria Creek is about an hour up the road, so carry water if the day is hot.

There is a good camping spot past an avalanche slope, between the slope and the next unnamed creek, on the left near the creek. Camping there is comfortable and it allows exploration of the mine site and Sockeye Lake.

Continuing west (straight) along the smaller trail leads to Sockeye Lake. The next junction off the main trail goes to either Johobo Mines on the left or Johobo Lake on the right. Johobo Lake is a muddy pond and not as pretty as Sockeye Lake. Johobo's shoreline is swampy, but abundant with moose tracks.

Going to the left are the remains of the old Johobo mine site and a boarded-up mine shaft on the side of the hill. Johobo was first discovered in 1950, staked in July of 1956, and re-staked in June of 1958. During that period, Johannes, Honing, and Boyed, the company from which the mine takes its name, mined 150 tons of ore from the southern area of the vein. In 1959, Honing discovered the north showing. In August and September of 1959, Conwest drilled four holes and then transferred the claims to the Johobo Mining Company. They shipped 750 tons of ore in December. The following May to November, Cerro de Pasco Corporation drilled seven holes into the north showing. Johobo mined 650 tons during 1960 and found a third deposit nearby. The new find produced 600 tons of ore by March of 1961. All in all, three deposits were found between 1959 and 1961 in an area a half

Brian Bakker, from Kluane's trail crew and Andrew Lawrence, Park Warden, are always ready to offer advice or assistance to hikers.

mile long, which produced 2,585 tons of ore containing 23% copper and 2 ounces of silver per ton. Most of the copper and all the silver was shipped to Japan. In 1961, 1,062 tons of ore was shipped to Tacoma, Washington and contained 20.2% copper and 1 ounce of silver per ton. The company continued to explore and survey until 1969, and in 1971 some trenching was finally done. The mining in the area was never a large moneymaker. This type of mining continued sporadically until the property was sold to the Crown in 1975.

Some of the old timbers around the mine site have been burned. Such things are considered artifacts and damaging them could net you a fine up to $1,000. Leave all man-made objects where you find them.

The trail continues through a spruce forest. The red-tinted trees are dying from an infestation of the spruce beetle. It is along the side of this hill that the mine shaft is located. There are carved wooden park signs indicating the direction of the Cottonwood Trail. These are the famous Henkel signs.

The next section is a pleasant stroll to the Cottonwood Flats where more of the famous Henkel trail markers show directions. Besides constructing the log church in Haines Junction, Henkel worked for the parks and made the signs with a chain-saw. In the 1980s, Parks Canada decided to replace his signs with the bright orange metal ones because they were easier to see. However, after complaints from park users, the Parks service is reverting back to the Henkel signs, which blend better with the environment.

Before the flats is a small creek with logs to walk across. This is the creek bed where I had my scariest grizzly bear encounter. Sitting in the creek bed, I was about to put a cup of coffee to my lips when I looked over my shoulder and saw a young grizzly also wanting a sip. He was no more than three metres behind me. I jumped to the opposite side of the creek and behaved aggressively by yelling, thus breaking all the rules I advocate. My companion did the same; if you are going to intimidate a grizzly, you may as well be unanimous. When the bear went back into the bush, we packed up, and I stuck the porridge, still uneaten and in the pot, into my pack. The bear followed the scent of the porridge down the trail until we met the trail crew who were working near the mine site. For obvious personal reasons, I do not recommend the creek as a camping spot.

Water is available at Cottonwood Flats [UTM (57-04) Cottonwood Lk] if you wish to camp there. Continue up the flats, around the first hill of the Dalton Range, to a large draw through which the trail obviously passes. There is a park sign at the end of Cottonwood Flats and another at the creek, indicating the trail direction. This is the beginning of the trail's alpine area. Before the alpine, the trail climbs up the draw to where the creek meanders through some willows. This is known grizzly area, so make lots of noise and always be alert for signs such as fresh scat or nipped-off fireweed flowers.

Fireweed, the Yukon's flower, and its brother the willowherb, both grow abundantly in the park. When the plant is young, the roots and stems are edible. Natives combined the flower fluff with dog or goat hair for padding and weaving. Some natives dried the stem peelings and twisted them into a twine that they used to make fishing nets.

Before turning up the hill, follow the creek to its confluence with Dalton Creek and the Cottonwood River. There is excellent camping at the confluence. The unnamed creek flowing from the opposite shore leads to the Lowell Overland route.

Continue following Dalton Creek until it meets the headwaters of

Victoria Creek, which is usually a trickle at this point and not the raging torrent crossed a few days earlier. However, it *can* be a raging torrent if the rains have been heavy.

The trail continues through meadows and balsam poplar forests above Victoria Creek. While hiking, check out the crevices on the right and to the south. There is a super rock glacier with its huge tongue spewing downward. The trail continues gently up the slope to the alpine. Camping in the alpine requires a stove. Since this area is so popular, try to pick a gravel (less fragile) spot.

Beloud and Virgin Creeks enter Victoria Creek near the beginning of the alpine area. Virgin Creek was originally mined by a man named Pringle and then, in about 1917, by a mining company from Haines, Alaska. After passing Virgin Creek, you will enter an alpine plateau.

In the alpine and near the plateau is a trench with Victoria Creek below, to the south. Do not cross the plateau; you will not only damage more of the alpine, but the descent will be steep and difficult compared to the west end of the plateau. There are numerous trails on this section where people have gone too far along the plateau. Instead, follow the trail to the right and down the gully to creek level. There are some wooden park markers, but they are difficult to spot. At the creek you will join the Mush Lake mining road. There are a few spots along the river to camp. The water in the river is clear, cold, and swift. If you plan to camp here, be aware of the soap berries and remember that bears love them. Many black and grizzly bears live in the area.

Soap berries form translucent-red clusters on a shrub with oval leaves. The Indians make "soopalalie" or "Indian ice-cream" from them. The berries are whipped into a white froth and then sugar is added. However, beside the fact that they are illegal to pick in the park, you won't be able to carry enough sugar to sweeten this berry to most people's tastes. I have a friend who made soopalalie and added a cup of sugar to half a cup of whipped berries, divided this in half and added another cup of sugar, then divided this in half again and added another cup of sugar. After all this mixing and dividing, she threw it out because the concoction was still too bitter to eat. I advise you to leave them for the bears.

The road follows Victoria Creek to a log crossing. If you stay beside the creek, there is a small lake around the side of the hill and about 2 kilometres (1.2 miles) beyond the log crossing. If you would like to go there, do not cross the creek but proceed along the road on the west side of it. The road continues beside the hill for 0.5 kilometres (0.3 miles) and then peters out. I am not certain if the bushwhacking is difficult, as I didn't hike to the lake.

Once you're across Victoria Creek, start up Dalton Creek. You must cross Dalton Creek twice: once at the bottom of the hill and again a few metres up the hill. Do not try to go up and over the hill before the first crossing, as it becomes steep and boggy. Once over Dalton Creek, the trail meanders along the alpine, crossing many little creeks until Mush Lake comes into view with the cold Kluane Range, far in the background framing the lush green valley of Mush Lake. There is also a rock glacier spewing out from between two mountains along this section of the road. To climb higher and have a better view of Mush and Bates Lakes, climb the last mountain in the valley that sits on the right (to the west). Take either the second last or last large draw for easy access to the top of the mountain. It is not a long climb and it is well worth the effort. The rest of the valley consists of tundra vegetation, low bryoids mixed with *Dryas integrifolia, Cassiope, Mertensia paniculata,* and an abundant number of different grasses.

Once you see Mush Lake and leave Dalton Creek, there is no water again for about 4 kilometres (2.5 miles) until you join Dalton Creek again. This section of the trail is pleasant. At the bottom of the hill, there is a trail sign that gives distances. Going right leads to Mush Lake, where there is a comfortable campsite (see Mush Lake-Lowell Glacier trail description, p. 46). The road is used by trucks and mountain bikes. Going left takes you to Dezadeash Lake and the highway.

To cross Dalton Creek use the log bridge on the left, which is not visible until you're near the water's edge. Don't ford the stream; many people do not see the bridge until after they have crossed the creek. Across the bridge there was once a convenient campsite for those going either way along the trail. There were about five fire rings and lots of driftwood along the river. It is no longer recommended to camp at this site during berry season, as the shepherdia berry is ubiquitous and bears haunt the area looking for the food. However, the fresh water is a treat, especially if you have spent some time camping on the muskeg or near a swamp. The site is close to civilization and a wash may be in order.

Remember to carry all wash water at least 30 metres (98 miles) away from the stream before discarding.

The trail from Dalton Creek follows the Mush Lake Road. This can be a long, boring walk and you may be plagued with mosquitoes. It is about 12 kilometres (7.5 miles) to the highway. There is another creek-crossing with a walking bridge and campsite. The area on the west side of the second creek is more comfortable than the area on the east side.

The last challenge of the trail is at 68.8 kilometres (42.8 miles). This is where Alder Creek drains onto the road. There are about 2 kilometres (1.2 miles) of creek bed and crossings that must be passed. Alder Creek was the first creek to be mined in the park in the late 1800s. The creek was mined all the way to Shorty Creek.

Before the mining days, Alder Creek was a route the natives followed in search of moose. The Tutchone usually boiled the meat of large animals in birch bark containers, in which water was kept hot with heated rocks. Only small game was cooked directly on an open fire.

Along the creek there is a Youth Corps marker carved into a burl. This is where the kids built the first bridge in the park in 1977, but the bridge has long been washed out and only the marker is left. The Youth Corps has done a lot of work in the park, including the construction of two of the warden's cabins. From the marker, continue down the creek, crossing about three times. It is cold water and often the crossings are long. If you have neoprene booties, you can save time by keeping them on instead of changing back and forth to your boots. Find the widest spot on the creek before crossing. Wider equals shallower. There are trail post markers along the creek that show the recommended route to follow, or during lower water levels you can follow the truck-tire tracks.

Once across Alder Creek for the last time, you will meet the Mush Lake Road again. This is a popular place for people to camp if they do not want to arrive at the highway late in the day.

Next along the road is a fork with a Parks Service sign indicating the start of the Shorty Creek Trail. You are a mere 5.5 kilometres (3.4 miles) from the highway. There is a parking area a few hundred metres before the abandoned Dezadeash Lodge and the highway, but there is no water along this last 5 kilometres (3 miles).

Beloud Post, the abandoned lodge at the end of the trail, was the site of a small mining camp and trading post built by Ben Beloud in the 1930s. Beloud Creek, passed earlier on the trail was named after him.

S8 SOCKEYE LAKE TRAIL (side trip)

Time: *2 to 4 days from Kathleen Lake campsite, returning the same route*
Distance: *56 kilometres (34.8 miles) return trip*
Difficulty: *Easy to moderate*
Change in elevation: *92 metres (302 feet)*
Maximum elevation: *854 metres (2,802 feet)*
Topographical maps: *Kathleen Lakes 115A/11, Auriol Range 115A/12*
Equipment needed: *Creek-crossing shoes and overnight gear are needed. A stove is recommended.*

The route: This is an easy hike that may be continued along the Cottonwood Trail to Dezadeash Lake and the highway if you have time and energy (see Cottonwood Trail). Sockeye Lake is designated a Zone 1 protection area, so camping on the lake shore is not recommended.

26.0 km   Follow Cottonwood Trail to Sockeye Lake turnoff
28.0 km   Sockeye Lake

Trail access: Follow the instructions for the Cottonwood Trail to the 26.0-kilometre mark at the Sockeye Lake turnoff. If this is a side trip from the Cottonwood Trail and if you are continuing to Dezadeash Lake, add only one day to your total time. Only minimal or no public use is permitted at Sockeye Lake. The marshland around the lake is delicate vegetation and should not be walked on.

The trail: Once you cross the unnamed creek at 26 kilometres (16.2 miles) on the Cottonwood Trail, the trail to Sockeye Lake goes toward the right while the main trail swings to the left. It is not really a trail but an open burned area that has, in the distant past, been cleared by a bulldozer. It was cleared for the miners so they could get to the lake to fish. Now the miners have been replaced by hikers but, even though there is great fishing in this lake, it is *not allowed.*

Sockeye Lake is at the top end of the run for landlocked salmon, which were trapped there when the land formations changed due to glacial activity. Before the changes, sockeye salmon spawned in Sockeye Lake and then returned to the sea through the waterways present at that time. After a glacial surge, the fish still spawned in Sockeye Lake and the Sockeye River, but they returned only as far as Kathleen Lake. This short run is still used by sockeye today.

Another fish found in Sockeye Lake is the rare pygmy whitefish, which grows to a maximum size of 5 inches. This rare fish, which is sparsely scattered around North America, is of special interest to biologists. The pygmy whitefish co-exists with the round whitefish, double in size to the pygmy and abundant in the deep lakes of the park. The Arctic grayling and the burbot, or freshwater cod also live in this lake. Too bad for all you fishers: *the lake is a protected area.*

Sockeye Lake has a few pebbly spots and water that is Caribbean blue on sunny days. Camping spots are hard to find close to the lake because it is surrounded by the largest marsh area in the park. There is a decent place off the bulldozed road, near a pile of logs and old railway ties 100 metres (328 feet) above the lake. This would be a nice place to spend a rest day. It is peaceful and pretty, but remember that there are salmon in the lake and grizzlies like salmon. There is an old barrel by the lake that some people have used as a garbage bin. Please do NOT use this barrel for that purpose. It only endangers those who would like to spend time near the lake.

Kinnikinnick or bearberry is common around the area. The word "kinnikinnick" originally meant "mixture" and the plant was often used as a topical antibiotic by native people. The berries were also fried in oil or boiled in stews. The natives called the plant "sacacomis." There is a similar-sounding word in French that means "a clerk's sack of tobacco": this amused the French because the Hudson Bay Company clerks always carried a sack of sacacomis leaves so they could smoke them. Of course bears love the fruit of this plant.

Climbing the mountain [UTM (56-07) Cottonwood Lk] between the Cottonwood River, Sockeye Lake, and Johobo Lake is recommended. The bushwhack takes about twenty minutes before you reach subalpine scrub.

 ## CAMPSITE LAKE (side trip)

Time: *5 to 6 days, returning by the same route*
Distance: *14 kilometres (8.7 miles) past Cottonwood Flats, return trip*
Difficulty: *Difficult bushwhacking*
Change in elevation: *92 metres (302 feet)*
Maximum elevation: *945 metres (3,100 feet)*
Topographical maps: *Cottonwood Lakes 115 A/5*
Equipment needed: *Leather boots are required for this section of the route. A map and compass, rain gear, and bear protection are also required.*

The route: This is not a trail, it is a route. That means bushwhacking, and bushwhacking in the southern area of the park is difficult. The rewards, however, are superb. The route passes the nicest rock glacier in the park and leads to views of the Alsek River with the cold icefields in the background. Some have tried to reach the Lowell Glacier by this route, but it is extremely difficult. Instead, try the Lowell Glacier Overland route.

Continuing along the Cottonwood Trail to the highway and Dezadeash Lake after making the side trip to Campsite Lake is possible if you have the time and energy.

0.0 km	Kilometre 33.9 on Cottonwood Trail at Cottonwood Flats
1.9 km	Cottonwood River
4.5 km	Small unnamed lake [UTM (54-05) Cottonwood Lk]
2.5 km	Campsite Lake [UTM (51-06) Cottonwood Lk]

Trail access: Follow the Cottonwood Trail to the Cottonwood Flats as far as the Henkel sign.

The trail: After leaving the Henkel sign on the Cottonwood Flats, [UTM (57-04) Cottonwood Lk], head northwest up the valley toward the Cottonwood River. The distance from the sign to the Cottonwood River is just over 1 kilometre (0.6 miles), but it is thick with willow. Another alternative is to go directly across the Cottonwood Flats to the river and then walk up the riverbed. It is a gravel-bottomed stream, which allows easy walking. The Cottonwood River is flat and shallow so it is easy to cross – but it is cold. The river is an excellent place to camp because there is clear water, lots of flat spots for a tent, and driftwood on the creek for a fire.

Once you're past the Cottonwood River, head up the western slopes of the hills and get above the tree line. This is easier than going straight through the bush – which is more like forest here with larger trees and less willow, making most of the bushwhacking moderately difficult. Either way, you will see a rock glacier spewing its tongue out from between two hills. It reminds me of the rock star from the group Kiss who has a long tongue. For this reason, I call it the "Kiss Glacier."

If walking on the slopes, go to the rock glacier and then follow its drainage creek down into the valley. Campsite Lake is visible from above. The walk down is not difficult, but it is steep in places and it may be necessary to hang on to the vegetation in order to descend. The bushwhacking to the lake (after the descent) takes about half an hour and is fairly easy.

If you are bushwhacking through the valley instead of taking the high ground, you will be close to the lake when you spot the rock glacier. The bushwhacking becomes more difficult again just before the lake. Cross a marsh, then work your way up the creek that flows out of Campsite Lake. The area about 2 kilometres (1.2 miles) before the lake is spotted with white rocky cliffs with many lookout points for reconnoitring. Walk carefully, as some of the hills have steep cliff edges.

Once you're at the lake, it is best to camp beside the beaver dam. There is lots of wood nearby and the bank above the lake makes a pleasant backrest. Tent sites are plentiful. I did not find any flat spots on the north side of the lake, as the vegetation is too thick.

SHORTY CREEK

Time: *8 to 10 hours to the confluence of Shorty and Alder Creeks; 2 to 3 days to the lakes and headwaters of the creek*
Distance: *31 kilometres (19 miles) return trip*
Degree of difficulty: *Moderate*
Change in elevation: *1,097 metres (3,600 feet)*
Maximum elevation: *1,829 metres (6,000 feet)*
Topographical maps: *Mush Lake 115 A/6*
Equipment needed: *Running shoes are sufficient if you are going only to the confluence. Boots are needed for the circle trip and rain gear is essential. You may walk or bicycle along the road. If going to Mount Barker, you will need a stove.*

The route: This is another interesting trip that passes mining artifacts and perilous canyons, before reaching alpine lakes tucked under craggy peaks. The route finally circles to a moonscape plateau under Mount Barker and overlooks the icefields across the way. There is high bear activity in this area so be aware of smells. *Read the entire section on bears.*

0.0 km	Suspension bridge over Alder Creek [UTM (94-81) Mush Lk]
0.1 km	Parks service gate
2.3 km	Unnamed creek [UTM (96-81) Mush Lk]
2.5 km	Viewpoint of Alder Creek Valley [UTM (97-80) Mush Lk]
4.5 km	Alder Creek
5.5 km	Shorty Creek; end of road
8.0 km	Shorty Creek mine site [UTM (99-76) Mush Lk]
12.0 km	Shorty Creek Lakes [UTM (97-74) Mush Lk]
14.5 km	Mount Barker Pass
15.5 km	Moonscape Lake [UTM (95-77) Mush Lk]
20.0 km	Alder Creek
24.4 km	Parks Service gate
31.0 km	Alaska Highway

Trail access: Drive south from Haines Junction along the Haines Road for 54.4 kilometres (33.8 miles). This is the site of the old Beloud Post. Buildings from Dezadeash Lodge still exist but the lodge is closed. The road turns right and follows the Mush Lake mining road. Drive about 1 kilometre (0.6 miles) past a park boundary marker and gate. Vehicles must have high clearance in order to go further. A small truck will make it but a small car might not. Continue along the road to the forks at the 2.8-kilometre sign. You may take either fork as they join again a short distance ahead. The junction at 5.5 kilometres (3.4 miles) has a sign indicating the Shorty Creek Trail. Go to the right about another kilometre and park. The suspension bridge over Alder Creek is obvious. Taking Shorty Creek as a side trip from the Cottonwood Trail is also recommended if you wish to extend your time in the park. In this case the 5.5-kilometre sign is just beyond Alder Flats.

The trail: Across from the parking spot, there is a suspension bridge that crosses Alder Creek. Fill water bottles here, as there is no more water for a few hours. Cross the bridge and pass the metal Parks gate that prohibits motorized traffic from entering. The trail is a wide, maintained mining road that steeply ascends over the hill and then returns to Alder Creek. The mountain reveals good views of Alder Creek and its valley going in both directions. At the summit, there is a viewpoint [UTM (97-80) Mush Lk] with a narrow trail that goes to the next gully. This trail has not been maintained by the parks and I advise staying on the main road. If you do follow the trail, it will end at a road above Alder Creek.

About two hours from the parking area is a creek with a log bridge. The trail starts to descend. The next creek has two bridges. This is the exit point if you're doing the circle route. Camping is not comfortable in this area so continue down the road to Alder Creek. Camping anywhere along the creek, or a few hundred feet up from the creek bed, is comfortable. The walk up Alder Creek to Shorty Creek is easy. There is a carved wooden sign indicating the confluence of Alder and Shorty Creeks. Driftwood for a fire is plentiful along the creek.

During low water, you may continue past Shorty Creek and up Alder Creek for another 6 kilometres (3.7 miles) to a long pass with two lakes. The area was once a sacred native campsite and nothing in the area should be touched. The walk up Alder is not possible during high water because the canyons are too steep to climb around.

In the summer of 1898, thirty-six men, led by Adair of the U.S. Cavalry, slogged 160 kilometres (100 miles) over the Dalton Trail to the "Last Chance Mining District." Known as the "Mysterious 36," these men established a mining camp on Shorty Creek, worked the creek in the summer, and pulled up stakes in the winter – never to be heard of again.

Follow Shorty Creek up the valley, staying on the left-hand side. There are many signs of mining activity along the lower end of the creek. Continue up the valley to where Shorty Creek divides [UTM (99-78) Mush Lake], passing one tributary creek on the south (left) side. Stay on the south side of Shorty Creek for the rest of the way. There is some easy bushwhacking in this section of the hike; the creek flows through canyon-like walls, but it is passable. The camping is good in this area.

There is a lot of ground pine in this area. At one time photographers used the spore powder produced from these plants, which look like miniature pine trees, for flash photography.

About 1 kilometre (0.6 miles) past the junction are the remains of a mining camp with stoves, beds, pans, and wooden furniture. The cabins once held dynamite left by the miners. Over the years, the dynamite turned to gel. When it was eventually found, the RCMP bomb squad had to be called in to get rid of the material. Although the gel would not explode, the RCMP conducted a controlled burning. What you see are the remains.

If water levels allow walking along Shorty Creek all the way to the lakes, then do so. The walk is not as steep as going over the hills, even though it is a bit longer. If the water levels are too high, continue along the creek to an alluvial fan, then ascend while veering to the south (left). Continue in a southwesterly direction, heading for the area below or between the two bald peaks above. If you're staying at the lakes for the night, head west and to the pass below the bald peaks. If you are going to the moonscape, walk between the peaks, east of the lakes. The landscape undulates steeply at times, but the ground is grassy and the walking is pleasant.

Once on the pass between the two bald peaks, the lakes can be seen below [UTM (97-74) Mush Lk] tucked underneath the craggy peaks that guard other passes leading to viewpoints above Victoria and Dalton Creeks on the Cottonwood Trail. The lakes are the headwaters of Shorty Creek. The foreboding "fang" mountain directly across from the pass is my favourite mountain in the area. There is no wood near the lakes, but there are flat spots for a tent. The valley floor is wet early in the season. If you walked up Shorty Creek to the lakes, continue along the valley in a southeasterly direction, past another small lake and the formidable fang hovering midway in the valley. The pass below Mount Barker [UTM (96-77) Mush Lk] is the one leading to the moonscape. There is a 60-metre (200-foot) incline to the top of the pass, but it is not difficult.

If you're walking to Mount Barker Pass from the two bald peaks above Shorty Creek Lakes [UTM (97-74) Mush Lk], skirt around the sides of the rock glacier and Mount Barker, descending slowly onto the pass. The boulders on this glacier are loose and could slip, thus pinning you, so be extra careful.

Hikers cross one of the few bridges in Kluane on their way to Shorty Creek.

From the Mount Barker Pass a lake [UTM (95-78) Mush Lake] comes into view about 60 metres (200 feet) down a gentle slope. Skirt this lake and continue to the left until you arrive at a second, higher lake. It sits under Mount Barker on a moonscape with the icefields glittering away to the south. This is one of the most spectacular sights in the park. Climbing Mount Barker will give you a better view of the icefields. There is no wood on the moonscape, so bring a camp stove.

Although not officially named, Copper Mountain is located in the icefields and is visible from the moonscape. Its openings lead down shafts 548 metres (1,798 feet) into the mountain, where passages contain mining equipment such as shovels, wrenches, and picks left by early explorers.

To leave the moonscape, walk beside Mount Barker and head toward the arm on your left. Once at the creek, beside the arm, continue down that draw for about 1 kilometre (0.6 miles) before crossing over and bushwhacking down the hill. Along the creek there are camping spots beside a grey and brown striped rock face. It takes about two hours to arrive at the Alder Creek Road from the lake on the moonscape.

Shorty Creek has a long and interesting history, starting in 1896 when "Long Shorty" Bigelow found gold there. He was a pioneer in the area and helped to drive cattle over the Dalton Trail. Later, he had a forced vacation in San Quentin for robbery. He was pardoned within six years, however, when the story of him saving a crippled woman was brought to the attention of government officials. He returned to the Yukon after being released but did not go back to gold mining or robbery.

In 1898, Shorty Creek was worked by prospectors after they had worked Alder Creek. In the 1930s, McCaully and Vass worked the creek. In 1946, two other prospectors, Banker and Rae, moved in with five large cats. They stripped a huge area of the surrounding mountains with hydraulic hoses, but did not get much gold. In fact they lost money. Tailings can still be seen today, along with cat treads, pieces of porcelain, old wire, and (about 1 kilometre up the creek) the sad remains of an old sluice box.

Alder and Shorty Creeks make a scenic and interesting hike, either for the day or for a few nights. Going into the meadows and headwaters of Shorty Creek is highly recommended. On our way up to the pass above Shorty Creek, we watched a blond grizzly sow and her kids. They appeared to have a kill on the opposite slopes above Shorty.

 ## S11 LOWELL GLACIER OVERLAND

Time: *8 to 10 days, but longer would be better*
Distance: *65 kilometres (40.5 miles) one way*
Difficulty: *Moderate*
Change in elevation: *1,538 metres (5045 feet)*
Maximum elevation: *2,300 metres (7,546 feet)*
Topographical maps: *Kathleen Lakes 115/A/11, Cottonwood Lakes 115/A5*
Equipment needed: *This is one of the most spectacular hikes in the park, so take the time to enjoy it. Although it is long, there are no difficult passes to cross and almost no way of getting lost. You will need leather boots, bear canisters and bear spray, a stove, and skill with both map and compass. A tent and rain gear are also essential because the route offers no protection from the forest for days and if you get wet, there is no way to make a fire. Water is plentiful, but wood is scarce.*

The route: It is an easy walk along the Cottonwood Trail. A map is needed only for interest's sake. However, once over the Cottonwood River, a map and compass is essential. You must spend two hours of moderate bushwhacking on the far side of the Cottonwood River before entering the alpine, where you will stay until just before climbing the ridge in front of the glacier. Hiking the Cottonwood Trail to the Cottonwood River from either Dezadeash Lake or Kathleen Lake is possible. The distances described here are charted from Kathleen Lake to the Cottonwood River and then to the ridge. From the Kathleen Lake campsite, it is 65 kilometres (40 miles) one way to the Lowell Glacier, but if time is short you can see the glacier from the black-tipped hills just behind campsite ridge, thus saving about 25 kilometres (16 miles). These hills could be reached during a day hike from Shaft

Creek, which is one day past the Cottonwood River. Before making any decisions, read the entire route description. There are many options.

There is a lot of bear activity in this area and it is a long trip. Always be bear-anoid. Couples should remember to abstain from sex. *Read the entire section on bears.*

35.2 km   Cottonwood River and unnamed creek
37.8 km   Out of tree line [UTM (99-55) Cottonwood Lk]
40.6 km   Unnamed creek; possible campsite
          [UTM (97-55), Cottonwood Lk]
44.8 km   Unnamed Lakes; excellent campsite
          [UTM (94-53) Cottonwood Lk]
45.5 km   Shaft Creek [UTM (94-53) Cottonwood Lk]
49.9 km   Glacier Pass [UTM (90-51) Cottonwood Lk]
53.3 km   Black-tipped hills [UTM (88-47) Cottonwood Lk]
55.7 km   Campsite Ridge [UTM (87-47) Cottonwood Lk]
60.5 km   Skookum Creek [UTM (86-44) Cottonwood Lk]
65.0 km   Vingborg Ridge [UTM (87-41) Cottonwood Lk]

Trail access: See the Cottonwood Trail for the first 35 kilometres (22 miles) of this route.

The trail: After crossing the Cottonwood Flats, the trail enters the bush for a short distance. At the next creek wash-out, turn right. The creek is silty here so it is not a good camping spot. There is an arrow pointing upward, carved into a cottonwood tree just before the creek. Across the creek is a trail marker indicating the continuation of the trail through the bush to the Dalton Range along the Cottonwood Trail. Do not go that way; instead, turn right.

Walk down Dalton Creek for 30 metres (100 feet) or so to the confluence of Dalton Creek, the Cottonwood River, and another creek coming in from the south [UTM (01-57) Cottonwood Lk]. The unnamed creek is where the bushwhacking will start. The Cottonwood River has clear water, lots of driftwood, and flat gravel spots for camping. However, this is a popular grizzly hangout, so watch for signs. It is better to camp down the Cottonwood 1 kilometre (0.6 miles) or so and return in the morning to cross the river. There are also numerous flat spots across the Cottonwood on the unnamed creek, some tucked into poplar groves. Crossing the Cottonwood River seldom presents a problem. This does not mean you can be careless, it just means that you will not have to wait for days for the water level to recede.

Follow the creek flats toward the green ridge in the southwest, between the obvious canyon and a smaller creek. This is south of the sand-coloured mountain across from the Cottonwood Flats from where you just came [UTM (99-55) Cottonwood Lk]. The creek forms a large "U" close to the Cottonwood River so feel free to cut directly across, thereby meeting the creek farther up. We found easy walking on the south side (left) of the creek. If starting on the north (right) side you will have to cross partway up the creek.

Across from the first sandy cutbank on the creek, there is a knoll. We found walking along the base of the knoll quite civilized. Regardless of which side you start on, be certain to be on the south (left) side of the creek by the time you come to a set of gravel covered cutbanks. Bushwhack across to the lowest set of cutbanks coming from the canyon just below the creek bed. The bush becomes thinner if you stay away from the water by 30 metres (100 feet). There are also some game trails to follow, which makes the walking easier. From the Cottonwood River, it will take two to three hours to reach the ridge above the tree line. The rest of your hike is in alpine.

There are three large slabs of rock fallen upon each other to form a den or hollow, which could be used as shelter in foul weather [UTM (00-56) Cottonwood Lk]. Once past the hollow (if you find it at all), walk upward, skirting the creek beside you. Going over the hill on the left, the distance is shorter but up-and-down, therefore requiring more energy. Skirting the hill is easier.

Continue past the brown, pyramid-shaped mountain [UTM (00-54) Cottonwood Lk] on the right. It is followed by a row of three grey, pyramid-shaped mountains. There is a round, tree-covered mountain on the left. Follow the valley between the pyramids and green mountain constantly veering slightly to the right. It is a pleasant stroll with gentle ups and downs, but more ups than downs. It will take two to three hours to reach the first unnamed lake [UTM (94-54) Cottonwood Lk], where camping is excellent. The boulder-dotted lakes have relatively warm water and there are many flat spots to pitch a tent. A stove is needed for cooking. The lake seen when looking down Shaft Creek valley is the top end of Mush Lake.

The alpine meadows around the unnamed lakes are rich with my favourite flower, the inky gentian: a tiny greenish-blue flower that appears to be illuminated. Its European counterpart was named after an Illyrian King Gentius, who used the root of the plant as a tonic and for flavouring in his liquor.

Standing directly in front of the last lake, looking across Shaft Creek, a lush green valley with a creek flowing down its centre is visible. On the left of the valley there are two scree mounds with some vegetation in the foreground. The first mound has a scree, sloped pass between it and the next rocky mound. Below the pass is a favourite spot for grizzly bears to graze. I call this place Grizzly Valley.

Pass the three unnamed lakes and head north for half a kilometre (a quarter-mile) before attempting to cross Shaft Creek. The canyons are steeper farther down the creek, so go up. Look for a rocky gravel bar and cross on the flat spot just before it. The creek can be tricky to cross so use creek-crossing shoes. Since sticks are in short supply, making a human chain to get across may be necessary. Crossing is best done in the morning when water levels are lower and you have more energy. Grunt up the hill on the opposite side and start across the slope, crossing behind the small knoll on the left. The descent and ascent from Shaft Creek is the steepest hill you will encounter before getting onto Vingborg Ridge.

If time is short, make the lakes a base camp. Climb to the black moss-tipped mountains [UTM (90-48) Cottonwood Lk] on the far side of the next pass above Grizzly Valley. There are distant views of the Lowell from there. Read the entire route description before making any decisions.

Walk up Grizzly Valley. Stay on the valley floor, but scan the area for bears before entering. I saw a sow with two cubs from the side of a hill in this valley and watched her feed her young, play with them, and then graze while they slept. If you see one or three bears, pass high on a side hill on the opposite side of the valley and leave the animals undisturbed.

Follow Grizzly Valley to the lowest pass [UTM (90-49)

Cottonwood Lk] at the top end of the creek. Continue straight ahead to the sandy-red-coloured hills in front of you. Although the map shows the top of the valley to have glaciers, this is not so. There is only a patch of snow, which does not block the pass in mid summer. After a heavy snowfall, however, you may have to cross some snow. It is safe. While sitting on this pass, notice Bates Lake to the left.

Continue across the lush green meadow below and to the right. While still on the pass, notice a reddish ridge slightly to the right, with some hoodoos partway down. Eventually, you will be in the valley behind that ridge [UTM (91-48) Cottonwood Lk]. Continue along the valley toward the large creek continuously veering to the left of the creek. Then grunt your way to the top of the hill.

Cross over the scree slope to the left of the hoodoos. The scree slope is stable and it is fascinating to see the stones at different ages of development. Some are still layered together, some are different types layered together, and some are cut and scraped where the glacier passed a few thousand years ago.

After crossing the top of this hill, where the next valley comes into view, notice a gorge leading to Bates Lake with a green swamp in front. At the pass, there is an arm of a ridge with a small creek flowing down the centre. This is where you want to be [UTM (88-48) Cottonwood Lk]. There is also another creek at the bottom of the valley. I suggest making camp on the ridge, keeping the black, dried moss-covered hills behind you. These black hills are the ones suggested for a day hike from the lakes at Shaft Creek. The views in the next valley present a rugged landscape in every direction. The wardens had previously flown over this route in a helicopter and did not think it would be an easy route to walk.

From a base camp on the suggested ridge, it is a twelve-hour day hike to Vingborg Ridge and back. However, climbing to the black-tipped hills for a view of the glacier is suggested. Although the glacier is visible from the hills, Alsek Lake or River cannot be seen.

About two hours farther down the valley and past the canyons on the creek, there are some excellent campsites. Standing on the high slopes before going down to the creek is a grey, triangular mountain in front of the icy ridges to the southwest. This is Goatherd Mountain and the general direction you want to travel. Goatherd is 2,300 metres

(7,545 feet) high and 700 metres (2,296 feet) from the valley floor. It is almost a 2-kilometre (1.2-mile) grunt from its base to the summit.

The creek flowing toward Goatherd has steep-walled canyons that make travel difficult at high water. Stay on the hills to the right-hand side of the creek when looking toward Goatherd. The choice is walking high and along loose scree, which I find dangerous, or skirting the scree and passing over grassy meadows that are interspersed with willows. Your last option is to stay in the willows and beat your way along, eventually joining the creek after the canyons. However, if you do get into the canyons on the creek during high water, you should backtrack to get back onto the hills.

Walking down the valley, you will see a semicircular clay bank on the left side of the creek [UTM (86-45) Cottonwood Lk], where a tributary creek flows. Pass the tributary and climb onto the grassy slope above the bank. Your most difficult part of the day is now over. Continue along this hill to the creek coming from around Goatherd Mountain.

I call the creek running from Goatherd "Skookum Creek," because that's what it is. Go up the creek for a bit before crossing. It was crotch-high on me and very swift during low water, so in high water you may have to go even farther up the mountain before crossing.

You now have a choice of climbing Goatherd or going up Vingborg Ridge. I do not recommend Goatherd because it is a steep scree slope and slippery during wet weather. However, if you want to climb Goatherd, follow Skookum Creek uphill until you are beside Goatherd Mountain. Find an inviting draw and grunt away. If you're not going up Goatherd, cross Skookum Creek and head downstream, toward the junction of the creeks.

Vingborg Ridge is not the official name of the ridge that I suggest you climb. I first discovered this route with a young lady named Elsebeth, who had come from Denmark especially to hike with me for a summer. She was so taken with the view of the glacier from this ridge, and so thrilled to have explored the route with me, that I named the ridge after her. If the ridge ever receives an official name, I hope it will be Vingborg Ridge.

Vingborg Ridge is three quarters of a kilometre (half a mile) closer to the Lowell Glacier and only 60 metres (199 feet) lower than the summit of Goatherd. To climb Vingborg, go downstream to the junction of the creeks after crossing Skookum Creek. Go up the first clay bank on the right from the junction of the creeks. Once past the first steep slope of this hill, there is a rocky knoll away from the main peaks. Go toward the knoll and continue along the alpine carpet. The front of the mountain is your destination, so go gently and enjoy the views of the Alsek Valley to the right. The blue-green lake below and to the side looks inviting, but getting to it would require bushwhacking. Once past the lake, the Lowell Glacier will soon appear. There are many false summits, but once you're over the last hump the view is breathtaking. Getting from Skookum Creek to the ridge, at a slow pace, takes about one and a half hours.

Glaciation occurs when snow crystallizes and moves, causing erosion and deposition that alters the landscape. Kluane's glacial landforms originated between 29,000 to 12,500 years ago and minor glacial advances have occurred as recently as 2,800 years ago. Due to friction, the centre of a glacier flows faster than the bottom where it is in contact with the earth, so that it is squeezed like toothpaste through gaps in the mountain range by the weight of the snow and ice of the icefields.

There are always icebergs in Alsek Lake and occasionally you will hear the glacier gods pontificating. Some hikers fly to the lake and hike to the ridge for the views. However, float plane operators do not like to book flights to Alsek Lake because landing between the bergs is dangerous. A helicopter is the other option – but it is expensive. If you are interested in a flight to the Lowell, talk to Kluane Park Adventure Centre in Haines Junction and they will quote prices and possibilities. The foot of the Lowell is one of three official landing spots in the park.

The Lowell, called "Naludi" in Tutchone, is 72 kilometres (45 miles) long and has surged numerous times during its lifespan. The reason for the surges are unknown; they are rare throughout the world. During one of its surges, the Lowell's tongue, standing 200 metres (656 feet) high, butted against Goatherd Mountain and backed up the Alsek River – flooding the Alsek, Kaskawulsh, Dusty, and Dezadeash valleys. When the water reached nine tenths of the toe's height, the trapped water lifted the glacial dam, causing the glacier to break and the water to drain. This left beach lines as far away as the north side of the

From Black Hill, Elsebeth Vingborg spots the Lowell Glacier in the distance.

Dezadeash River, west of Haines Junction. The higher lines were formed either 2,800 or 1,250 years ago. The lower beach lines were formed during surges 320 and 125 years ago.

There was another small surge in 1953. One village was at the junction of the Tatshenshini and Alsek Rivers when the glacier gave way. According to Kittie Smith, a Tutchone, the people of the village could see the water coming halfway up the mountain. Everyone except one man was killed.

The Alsek River, a Canadian Heritage Site, flows approximately 250 kilometres (155 miles) across the southwest corner of the Yukon, the northern tip of B.C., and the Alaskan panhandle, finally emptying into the Pacific Ocean at Dry Bay, Alaska. The Alsek was first explored by Edward Glave, who had also travelled in Africa and testified against missionary atrocities committed there. In Canada, Glave worked for Frank Leslies at the *Illustrated News*, on an expedition to Alaska. His excellent descriptions brought the beauty of the Yukon to the attention of the United States. In 1890, Glave and Dalton walked over Chilkat Pass and down to the Tatshenshini, where they took a dugout canoe down to the ocean. They returned to Dalton Post in 1891 with four packhorses. These were the experiences he wrote about for the *Illustrated News*.

The landscape looks different on the way back, so pick your return route while you're still on the ridge; it can be confusing once you're back on the valley floor. The "Y" junction is obvious from the top of the mountain; one creek comes from around Goatherd, one goes toward the Alsek River and the leg of the "Y" comes from where you want to go. The walk from the ridge to Skookum Creek takes about one hour. However, returning to your camp will take longer than it took to get to Goatherd because it is upstream.

Climb the grassy ridge above the half-circled cutbank. There is a waterfall in the centre of the half-circle. This is a nice lunch spot or campsite if you want to be closer to Vingborg Ridge. Continuing your exit, cross the main creek at the half-circle cutbank and climb the slope on the opposite side. From there pick your poison: go high and along the scree, stay low and bushwhack through the willows, or go somewhere in between. Returning to ridge camp from the waterfall will take three to four hours. Once past the red clay slopes on the main creek, it is safe to return to the creek bed and saunter upwards toward ridge camp. Take the second tributary on the left after the red clay slopes. It looks narrow and impassable, but it is an easy walk. You will be within ten minutes of the alpine slope where the camp is located.

This day hike took me twelve hours. Camping closer to the creek may save forty-five minutes on your day. Camping close to Skookum Creek enables early morning crossing, thus avoiding a bit of high water. However, there are no comfortable campsites between the suggested one on the ridge in front of the black-tipped mountains and the half-circled cutbanks close to Skookum Creek.

On the return trip, cross the pass beside the black-tipped mountains and head for the green pass on the right. Do not go down the inviting valley of scree slopes. The green pass is a piece of cake. Follow the creek partway down Grizzly Valley toward Shaft Creek, veering to the left and onto the side of the hill, so as to avoid the steep gullies of Shaft Creek and the swampy spots in Grizzly Valley. Once back at the alpine lakes, keep to the left, passing fairly close to the pinkish-white mountains rather than the green one on the right. Once past the last pinkish-white pyramid, stay on the right-hand side of the creek and gully. The closer you stay to the pyramid mountains, the fewer gullies you will encounter.

Johobo Lake and the Cottonwood Flats will soon come into view. Note the gouges, formed by switchback roads on Johobo Mountain, to the right of the lake. Sometimes civilization is a comfort, even if it is a mess. Return to the Cottonwood Trail by the same route that you came.

 ## QUILL CREEK (South)

Time: *2 to 3 days*
Distance: *37.0 kilometres (23 miles) return*
Difficulty: *Easy to first canyon, difficult past canyon*
Change in elevation: *370 metres (1,214 feet)*
Maximum elevation: *1,200 metres (3,937 feet)*
Topographical maps: *Kathleen Lakes 115 A/11, Auriol Range 115 A/12, Dezadeash Range 115 A*
Equipment needed: *This is an easy hike if you are going only to the canyons. You need runners, a snack and a jacket. If you're going all the way to the headwaters of Quill Creek, leather boots, rain gear, and a tent are needed. Water is plentiful, but there is little firewood at the top.*

The route: Weather conditions can change rapidly in this area so take waterproof gear. The trail crosses scree and talus slopes. The upper valley is famous for its rock glaciers. Once there, you will find spectacular scenery and numerous exploration routes. A recommended over-nighter, if you are not going all the way to the end of the valley, is to camp at the beginning of the canyon section, go into the alpine for the day and return in the evening. There is bear activity in the area so keep odours to a minimum. *Read the entire section on bears.*

0.0 km   Quill Creek bridge
2.5 km   Cutbanks; view of canyon
5.5 km   Second canyon

7.0 km   End of canyons
8.5 km   Rock Glacier Plateau [UTM (59-23) Auriol Range]
11.0 km   Headwaters of Quill Creek [UTM (60-24) Auriol Range]
18.5 km   Headwaters of Beachview Creek (11.5 miles)
           [UTM (57-23) Auriol Range]

Trail access: Drive south from Haines Junction on the Haines Road for 13.2 kilometres (8.2 miles) to the Quill Creek Bridge. There are signs indicating the trailhead. Take the first right turn past the bridge and follow this road for about five minutes. The trail begins there.

The trail: The Tutchone Indians called this creek "Natan Chu," which means "glacier creek." This tells you what to expect for water conditions, especially near the headwaters. If you're on the north side of the creek, walk along the flat plateau over the cutbank to see the first canyon. You cannot proceed past here, as the cutbanks are steep and eroded. To continue, you must cross the creek.

If you are travelling along the recommended south side of the creek, the walking is easy beside its shore or, when the creek runs too close to the bank, along game trails through the bush. Before the first canyon, there are numerous campsites with wood, clear water, and trees for shelter.

At the end of the flats, continue past the first creek and an alluvial fan. The fan is directly across from the rocky bluffs seen on the opposite shore. The first canyon starts here. Take a look upward to the south and plan your route along the moss and low, vegetated areas. After the alluvial fan, follow the first clear creek up the mountain. It is steep but stable. Do not attempt to go through the canyons along the creek because the water is deep, cold, and swift.

Do not go up the hill directly across from the rugged rocks at the end of the cutbanks, as the willows are far too thick to beat against. Continue up the little creek, veering slightly to the right once you are beyond the creek bed. Take water as there is none until you return to Quill Creek. Get high and stay out of the bush. Once in the open, go over the hill and head up the valley.

If you are doing the day hike, continue up the valley (as described above) to the first nonvegetated gully and turn away from Quill Creek.

Follow it to a cirque and numerous grassy eskers. The walk takes about an hour. There are rock rabbits or picas in the area, which live on the steep talus slopes above the timberline. Although these animals are hard to see, they keep neat stacks of vegetation outside their nests from which they nibble during the winter.

This valley was once a favourite for sheep poachers but, between the wardens and the RCMP, the poachers were all chased, caught, and convicted. When you return to the creek after passing the first canyon, there are remains of sheep horns sitting beside a rusting tin can. I suspect these would be remnants of the poaching days. If caught, anyone harming animals in Kluane can be fined up to $150,000. If you see anything suspicious, please report it to the wardens.

The Tutchone women came to this area to pick blackberries and mossberries (men did not pick berries) which they used as a decorating dye for their baskets. They also used the berries for tea to cure diarrhea.

If going all the way to Rock Glacier Plateau, return to Quill Creek along this gully, instead of going up to the cirque, and pass the first outcrop before heading up again. You are now above the first canyon. Go high to avoid impassable willows. Stay high until you pass the sharp "S" curve being carved by Quill Creek then return to the creek after crossing the small scree slope just beyond the "S." The slope is low and stable.

The second canyon must also be passed by climbing the steep vegetated slope and then by gouging the side hills along the subalpine. The two canyons take about four hours to pass and each climb is about 60 metres (200 feet). The canyons resemble a miniature Nahanni River. For anyone who has been to the Nahanni, the thrill of seeing a similar but younger (and much smaller) river in its beginning stages awaits you.

After passing the second canyon, a V-shaped plateau [UTM (61-23) Auriol R] comes into view. Head for it. Return to the river and bushwhack to the upper end of Quill Creek. The willows are thick and travel is difficult, but there are a number of places to camp – the best being at the fork of Quill Creek. However, it is also nice on Rock Glacier Plateau. While travelling along the creek, be aware that it gains many channels and swallows the bank, forming cornice edges. Be careful not to walk too close to the edge.

Once at Rock Glacier Plateau, [UTM (59-23) Auriol R] continue in a northwesterly direction past a rock glacier and then go directly north (right) to another rock glacier at the headwaters of Quill Creek [UTM (60-24) Auriol Range]. However, do not ascend the rock glacier at the headwaters of Quill Creek. Instead, turn west (left) once you have gone far enough around the corner of the hill and toward Quill Creek headwaters to be able to clearly see the toe of the rock glacier in front. Then head for the pass and third rock glacier to the northwest (left). This area is definitely Rock Glacier Plateau. Once you're on the plateau, views of the icefield ranges appear and walking is easier. Continue along the valley toward Beachview Creek. The deep canyons of Beachview Creek are caused from melt water erosion. These are even more spectacular than those on lower Quill Creek.

From the pass, you can see the Dezadeash and Kaskawulsh Rivers meet the Alsek and flow around Profile Mountain. You are in the heart of the Auriol Range and though the travel has been difficult, the views are worth it.

Although I have never found it, scout around for the remains of a Tutchone raft that was left when Lake Alsek drained after an 18th century glacial surge. The lake had risen 81 metres (265 feet) above present water levels. There are faint signs of the lake's presence on the landscape. In 1978, a 4.5-metre (15-foot), axe-hewn oar was found, 24 metres (80 feet) above the Alsek River. The rumour attached to the oar was that it was Russian-made. It is in the display case at the Haines Junction Interpretive Centre.

If you're camping on Rock Glacier Plateau, there is an interesting day hike toward Mount Martha Black, over the rock glacier in the last valley to the right, beside a tiny lake that appears before you descend toward the Alsek River. If you go as far as the lake, you have gone too far. It is best to camp beside the lake and hike over the rock glacier toward Mount Martha Black with a day pack. It is about five kilometres to the mountain, but your best views are from the summit of the hills beside the rock glacier.

Since it is only a one-day hike to the highway from here, staying until you are almost completely out of food is okay.

There are three species of ptarmigan in Kluane: rock, willow, and white-tailed. They change colour from white in winter to black and grey in summer. Camouflage is the only defence these birds have, so they are often found near the willows.

When travelling in willow, make lots of noise – as this is a favourite hangout for bears too. They may be unable to hear anyone because of the river noise and the muffling effect of the willows. Keep all food in a canister, carry a pepper spray and sing as if you were in the shower. Always keep smells to a minimum.

Dick and Polly Mahoney ran the Kluane Huskies and lived in a cabin on Quill Creek until their government lease ran out. After the Mahoneys left, park management said the improvements had to be moved so Brent and Wenda Liddle bought the Mahoney cabin and moved it to their property across from Kathleen Lake. The cabin had been built so that dismantling would be easy. Each plank was numbered. Building and dismantling was done in numerical order. Guests staying at the Cabins B&B can now rent this historical little building.

After Polly left the Yukon, she was commissioned by the American government to remove dogs from the Antarctic. It seems the dogs, not

Cutbanks along Quill Creek.

being indigenous to the area, were leaving poo piles that were damaging the delicate ecological system. Polly helped relocate the animals in Canada's North.

 AURIOL TRAIL

Time: *4 to 6 hours or overnight*
Distance: *15 kilometres (9.3 miles) round trip*
Difficulty: *Easy*
Change in elevation: *550 metres (1,805 feet)*
Maximum elevation: *1,300 metres (4,265 feet)*
Topographical maps: *Kathleen Lake 115 A/11, Auriol Range 115 A/12*
Equipment needed: *For a day hike, a picnic lunch and running shoes are sufficient. Also tuck a raincoat into your pack because the area is wetter than those in north Kluane. Otherwise, enjoy this delightful, easy trail. Overnighters will find a primitive campsite on the trail near the alpine, but a stove is required because firewood is sparse. A map is needed for interest's sake only.*

The route: This is a maintained trail that most people can enjoy either in whole or in part. Since it is close to Haines Junction, those without a vehicle could walk to the trailhead. I do suggest taking a map and going farther into the park on an exploratory mission, after making camp at the primitive campsite. The rewards are extraordinary.

0.0 km	Parking area; trailhead
2.0 km	Fork
3.0 km	Creek and water
5.0 km	Small lake
7.0 km	Small stream with drinking water
7.3 km	Primitive campsite
8.2 km	Fork that goes up or down the hill
10. km	Viewpoint
11.6 km	Viewpoint (7.2 miles)

Trail access: Drive south from Haines Junction along the Haines Road for 7.2 kilometres (4.5 miles). There is a park trail sign and parking area on the right-hand side of the road. Parks Canada has placed a sign inside the gate with a map of the trail.

The trail: Maintained by Parks Canada, the trail was established in 1983. The Auriol Range was named in honour of the French president Vincent Auriol, after his visit to Canada in 1952. This trail goes into the Auriol Range and has the same name.

This is an excellent trail for those wishing to spend a night inside the park. The campsite can be reached from either direction on the trail, but the north-to-south direction is a bit steeper. I recommend taking pre-teens on this trail because it is an easy walk with many rewards. You need only a few chocolate bars to entice them.

Taking the long loop, you will pass through three zones: boreal forest, subalpine, and alpine – all within 8 kilometres (5 miles). From the top of the trail, access to the mountain cirques is easy, but there are no maintained trails. Use a map and explore an area that appeals to you.

It takes ten minutes to reach the 1-kilometre sign on the trail. Veer to the left along the main trail unless you are taking the steeper climb to start the hike. In that case, go to the right. The 2-kilometre sign appears in about twenty minutes. It is easy hiking to here. The next half hour is spent going up and down gentle slopes. A bridge over a creek is the next landmark.

Yarrow is common in the area. It has fern-like leaves and a cluster of white flowers on the top of the stem. Tea made from dried leaves is a cure for constipation. The tea is also reputed to be a coagulant and antiseptic. Mash the leaves and put them on a wound. Old-timers claim it speeds healing and it also relieves the itch from insect bites.

The next stream is about fifteen minutes farther, so carrying water is not essential. There is another one twenty to thirty minutes on in a dwarf birch and willow meadow. This stream may dry up during hot weather or late in the season.

Ten minutes after the meadow is a small lake that is nice to rest beside but not recommended for camping. There is a stream running into the lake with fresh water for drinking. An old rock glacier, now partially covered with vegetation, is visible directly ahead.

Fifteen to twenty minutes past the lake is the 6.1-kilometre sign. The left-hand fork of the trail goes to a meadow and around the hill, revealing pleasant views. The right-hand fork is the main trail. There is another stream with drinking water about ten minutes past the fork. Follow the rocky trail beside the stream to the 7.3-kilometre sign where a primitive campsite is located. The Ruby Range, across the valley, often glows in the evening light.

The campsite is about 30 metres (100 feet) off the trail to the right. There is room for four or five small tents. There are three tent pads with a stone base for drainage during the rainy times. The unisex outhouse is on the hill to the right. There is a fire pit with logs to sit on and a bear rack for backpacks. This is a well-sheltered campsite. It is a good base from which to explore the mountain cirques and the rock glaciers farther into the mountains. However, getting there requires bushwhacking as there are no maintained trails above the Auriol Trail.

When continuing along the trail, stay on the right-hand side of the creek. Within a kilometre, a bridge crosses the creek and then, a few hundred feet up the creek, just past a signpost, another bridge crosses back again. Once across the second bridge turn downstream a bit before going up the hill. There are park markers. One park marker to the left is used in winter for skiing. At the next fork in the trail is another marker, which should be ignored. Veer to the right and follow the markers down the hill.

After twenty to thirty minutes you should arrive at the 9.4-kilometre sign. This is the subalpine area. The next park marker points to a viewpoint on the hillside where park benches may be enjoyed. The views are of Haines Junction and the Dezadeash River wandering through the bush. The King's Throne is on the mountain to the southeast. Looking toward Haines Junction, the Shakwak Trench created by the Denali Fault is visible. It displays the magnificence of the trench. Golden eagles have been seen soaring in this region.

Another viewpoint is at the 11.6-kilometre sign. Fifteen minutes later is a bridge over a creek where water can be obtained. The original trail is then joined at the 2.0-kilometre point.

DEZADEASH WETLANDS TRAIL

Time: *2 hours round trip*
Distance: *5.5 kilometres (3.4 miles) return trip*
Difficulty: *Easy*
Change in elevation: *15 metres (50 feet)*
Maximum elevation: *640 metres (2,100 feet)*
Topographical maps: *Auriol 115 A/12, Kathleen Lake 115 A/11*
Equipment needed: *Comfortable shoes and a bit of drinking water are all that is needed for this walk. A map is required for interest's sake only.*

The route: This is a trail interesting to everyone from the gung-ho back-country traveller to the motor home crowd – and especially the bird-watchers. Because of the boardwalks, 300 metres (984 feet) of the trail is wheelchair-accessible. The trail passes through wetlands meadows, and forest along the Dezadeash River. The trail is well-maintained and interspersed with viewing benches, so it is also recommended for small children.

0.0 km   Parking area; trailhead
0.5 km   Bench
1.4 km   Fork in trail with signpost
2.8 km   End of loop
3.5 km   "T" in trail; to RV Park
4.5 km   RV Park
5.5 km   Parking area

Trail access: Follow the highway from Haines Junction south to the Dezadeash Bridge less than half a kilometre from the town's centre. The trailhead is on the north side of the bridge. There are highway signs indicating the Dezadeash River and the Wetlands Trail. The parking area has a picnic table and garbage disposal unit.

The trail may also be started at the Haines Junction Information Centre. Beside the parking area is a trail that goes through a treed area and then across the highway past the Kluane RV Park. The trail may also be picked up at the RV Park. Regardless of where you start, it is an easy stroll that should not be overlooked by anyone.

The trail: The trail is well-maintained with bridges and boardwalks, and is covered with sawdust or wood chips. Parks Canada has built benches at lookout spots.

The word "Dezadeash" comes from the Chilkat Indian word meaning "lake of the big winds." This river drains from Dezadeash Lake to the Alsek River, now a World Heritage River.

This trail is described from the bridge on the highway.

The first kilometre (two-thirds of a mile) of the trail passes through the swampy wetlands over which Parks Canada has built boardwalks. The trail reveals sections of the river; the first viewing bench is situated 1 kilometre (0.6 miles) past the boardwalk. Here the lucky hiker can see moose chomping on fresh water shoots. The Auriol Range can also be seen.

Veer slightly to the right and avoid going down the pipeline cut straight ahead. In twenty to thirty minutes, take a horse trail to the left.

Park signs at the junction of the trail are next. The signs say 0.9 km and 2.8 km, which means you have come 0.9 kilometres from the parking area and if you continue around the loop, you have an additional 2.8 kilometres to go before returning to the signpost. Walking in either direction brings you back to the same spot. The loop takes about an hour. The scar of the pipeline can be seen from this part of the trail (the actual pipes have been removed). The pipeline was built above ground because it is not possible to sink pipes into permafrost.

The next section of the trail passes through aspen forests and grassland meadows. Once back at the "T" junction, go right through the spruce trees to the parking area. Walking straight ahead will take you to another section of the pipeline and the Kluane RV Park on the Alaska Highway, where you will find a store that sells ice-cream.

Routes and Trails

Central

SECTION

Trail Legend

C1	Alsek Trail to Thundegg Creek and Ferguson Creek
C2	Mount Decoeli
C3	Kimberley Meadow to Alsek Trail
C4	Kimberley Meadow to Jarvis River
C5	Jarvis River
C6	Silver Creek to Outpost Mountain
C7	William's Horse Trail to Kluane Plateau
C8	Vulcan Creek
C9	Slims River East
C10	Soldier's Summit
C11	Sheep Mountain
C12	Slims River West to Observation Mountain
C13	Bullion Creek
C14	Sheep-Bullion Plateau to Sheep or Congdon Creeks
C15	Sheep Creek to Congdon Creek
C16	Fisher Creek
C17	Williscroft Canyon
C18	Congdon Creek
C19	Dickson Creek
C20	Nines Creek (North)
C21	Nines Creek (South)
C22	Bock's Brook

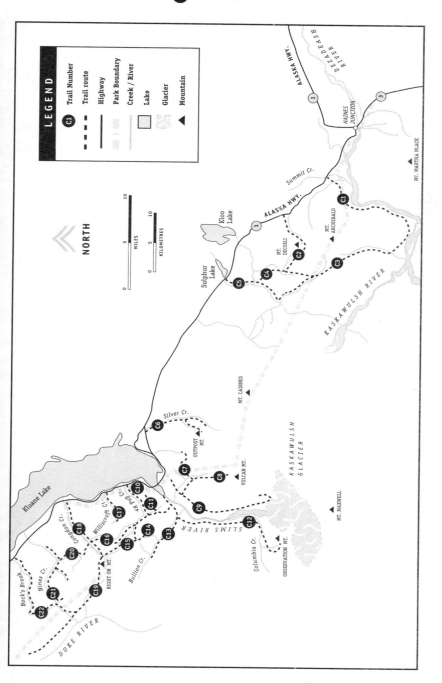

ALSEK TRAIL TO THUNDEREGG CREEK AND FERGUSON CREEK

Time: *2 to 3 days, if walking to Ferguson Creek (Sugden). This trail may also be cycled. Thunderegg Creek is an hour or two from the car.*
Distance: *58 kilometres (36 miles) return trip*
Difficulty: *Easy*
Change in elevation: *40 metres (131 feet)*
Maximum elevation: *640 metres (2,100 feet)*
Topographical maps: *Kloo Lake 115 A/13, Auriol Range 115 A/12*
Equipment needed: *Running shoes and a picnic lunch will suffice for a day hike or a walk to Thunderegg Creek (to find thundereggs). However, if you're going to Ferguson Creek, creek-crossing shoes plus walking shoes are needed. Runners are sufficient for the entire trail. A map is needed for interest's sake only. All overnight equipment is required if you're going to Ferguson Creek.*

The route: This is an easy but interesting hike, as you will pass the shores of Recent Lake Alsek that flooded the area a century ago. There are historical cabins and a large number of wild animals – including grizzly bears, so carry pepper spray and a canister. *Read the bear section.*

0.0 km   Turnoff at Mackintosh Lodge
1.5 km   Summit Creek
5.0 km   Thunderegg Creek [UTM (40-52) Kloo Lk]

6.2 km	Park boundary sign
8.0 km	Last water fill-up until the silty Dezadeash River
10.6 km	Park signpost before open flats
15.4 km	Park gate; no vehicles allowed past here
18.0 km	Sand dunes and old river eddies
20.9 km	Horse campsite
22.5 km	Profile Mountain
25.9 km	Horse campsite
29.0 km	Ferguson Creek and cabin

Trail access: Drive north from Haines Junction Information Centre along the Alaska Highway for 10.7 kilometres (6.6 miles). Turn left on the road across from Mackintosh Lodge and drive past a log cabin. If the road conditions are dry, a car can go to Summit Creek where people have camped in the past. However, camping at least 2.0 kilometres from your vehicle is mandatory when in the park. Should you park at Summit Creek, park off the road so as not to block the way for other vehicles. If driving to the 15.4-kilometre mark at the park gate, a four-wheel-drive vehicle is required. Mountain biking along this trail is recommended, but make noise as there are bears in the area. Bells, whistles and loud shouting are necessary. We once rescued a cyclist on this trail who had been clawed by a bear when he surprised her and her two cubs. Do not cycle alone. Two people can make far more noise than one person.

The trail: The Alsek Trail is an easy two- or three-day, roundtrip hike from Summit Creek to Ferguson Creek. Children can manage this trail because there is almost no elevation change and you are always on a road (built by Parker and Rae). The landmarks are historically interesting. There is a cabin at the end of the trail and the scenery is pleasant. The Dezadeash River joins the Alsek and is the only river in the Yukon to flow into the Pacific Ocean.

If doing a day hike, this trail is close to the amenities of Haines Junction. The hike is highly recommended. I find that this trail is not used as much as it should be.

Starting at Mackintosh Lodge, there is about 1.5 kilometres (0.9 miles) of boring road to walk along before reaching Summit Creek.

John Harris at the Alsek Trailhead where he will look for thundereggs (concretions) before continuing to Ferguson Creek.

There is no elevation change. If driving to Summit Creek, park your vehicle in the open field just before the creek. The start of the hike requires a creek crossing. The water from this creek can be silty.

An open meadow and forested area are your next landmarks. Continue to the large washout area which is Thunderegg Creek. This will take less than an hour to reach. Turn to the right if going up Thunderegg Creek to look for thundereggs.

Concretions known as thundereggs, or nature's bowling balls, can be found along this creek bed. The sandstone balls were formed in the glacial lake delta. Leaves, twigs, and small animal pieces were deposited on the bed of sediment. Negative charges of matter attracted positive charges of minerals. They bonded together and then were tumbled in the glaciers, thus forming the balls.

The thundereggs are difficult to spot because they are usually half-buried in the creek bed under silt deposits. If you don't see any, examples of the concretions are on display at the Haines Junction Visitor Information Centre and at Cabin Crafts, next to the bakery in Haines Junction.

Continuing along the Alsek Trail, the Dezadeash River is to the south (on the left). There are wave lines along the hills which were formed when the Lowell Glacier surged and blocked the flow of the Alsek River, creating the lakes. The lines go as high as 90 metres (300 feet) up the hills. This has happened many times in past years, but the most recent lake was formed about 150 years ago. There was a native settlement below the glacier, close to the lake. The settlement was washed away when the ice dam broke and the lake drained. It is believed that the entire lake drained within one day. There is speculation that Recent Lake Alsek was explored by Europeans. An oar hanging in the Haines Junction Information Centre was found in the driftwood left by the lake. The oar exhibits signs of being axe-hewn and is a style used by the Russians.

Thunderegg Creek is recommended for an afternoon of exploring. Although I have never done it, I think going up Thunderegg Creek could get you near the summit of Mount Archibald, where the view of the Icefield Range would be the best in the park.

Continuing along the trail, the park boundary sign at the 6.2 kilometre point is next. There is water along the trail up to the 10.6-kilometre sign. Notice the beach lines along the side of the hills up to this point. At present they are obvious but vegetation is growing over and covering the lines.

The trail veers slightly to the right and then follows the Dezadeash River. A creek must be crossed once before the park boundary and, if water levels are high, it will be more than just a wade. Rafts are put into the Dezadeash River at this spot so vehicle traffic is common.

One hour past Thunderegg Creek will take you through a wooded area and beside the foundation hole of an old cabin. Just beyond is the park gate at 15.4 kilometres. No motorized vehicles are permitted past this point. Continue up the hill for a couple of minutes to a well-protected camping spot with a clear stream and plenty of wood.

One hour past the gate are sand dunes where back eddy swirls are visible. These were left by Lake Champagne. When this lake receded, the back eddies that formed were quite large. Just beyond the eddies is the first view of the Alsek River. Continuing along the trail, look across the river between two rock walls where there are prominent wave-action lines along the hills. Like the rest, these are starting to grow over.

Just past the 20.9-kilometre sign is a clear creek and an open-area horse camp with plenty of places across the road to pitch a tent (away from the camp fire). There are boards, left from an old corral, that can be used as chairs. This campsite makes for a wonderful day's end.

At kilometre 22.5 is the junction of the Alsek, Dezadeash, and Kaskawulsh Rivers. The Kaskawulsh is running the fastest because at this point it has a 28-foot-per-mile downgrade. The river flats cover an area over 2 kilometres (1.2 miles) across with many signs of wave action along the hillsides. On the other side of the Dezadeash River is Profile Mountain, which looks like a blown-out volcano. From here the road is washed out so go up the hill along the trail to the 25.9-kilometre sign.

Just past the 25.9-kilometre sign is an unnamed creek with clear water, a fire ring, and flat tenting spots. All three rivers are visible from this spot. It takes about another half an hour to reach Ferguson Creek, or Sugden Creek as it used to be called. The creek was originally named after Dr. Sugden who practised medicine in Silver City during its peak.

To get to the cabin, cross Ferguson Creek by walking downstream to where it fans out. Choose the crossing carefully as the water is cold and swift, even during low water. Once across go up the creek to the cabins. They are not habitable but there are interesting artifacts to look at. Inside the main cabin is a stove, with pots and kitchen utensils hanging from the rafters, plus a cork screw for anyone who brought a bottle of wine. There is one box dated 1953 and the hand-hewed sawhorse is a work of art – not to mention a photographer's delight. It is illegal to remove anything in or around the cabins.

Return by the same route.

 ## MOUNT DECOELI

Time: *Day hike to the pass and summit, overnight to the valley*
Distance: *7.5 kilometres (4.7 miles) to Decoeli Pass; 17.8 kilometres (11.1 miles) to Kimberley Meadow*
Difficulty: *Moderate*
Change in elevation: *879 metres (2,884 feet)*
Maximum elevation: *1,860 metres (6,102 feet)*
Topographical maps: *Kloo Lake 115 A/13*

Equipment needed: *Leather boots are a must and if you're going beyond Decoeli Pass, a map and compass are recommended. Rain gear should always be carried and creek-crossing shoes could be necessary during high water. A stove is needed for overnight trips.*

The route: This is a scenic route that is steep but requires no bushwhacking. The route follows rock glaciers for more than half the way. If the weather is bad, views may not be possible. This is one of the routes in the park where llamas may be used as pack animals for hikers. Their split hoofs do not damage the vegetation and when they eat, they snip off the greenery instead of pulling it out, thus causing less damage. Bears, unfamiliar with the scent of llamas, seem to ignore them. Contact the Kluane Park Adventure Centre in Haines Junction for more information.

The summit of Mount Decoeli reveals views of the Shakwak Trench and the icefields. If going to Kimberley Meadow, the hike has only moderate challenges in store. Spending a week in the area just exploring would be rewarding. Some people have crossed from Kimberley Meadow over to the Alsek Trail, but I recommend exiting by the Jarvis River route if a circle trip is desired.

0.0 km	Parking area and Summit Creek	[UTM (50-50) Kloo Lk]
5.0 km	Toe of rock glacier	[UTM (45-46) Kloo Lk]
7.5 km	Decoeli Pass	[UTM (43-46) Kloo Lk]
10.8 km	Toe of rock glacier; campsite	[UTM (41-49) Kloo Lk]
15.6 km	Alpine Lake	[UTM (38-47) Kloo Lk]
17.8 km	Kimberley Meadow	[UTM (38-45) Kloo Lk]

Trail access: Drive along the Alaska Highway 20 kilometres (12.4 miles) north from the Haines Junction Information Centre. There is a sign marking Bear Creek Summit. The parking area is on the south side of the creek. Turn left and park. Walk along the access road beside the creek.

The trail: This trail starts at the summit of Bear Pass at 1,004 metres (3,294 feet), which means you are soon in subalpine meadows. In the South Tutchone language "Decoeli" means "weather indicator," so expect colder, wetter weather here than you would farther north, where the average precipitation is 22 centimetres (8.7 inches) per year. From Decoeli south, the park is in the Pacific rain belt.

Follow the access road from the parking area for about twenty minutes. It soon becomes a narrow trail beside the creek. During high water, walk on the tundra on the south side of the creek. The walking is easy either way. Cross to the north side of the creek when you reach the toe of the first rock glacier, near the top end of the creek.

It takes about two hours to reach the toe of the rock glacier. Once there, climb the hill on the north (right) and continue above the rock glacier. Although a fire pit can be found on the side of this hill, I don't know what was burned as there is no wood in the vicinity. Do not make fires in the alpine.

To reach the pass or the summit of Decoeli, continue walking past three gullies that may or may not have water in them. Walk until almost at the top end of the rock glacier. There is ice and a sawtooth mountain just past the draw leading to Decoeli Pass. The draw with

Lorne LaRocque takes llamas to Mount Decoeli. The animals do not attract bears, they can carry heavy loads and, because they have split hoofs, they do not damage delicate vegetation.

brown rocks on the slope is not the draw to follow. Continue to the next draw where the rock is dark grey or slate in colour. Turn northwest (right) up the slate-coloured draw and slug your way up the scree. It is not too steep and it will take about a half hour to reach the top of the pass from the turn at the rock glacier. If going to the summit of Mount Decoeli, turn east (right) at the pass and continue upward.

Start the descent from Decoeli Pass along the east (right) side. The pass is often socked in with clouds but, due to winds, the clouds dissipate quickly. To the north are two humps on the side of the ridge, just east (right) of the rock glacier. The humps, which appear in front of you, are good landmarks to head for. Descending on the right-hand side of the glacier is easier than on the left. Getting off the rock glacier requires a steep descent into the creek bed. Reconnoitre carefully before descending, but do not go all the way to the toe of the glacier before getting off. Following the stream at the side of the glacier is safe and easy. It will take about two and a half hours to cross this glacier.

If returning by this route, take water as it is difficult to find on the glacier. On the return, do not follow the draw between the grassy slopes below the brown rocky outcroppings. Continue to the next draw where the shale is slate grey or return the way you came.

About 500 feet past the toe is a meadow that is recommended for camping. Clear water is close but flat spots are at a premium. Do not build a fire in this area.

To go to the alpine lake, veer to the west (left) and follow the valley. Stay partway up the grassy hills on the west side of the valley. Contour around the mountain to the rocky outcroppings where Kloo Lake and the icefields come into view. Walking in the valley rather than up on the hills may result in puddle-jumping, as the valley is usually wet. It also takes longer to walk on the valley floor.

After passing the rocky outcrop on the curve of the valley, continue in a southerly direction, moving slowly down the hills. There is little or no firewood at the lake so stoves are essential. The lake is pretty, but I prefer the toe of the rock glacier for camping. Climbing the unnamed ridge to the north, above the lake, leads to Kimberley Creek and the Jarvis River route. Once on the ridge, Kimberley Creek, Kaskawulsh River, Telluride Creek and peaks in the icefields come into view. The pink cirque across Kimberley Creek to the north has been dubbed the Queen's Throne.

Anemones are common in the region early in the year. Natives used the plant to kill fleas, and some drank anemone tea to rid themselves of rheumatism. The tea is now believed to be poisonous – the natives did say the tea burned like whiskey going down.

Continuing along the valley past the lake and across or around the bottom of the rock glacier leads to Kimberley Meadow. The ramp leading off the glacier was caused by an underground river before the ice melted. Follow the ramp partway, turning south (left) when near the meadows. Staying on the ramp will take you to Kimberley Creek.

KIMBERLEY MEADOW TO ALSEK TRAIL

Time: *3 to 5 days from the Alaska Highway*
Distance: *26.1 kilometres (16.2 miles) to headwaters of Ferguson Creek from Bear Pass*
Difficulty: *Difficult*
Change in elevation: *879 metres (2,884 feet)*
Maximum elevation: *1,860 metres (6,102 feet)*
Topographical maps: *Kloo Lake 115 A/13, Auriol Range 115 A/12*
Equipment needed: *Leather boots, a map and compass, and extra food (in case the weather socks in) are needed if you're going beyond Kimberley Meadow. Overnight gear and rain gear are essential.*

The route: This is a difficult route through isolated terrain. A few hikers have gone this way, but it is not recommended unless you have a lot of experience and you want a challenge. Bushwhacking through thick alders and descending from a steep ridge are two of the challenges. Bushwhacking down Ferguson Creek includes passing a box canyon that could prevent passage in high water.

5.0 km   Toe of first rock glacier [UTM (45-46) Kloo Lk]
7.5 km   Decoeli Pass [UTM (43-46) Kloo Lk]

11.0 km   End of second rock glacier [UTM (41-49) Kloo Lk]
12.0 km   To ridge above Kimberley Creek
15.6 km   Alpine lake on Mount Decoeli Trail
          [UTM (38-47) Kloo Lk]
16.6 km   Ramp on rock glacier
17.8 km   Beginning of Kimberley Meadow
20.1 km   Beginning of long rock glacier crossing
          [UTM (39-43) Kloo Lk]
25.6 km   End of glacier crossing
26.1 km   Headwaters of Ferguson Creek

Trail access: Follow the Mount Decoeli Trail to the alpine lake [UTM (38-47) Kloo Lk]. Kimberley Meadow is highly recommended for a day of exploration.

The trail: After leaving the alpine lake, continue south down the valley. There is a rock glacier with a ramp ahead. The ramp is an old riverbed where water flowed from the glacier. The rounded river stones are different from the surrounding sharp glacial stones. Follow the ramp down to the toe of the glacier, rather than climbing onto the glacier. Skirting the glacier will take about two hours. The route over the glacier is steeper and more difficult. However, if you're crossing the glacier, there are green patches on which to rest and the view is better.

The ramp follows the toe of the glacier and descends to the meadow. Originally, the glacial river flowed into Kimberley Creek and this route could be taken if going out the Jarvis River. Once around the toe of the glacier you will be heading south again. Kimberley Meadow is one of the nicest meadows in the park.

Although the meadow is only 2 or 3 kilometres long, there is fresh water and numerous campsites are available. Continuing south, there are rock glaciers leading to Kimberley Pass and the headwaters of Ferguson Creek. From Kimberley Meadow I suggest climbing Mount Archibald for the icefield views. However, I cannot suggest an easy route up Archibald, as the climb has always been too ambitious for me.

Once you're over the rock glaciers and at the headwaters of Ferguson Creek, there are campsites for about 2 kilometres (1.2 miles). From the headwaters to the Alsek Trail, hiking is suggested only for those adventuresome spirits with lots of experience. I have not done this section of the trail; the following directions were provided by Sean Frey.

Continue down Ferguson Valley for 3 kilometres (1.9 miles) until the bushwhacking starts. After the willows become thick, look for the second saddle or notch to the northeast (left) and head up there. Descending the creek is not possible because a canyon prevents crossing. Going to the notch are three steep gorges and thick willows where the potential for a bear encounter is extremely good. The willows grow up to 2.7 metres (9 feet) high. Climb high to get around the bush and then descend to pass the gorges.

Past the last (third) gorge is a flat, grassy area where rest is recommended before conquering more willows. Continue to a rock outcrop and then further up the notch. The notch is dangerous and requires reconnoitring before going over.

After crossing the notch, walk along the ridge to a small creek on the east (left). This is the best way down to the Alsek Trail and the Dezadeash River.

I walked up his small creek from the Alsek Trail to see if I could get into Kimberley from that direction, but I gave up. The bushwhacking was easier than it was on Ferguson Creek – the creek never gets too big and the underbrush never gets too dense – but the snags across the creek are a nuisance.

If you're going out along the Dezadeash River, see the Alsek Trail description. If you came over the notch, the rest is a cakewalk.

 ## KIMBERLEY MEADOW TO JARVIS RIVER

Time: *2 to 3 days*
Distance: *15.8 kilometres (9.8 miles) from Kimberley Ridge to road*
Difficulty: *Moderate to easy*
Change in elevation: *522 metres (1,713 feet)*
Maximum elevation: *1,402 metres (4,600 feet)*
Topographical maps: *Kloo Lake 115 A/13, Jarvis River 115 B/16*

Equipment needed: *Boots with a good grip and all overnight gear are needed. One creek crossing on the Jarvis Road could be difficult, so creek-crossing shoes should be carried.*

The route: If you have made it to the ridge above Kimberley Meadow, the most difficult section of the hike is over. Even the bushwhacking down to Kimberley Creek is not difficult as the vegetation is low and the trees are sparse. This exit makes a nice circle route from Mount Decoeli.

12.0 km   Ridge above Kimberley Creek
15.4 km   Mine site on Kimberley Creek

Vivien rests on the ridge near Kimberley Meadow. The Queen's Throne glistens in the background.
Photo by Joanne Armstrong

17.6 km Jarvis River Road
27.8 km Alaska Highway

Trail access: Follow the Mount Decoeli trail to the end of the second rock glacier that is situated 4.6 kilometres (2.9 miles) before the alpine lake. Or go as far as the riverbed at the toe of the glacier and follow it to Kimberley Creek. Kimberley Creek has wide gravel beds so walking is easy.

The trail: If you're going over the ridge, veer to the west (right) from the toe of the rock glacier toward the green knoll above the cutbanks. Cross the valley while staying between the two humps seen when descending from Decoeli Pass. Once on the ridge, walk to the top of the higher knoll for excellent views of Kimberley Meadow. Continue over the ridge and down to the cutbanks along the first creek ahead. Follow this creek for a minute, but be very careful as there is an 18-metre (60-foot) drop, with no guard rails. After finding a suitable spot, climb the hill on the opposite side of the creek. A view of the road along Kimberley Creek will become obvious. Continue in a westerly direction, avoiding the thick brush for as long as possible before dropping to Kimberley Creek.

There is an active mining site close to the Jarvis River Road junction. The mining site has an abandoned bus with 1979 Minnesota plates, a flotilla of bunkhouse trailers, a cabin, and some private trailers. The site is decorated with rusting junk and the side of the hill has been sluiced. The site gives me incentive to join the Canadian Wilderness Society who are fighting to change Kluane Sanctuary to park status. Mining is prohibited in parks.

Continue along the road to the junction on the right. It is a two- to-three hour walk to the turn-around spot on the Jarvis River Road and another 4.3 kilometres (2.7 miles) to the highway. See Jarvis River Trail for the remainder of the walk.

C5 JARVIS RIVER

Time: *3 to 4 hours*
Distance: *9.0 kilometres (5.6 miles)*
Difficulty: *Easy*
Change in elevation: *213 metres (700 feet)*
Maximum elevation: *1,036 metres (3,400 feet)*
Topographical maps: *Kloo Lake 115 A/13*
Equipment needed: *If you're going only to Kimberley Creek, the Queen's Throne, and the mine site, runners are sufficient. There is water at least every third kilometre along the road.*

The route: This is a pleasant stroll along a flat road with one creek-crossing, which is not difficult but requires boot removal. The Queen's Throne comes into view early in the walk and the view continues for the entire trek. If coming from Mount Decoeli, this is an easy walk to the highway. The river was named after A. M. Jarvis, an RCMP officer who lived and worked at Dalton Post from 1899 to 1902.

0.0 km	Alaska Highway
1.5 km	Jarvis Creek
4.3 km	Pullout
5.3 km	Creek-crossing
13.0 km	Fork
15.0 km	Kimberley Creek; mine site

Trail access: Drive 38.3 kilometres (23.8 miles) south from Sheep Mountain Information Centre. The road is 2 kilometres (1.2 miles) north of where the Jarvis River crosses the highway. There are deep ruts in the Jarvis River Road and if there has been any rain, do not attempt to drive more than 1 kilometre (0.6 miles). Even vehicles with four-wheel-drive have been known to spend an entire summer on the trail because they were stuck. During dry weather, it is possible to drive 4.3 kilometres (2.7 miles) to a pullout area.

The trail: Park near the highway and follow the road. It crosses a small creek. The meadow at the beginning of the trail has many gophers. Female gophers get rid of their mates early in their relationships and share rearing responsibilities with other females.

Continue to a creek with an obvious car pullout area. This creek is not difficult to cross. The next creek, 1 kilometre (0.6 miles) farther, is swift and cold. If there has been a lot of rain, it may present a problem.

The next landmark is the fork in the road. The fork on the right goes to the Jarvis River and the one on the left goes to Kimberley Creek. The Queen's Throne, across the river from the road, is in view for almost the entire walk.

The first gold found in Kluane Country was on the tributaries of the Jarvis River in the summer of 1903. By late autumn of the same year, there were stakes on the Jarvis, Ruby, Fourth of July, McKinley, Telluride, Gladstone, Bullion, Sheep, Vulcan, Metalline, Multi-metal and Canada Creeks – with Bullion Creek spewing 43 ounces of gold in nine days. Otherwise, hardship was the only thing offered by the land, and by the end of 1904 most of the rush was over.

Red and yellow Indian paintbrush is abundant in the area. It was once forbidden to pick the flower because some native peoples believed it to be sacred. Today, it is forbidden to pick the flower because it is against park regulations.

 ## SILVER CREEK TO OUTPOST MOUNTAIN

Time: *2 to 3 days*
Distance: *20 kilometres (12.4 miles) return*
Difficulty: *Moderate*
Change in elevation: *305 metres (1,000 feet)*
Maximum elevation: *610 metres (2,000 feet)*
Topographical maps: *Jarvis River 115 B/16*
Equipment needed: *Boots and overnight gear. Water should be carried on the mountain.*

The route: This creek should be called either Black Creek or Mud Creek because of its colour. However, clear drinking water can be obtained from the streams flowing into Silver Creek. The walk is easy with no creek-crossings, only a bit of bushwhacking. Outpost Mountain reveals views of the Shakwak Trench, Kloo Lake, Kluane Lake, part of Slims Valley, and Vulcan Glacier. Silver Creek Valley is attractive with hanging glaciers becoming more visible with each hundred metres walked.

0.0 km	Parking area
8.5 km	Curve [UTM (60-46) Jarvis Cr]
9.0 km	Ascent to Outpost Mountain [UTM (59-45) Jarvis Cr]
10.0 km	Outpost Mountain

Trail access: Drive south on the Alaska Highway from Sheep Mountain Information Centre 13.2 kilometres (8.2 miles) and turn left. There is a small area suitable for parking.

The trail: Start on the north side of the creek, even though the south side looks more inviting. The south side of the creek washes into a high bank that cannot be scurried around. Crossing this creek is dangerous. It is swift, boulders are bouncing along all the time and, because of the colour, it is not possible to see where you are stepping. When standing in the creek, the water rapidly washes the sand away from around your feet. Walking on the north side requires some detours through the bush, but it is not thick and travel is easy. Carry drinking water as there is none for three to four hours unless you find some settling pools where the black sand has precipitated.

Continue past the curve until the glaciers come into view. Shortly after the curve is a vegetated island with a clear creek flowing into Silver Creek from Outpost Mountain. This is the best campsite along the bottom part of the creek. There are two sandy cutbanks with jagged rocks poking through the vegetation. The creek flowing between these cutbanks is the one to follow to ascend Outpost.

Bushwhacking up the creek toward Outpost Mountain is difficult for about fifteen minutes. The creek splits and the left-hand fork soon opens into a four lane gravel highway which leads to the alpine on

Outpost Mountain. Once in the alpine, take the ridge to the right and follow it as high as you wish to go. It will not take you to the summit because the scree becomes fairly loose near the top. However, if you have time and energy, continue around the north side of the mountain and ascend to the plateau on top by the back door.

From the mountain Kluane Lake, Kluane Plateau, Red Castle Ridge, Right On Mountain and Sheep Mountain come into view. Looking in the opposite direction (south) you will see Mount Decoeli and Kloo Lake. From Outpost Mountain it will be obvious that you have entered the Kluane rain shadow. The vegetation is less lush (less alder) and clouds seem to gather around Mount Decoeli, while the northern skies are clear. North of Mount Decoeli the icefields catch most of the moisture, which results in an average precipitation of 22 centimetres (8.7 inches) per year in the area. The southern section of the park falls under the Pacific rain belt and gets well over 100 centimetres (39 inches) of precipitation per year.

Return as you came, being certain to carry water. The possibility of exploring as far as the headwaters of Silver Creek are excellent. The creek splits partway up and each arm leads to a rock glacier. The views are spectacular and the area is recommended. There are creeks with clear water at regular intervals along the way.

 ## WILLIAM'S HORSE TRAIL TO KLUANE PLATEAU

Time: *7 to 9 hours*
Distance: *14 kilometres (8.7 miles) return trip*
Difficulty: *Moderate to difficult*
Change in elevation: *900 metres (2,953 feet)*
Maximum elevation: *1,720 metres (5,643 feet)*
Topographical maps: *Jarvis River 115 B/16, Slims River 115 B/15*
Equipment needed: *Boots and rain gear are needed if you're doing the circle route. This is a strenuous day trip, so water and food should be carried. A map and compass are recommended.*

The route: The route follows a horse trail to the plateau. From the plateau to the exit route along the Slims River requires easy orienteering, but the descent could present some problems. Returning by the horse trail is the easiest route.

0.0 km   Horse trail
2.0 km   Rocky hill; start of climb
4.2 km   Knoll near top of hill
5.2 km   Ridge along plateau
7.0 km   End of plateau

Trail access: There are two approaches to the plateau but the William's Horse Trail is recommended. Drive 8 kilometres (5 miles) south from the visitor's information centre to the last creek before the Glacier Helicopter landing pad. There are two creeks within a few hundred feet of each other; you want the southern one. There is limited parking along the side of the road.

The second approach to the plateau is 3.4 kilometres (2.1 miles) south of the Sheep Mountain Information Centre. Turn right onto the side road (Slims East Road) where a sign indicates a ski trail. Vehicles with clearance may drive 3.2 kilometres (2 miles) before parking. On the left is an obvious signpost beside a horse trail going through the bush toward the east. Take this trail.

The trail: Taking the William's Horse Trail, follow the creek for about 100 metres and turn right onto the old pipeline road. Follow the road for about 50 metres and turn left onto a bulldozed track. Follow the track to the split in the creek then cross to the far bank. Follow the left-hand side of the creek until a flagged horse trail comes into view. Follow this trail for approximately two hours to the plateau. The trail is steep for a short distance. It is also often wet.

William's Horse Trail was originally called Mike's Trail, named after Mike Williams who owned Kluane Lake Lodge situated a few miles south of Sheep Mountain on the old Alaska Highway. When the new highway was constructed, Williams relocated to the lake, but eventually sold the property.

Going from the second access route on the Slims East Road, carry water and snacks as the route is difficult and dry. Walking toward Vulcan Mountain results in having to cross steep gullies. Getting lost could be a problem for those without expert orienteering skills. If doing the circle, the William's Horse Trail is difficult to find from this approach.

The Slims East Horse Trail becomes indistinct after 1 kilometre (0.6 miles). At the end of the trail, veer to the right toward Vulcan Creek. During wet years, Vulcan Creek takes more than one path; therefore crossing some tributaries may be necessary before getting onto the main creek bed.

Follow the creek bed for about one hour to the first outcropping on the north (left). There is a trail over the outcrop and to an old mining camp on the opposite side. This is a good campsite if you're camping overnight and starting the trail in the morning.

From the trail on the outcrop, continue up the hill. Carry water as there is none for at least four hours of walking. If you're returning the same way, make note of some landmarks you can use as guides. After passing the hill, turn left (the only possibility) and continue farther uphill, following the trail. This section is steep but the views are great. Halfway up the hill the remains of the old Alaska Highway Bridge crossing the Slims River come into view. Once at a large resting boulder, look across Slims, up Bullion Creek, or behind at Vulcan Mountain and Vulcan Glacier. Outpost Mountain is to the south.

Beyond the resting boulder, enter the bush along a trail, which eventually disappears after starting you off in the right direction. Continue this way for ten or fifteen minutes and then bushwhack for another twenty minutes or so, going in a northerly direction. Stay on animal trails as much as possible to save delicate vegetation and to help form a regular trail, which helps to prevent erosion.

Once in the subalpine, walk toward the rocky bluffs and the obvious rust-coloured knoll on the left. Continue keeping the knoll to the east (right) until you're in the meadow. Cross the meadow and follow the ridge on the opposite side. Kluane Lake and the Shakwak Trench come into view.

There are two lakes on the plateau where some camping is possible. The white clay rock face is above the larger lake, and the hill to the right has some flat camping spots.

Kluane Plateau is part of the Shakwak Trench, which is believed to be one of the first corridors travelled by Asians during their migration across the Bering Sea. The little arm on the southwest shore of Kluane Lake is where archeologists found signs of human presence dating back thousands of years. Old Crow on the Beaufort Sea is where a 27,000-year-old hide-working tool and immature human mandible were found. The Shakwak Trench and the Nahanni River region were never glaciated so the corridors were hospitable to human beings.

Crossing the plateau, Vulcan Creek Canyon becomes visible. From the trailhead, the canyon takes about three to five hours to reach. Do not attempt to return to Vulcan Creek by Jessie Creek, as the way is steep and the terrain is unstable.

You may continue across the plateau and find the William's Horse Trail but it is difficult. I recommend going up the William's Horse Trail and coming down by the route described, or by the route leading to the highway.

Going back to the highway, an alternative to taking the William's Horse Trail is to climb the ridge on the western side of the plateau, near the ridge's centre. Looking down, three ridges above steep creek gullies can be seen. The centre ridge is the easiest to descend, requiring moderate bushwhacking through willows and spruce. There are some game trails to follow. After descending a third of the way, enter the creek bed on the right for easier walking. This descent was recommended by Michelle Oakley of Haines Junction.

C8 VULCAN CREEK

Time: *Full day or overnight*
Distance: *20 kilometres (12.5 miles) return trip*
Difficulty: *Moderate*
Change in elevation: *780 metres (2,560 feet)*
Maximum elevation: *1,600 metres (5,250 feet)*
Topographical maps: *Jarvis River 115 B/16, Slims River 115 B/15*
Equipment needed: *Hiking boots and creek-crossing shoes are necessary. Rain gear is recommended.*

The route: There is little reason to walk this creek and encounter many crossings in icy water, unless you wish to climb Vulcan Mountain or see its hanging glacier. The creek bed is rugged and the creek often runs against a cliff edge, requiring many crossings in the swift, cold water. During high water levels, the creek may not be possible to cross. We tried going up and over some of the bluffs on the east (left) side of Vulcan Creek, but it was hard going.

0.0 km	Horse trail
2.0 km	Mining camp
3.2 km	Jessie Creek
5.5 km	Alpine ridge
8.0 km	Fork of Vulcan Creek
10.0 km	Vulcan Mountain and glacier

Trail access: Drive south 3.4 kilometres (2.1 miles) along the Alaska Highway from Sheep Mountain Information Centre. Cross the Slims River Bridge and turn right. A park sign indicates the turnoff. Continue along this road for 3.2 kilometres (2 miles) to a well-defined horse trail. Vehicles driven on this road should have high clearance.

The trail: Follow the horse trail while veering right, until Vulcan Creek is reached. It will take less than one hour. Continue to the first outcropping where a trail goes over a ridge. Remains of an old mining camp are on the opposite side. This is an interesting place to stop and poke around, or to make a base camp before exploring the rest of the area.

Continuing up the stream, cross whenever necessary. Water levels will come up during a hot day or during a hard rain so if crossing is difficult early in the day, it could be worse later. Past Jessie Creek is an alpine ridge that could be a campsite.

Vulcan Creek forks shortly after Jessie Creek. The area is dotted with uniquely coloured rocks. Either fork of Vulcan Creek is interesting. If going onto the glacier, ropes and climbing equipment are necessary.

C9 SLIMS RIVER EAST

Time: *2 to 4 days*
Distance: *40 kilometres (25 miles) return trip*
Difficulty: *Easy to moderate*
Elevation gain: *980 metres (3,215 feet)*
Maximum elevation: *1,800 metres (5,905 feet)*
Topographical maps: *Slims River 115 B/15, Jarvis River 115 B/16*
Equipment needed: *Light boots or runners are sufficient. Maps are needed for interest's sake only.*

The route: This is an alternative route when the Slims River West Trail is closed. The Kaskawulsh Glacier can be seen from this side, but you are across from it rather than above it as you are on Slims River West. There is an old road cut through the bush for most of the way. The road was originally made to take tourists in large-wheeled buses, like those used on the Columbia Icefields in Jasper, to the Kaskawulsh Glacier. However, due to adverse weather conditions and constant terrain changes, the road could not be maintained at a reasonable cost. It is now a hiker's paradise, even though some sections are overgrown. The trail is clear to the lakes, after which most hikers walk beside the river. The only challenges are crossing the alluvial fans, which make the trail hard to pick up on the opposite side. These melt water fans are among the best in the park.

0.0 km	Trailhead; end of road
1.5 km	Vulcan Creek
2.0 km	Freshwater spring [UTM (34-62) Slims R]
7.5 km	Possible campsite
11.0 km	Small lake
16.5 km	Larger lake [UTM (30-55) Slims R]
20.0 km	Lookout point

Trail access: Drive south along the Alaska Highway 3.4 kilometres (2.1 miles) from the Sheep Mountain Information Centre. Cross the Slims River Bridge and turn right along an access road. There is a park sign indicating the turnoff. Continue along this road for 3.3 kilometres (2.1 miles). The road once went farther, but in 1991 Vulcan Creek washed it out.

The trail: Walk towards Vulcan Creek in a southeasterly direction from the parking area. There are cairns and park signposts across the flats that lead to a trail on the hillside on the far side of the creek. Beyond the flats is a muskeg patch that must be crossed. The trail is not visible in the muskeg. Go in a southerly direction, away from the river, where the walking is drier. Continue to the trail which is made obvious by the red paint marks on the trees. To reach the trail on the hill will take one to two hours.

About fifteen minutes along the hill, between the trail and the river, is a spring coming out of the hill just above the river bank. Although the water is excellent, there is no place to camp.

Continue to the next washout about one hour farther. Camping is possible in the meadow beyond the washout, near a stream with clear water. After the meadow, the trail winds toward the river. The Kaskawulsh Glacier comes into view within two hours of leaving the meadow. Be certain to follow the trail after the washout, as it is easier than bushwhacking.

A small lake is reached fifteen minutes beyond the first view of the glacier. Camping sites with views of the glacier are abundant from here on.

It is two hours more to the end of the valley where you can ascend the mountain to see the glacier better. There are two options. If time is short, walk up the next alluvial fan while veering south (left) in order to cross the hill. Vantage spots soon become obvious. This climb takes about two hours going up and one hour coming down.

If time is not pressing, continue along the river past the end of the valley and the glacier's toe until around the corner and facing east. Ascend the hill on the left. It is not steep and the view is excellent. From the hillside, crevasses with moving water, pressure geysers and glacial lakes – some of which have trees near them – become visible. Occasionally a geyser-like fountain will emerge at the toe of the glacier. The fountains may be up to 3 metres (10 feet) across and 6 metres (20 feet) in height. The Slims River spews 216 million litres (57 million gallons) of glacial melt water into Kluane Lake every day. This water is an accumulation of melt water from the Kaskawulsh and Vulcan Glaciers plus the melt water streams flowing into the Slims.

Note that on this side of the hill you are on the Kaskawulsh River, which flows into the Alsek near Ferguson Creek. I have heard of people hiking to here and then following the Kaskawulsh River to the Alsek Trail. It would be a long hike.

If walking on the riverbed in front of the glacier, be aware of glacial goop or quick-mud. It is dangerous and falling into some could be frightening, if not deadly.

Returning, walk along the river past the lake. Near the cliffs turn inland as it is dangerous to scramble along the edge. Quick-mud or glacial goop is along this section of the river. The river got its name from Slim, a horse who died because his master could not get him out of the glacial goop after riding him across the river. Be certain to stay away from nonvegetated areas, or you could join Slim in a muddy grave.

Horsetail plants are common near the river. The plant was used by the South Tutchone as a sandpaper for scouring and the Tlingit made a tea that they drank for bladder problems.

 SOLDIER'S SUMMIT

Time: *1 hour*
Distance: *0.5 kilometres (0.3 miles)*
Difficulty: *Easy*
Change in elevation: *20 metres (65.5 feet)*
Maximum elevation: *853 metres (2,800 feet)*
Topographical maps: *Congdon Creek 115 G/2*
Equipment needed: *Runners are all that are needed for this short hike.*

The route: This is a historic stroll with excellent views of Kluane Lake and the Alaska Highway. The trail has interpretive signs that convey the history of the highway.

Trail access: Walk or drive one half a kilometre north from Sheep Mountain Interpretive Centre. Follow the interpretive signs. The photos on the signs, duplicated from archival copies, reveal the hardships endured during the highway's construction. Memorials along the highway do not have bodies under them. During the construction period, the dead were shipped back to their families living elsewhere.

The trail: The building of the Alaska Highway was proposed on February 12, 1942 and approved the next day. Eight months and twelve days later the 2,440-kilometre (1,525-mile) roadway from Big Delta, Alaska to Dawson Creek, B.C. was completed. 25,000 men and women worked with engineers, through temperatures so cold that antifreeze froze and diesel fuel turned to lard.

At the summit you can hear a replay of the radio broadcast that was recorded during the opening ceremony – complete with bars from "God Save the King" and "The Stars and Stripes Forever."

Because of the soldiers' indiscriminate hunting practices during that time, an ordinance was passed forming the Kluane Game Sanctuary. In June of 1942, Charles Le Capelain came to the Yukon from Waterton Lakes National Park, where he was the superintendent. Le Capelain and Commissioner George Jeckell, eventual rivals in the control of the Yukon, first met in August of 1942 and agreed that together they would work to establish national parks or game sanctuaries in selected areas of the Yukon. Kluane was one of the areas the two men agreed needed saving.

Le Capelain and Jeckell wrote to Mr. Gibson, their boss in Ottawa, stating, "the stretch of road running from the Dezadeash River to the White River offers something you cannot get anywhere else in Canada: a view of St. Elias Mountains containing the largest glaciers and mountain peaks in Canada."

In October, Parks Commissioner James Smart forwarded a memo to Privy Council, requesting wildlife protection at Kluane. Two weeks after the highway opened, the land around Kluane came under a government freeze, and in the spring of 1943 the area became a game sanctuary where hunting and fishing were strictly prohibited.

Below the summit, Kluane Lake has imprinted older, higher water levels on the surrounding hills. Three to four hundred years ago, the

Kaskawulsh Glacier surged across the Slims River. Prior to the surge, the Slims River drained in the opposite direction toward the Kaskawulsh River, and then the Alsek River. The surge closed the drainage and raised water levels on the lake by 9 metres (30 feet). An arm was carved at the northeast end of the lake, which now connects the lake to the Yukon River. The glacial surge caused the river to reverse its path into the Bering Sea, instead of flowing to the Pacific as it did before. Lake levels have since come down.

Kluane Lake is frozen from November until May or early June. Water temperatures rarely exceed 7°C (44.6°F) and frost around the lake is possible any time of year.

Edward Glave, the British explorer and journalist, was travelling in the area with Jack Dalton from Haines, Alaska. They took a dugout canoe onto Lake "Tloo Arny," but heavy winds came up and capsized the vessel – almost killing the explorers.

Sheep Mountain Information Centre was once directly below Sheep Mountain, but the centre was moved in 1996 because of the danger of falling rocks from the mountain. The park has up to four hundred minor earth tremors per year and one major tremor every five years. With all that shaking going on, officials thought it wise to move the centre to its present site on the flats before a disaster occurred.

C11 SHEEP MOUNTAIN

Time: *9 hours return trip*
Distance: *12.0 kilometres (7.5 miles) return trip*
Difficulty: *Moderate*
Change in elevation: *1,158 metres (3,800 feet)*
Maximum elevation: *1,950 metres (6,398 feet)*
Topographical maps: *Congdon Creek 115 G/2*
Equipment needed: *Running shoes are sufficient, but if the trail is wet wear boots. Carry water. A map is need for interest sake's only.*

The route: National parks in Canada have a zoning system that classi-fies areas according to the amount of protection they need. Sheep

Mountain falls into the Zone 1 classification. This means the area of the mountain above the Information Centre, plus a section facing the Alaska Highway, is to have limited or no public traffic. I have seen some hikers trying to get off the mountain by way of the restricted area. Please be sensitive to park regulations or the mountain may be closed to visitors altogether.

0.0 km	Warden's cabin
0.5 km	Sheep Mountain turnoff
3.8 km	Sheep Creek turnoff
4.8 km	Hoodoos and turnoff
5.0 km	Sign indicating you have gone too far
6.0 km	Ridge

Trail access: Walk or drive down the first access road north of Sheep Mountain Information Centre. There is parking at the warden's cabin. A gate closes traffic to motorized vehicles beyond this point. The road and trail are well maintained.

The trail: For those not going to the summit of Sheep Mountain, walking partway up the road reveals great views. Only after Sheep Creek turnoff does the trail become a bit difficult. Since the front section of Sheep Mountain is a Zone 1 area and may not be entered without a permit from the Superintendent of Parks, you must descend the same route by which you came. If weather is bad do not go up as there are steep drop-offs which may not be obvious. Besides, why climb for no view?

Walk past the gate and continue along the road to the 0.5-kilometre sign. Turn right and start up the hill. There are views of Vulcan Mountain, Slims River Valley, and the toe of the Kaskawulsh Glacier within half an hour.

Continue to the fork at the 3.8-kilometre sign. The road to the left branches off to Fisher Creek. Follow the right-hand fork until past the hoodoos before 48 Pup Creek. Climb the ridge past the hoodoos. If you pass the 5.0-kilometre sign, you have gone too far. The knoll beside the sign is too steep.

Follow game trails going up the ridge beside the hoodoos. Stay close to vegetation for safer footing. When choosing between the two ridges beside the hoodoos, take the one closest to 48 Pup as it is not as steep as the one nearer the hoodoos. Once on the ridge, it is difficult to get lost.

The colours of the Slims River delta emptying into Kluane Lake make the view more like a picture of the Caribbean Ocean than of Northern Canada. Also visible are the Kaskawulsh Glacier, Red Castle Ridge going towards Congdon Creek, Vulcan Mountain, Wallace Mountain, and most of the Shakwak Trench. The icefield ranges in the distance accentuate the vastness of the area. The insignificance of one human in this immense territory is overwhelming.

The Slims River delta formation, where the river enters Kluane Lake, has silt ten feet deep. The delta spreads a mile upstream and it advances 49 to 73 metres (160 to 240 feet) per year. It took eight thousand years for the Kaskawulsh Glacier to recede from the lake to its present position. The delta is under Zone 1 protection, which strictly limits public use.

Sheep Mountain is called "Thya-chul" by local Indians and means "the place where hide-scrapers are found." Needless to say, there is a good chance of seeing sheep on the mountain. Ewes have shorter horns; males have longer, curled horns. Sheep never shed their horns and the age of the animal can be determined by counting the rings on the horns. Freezing temperatures can damage the base of the horns causing a fatal ingrowth. During mating season, rams butt their heads against each other, creating loud crashing noises. Sheep have an air pocket between two layers of skull that partially absorbs the shock.

Sheep live on Sheep Mountain because the food supply is exceptionally rich. The dry flood plains of the Slims River have minerals ground from bedrock by the glaciers and deposited on the river during run-off. The winds carry these minerals, called loess, and deposit them on Sheep Mountain. The rich soil creates a haven for plant growth with sheep favourites like sage, saxifrages, willow and mountain avens. The salt lick beside a creek at the base of Sheep Mountain provides essential minerals for bone building in young sheep.

Do not disturb the sheep when on the mountain. There is plenty of room for everyone as long as respect is shown. If sheep or bear are along the ridge, turn back.

Return the same route as you came. Returning by 48 Pup Creek and arriving at the Bayshore Motel is another option. Coming down the face of the mountain is not permitted because of the delicate ecosystem.

SLIMS RIVER WEST TO OBSERVATION MOUNTAIN

Time: *3 to 5 days*
Distance: *60 kilometres (37 miles) return*
Difficulty: *Moderate*
Change in elevation: *120 metres (393.7 feet) to campsite, 1,314 metres (4,311 feet) to top of Observation Mountain.*
Maximum elevation: *2,114 metres (6,936 feet)*
Topographical maps: *Congdon Creek 115 G/2, Slims River 115 B/15*
Equipment needed: *Creek-crossing shoes are needed, as the trail is wet. Boots are recommended for Observation Mountain. It is mandatory to carry a food canister. If you are caught without a canister on this trail, the fine is $2,000 and will be strictly enforced. There is now a canister drop at the Kluane Park Visitor Information Centre, so you can de-register after hours by leaving the canister at the drop.*

The route: This route leads to the most accessible glacier in the park, but it is also the one most often closed due to bear activity. Because of the high bear concentration, be especially aware of creating odours. *Read the entire section on bears.*

The entire Slims River Valley is a Zone 1 protection area which means that there will be only minimal or no public use, depending on the need of the resource being protected. The bears in the Slims River Valley are the resource that is being protected and they have priority use of the trail. Therefore the trail will be closed any time a group of bears decide to hike or picnic on or near it.

This is an easy hike except for the stiff climb up Observation Mountain. Crossing Bullion Creek can also be a challenge during high water. Giardiasis has been reported in the Slims River area so water filters may be useful. The trail can be raced through in three days but is more enjoyable done in four or five days. By taking more time, explorations up Bullion Creek and to the toe of the glacier are possible. Regardless, the main objective, the view of the Kaskawulsh Glacier from Observation Mountain is second to none and probably the most photographed vista in Kluane National Park.

0.0 km	Warden's cabin
2.8 km	Sheep Creek
5.8 km	Bullion Creek
9.3 km	Sand dunes [UTM (29-60) Slims R]
12.0 km	Clear water; campsite [UTM (28-59) Slims R]
15.4 km	Clear water; campsite [UTM (27-56) Slims R]
20.3 km	Quick-mud area [UTM (29-52) Slims R]
22.5 km	Primitive campsite
30.4 km	Summit of Observation Mountain

Trail access: Turn left onto the first road north of Sheep Mountain Information Centre (at the base of Sheep Mountain) and follow it to the warden's cabin and parking area. The road is well maintained.

The trail: Follow the road beside the parking area, passing the Sheep Creek turnoff on the right. About 200 metres (656 feet) farther, a footpath branches to the left leading to Shepherd's Knoll, a vantage point for viewing the valley. Continue along the road to Sheep Creek, within half a kilometre (a third of a mile). Cross Sheep Creek; this can be difficult during high water. Fifteen minutes beyond is the plateau turnoff marked by a post, and then a swampy area must be crossed. Beyond the swamp, the trail cuts through some dwarf cottonwoods.

Bullion Creek, at kilometre 5.8, is recommended for exploring. There are remains of an old camp, plus some boards from the suspension bridge that crossed Bullion Creek before it was washed out in a 1988 flood. Those not going to Observation Mountain can climb the corner rock at the Bullion Creek junction and get a glimpse of the Kaskawulsh Glacier. Even at this vantage point, the glacier is a thrill to see.

Crossing Bullion Creek can be difficult. Rain, snow, and hot weather all cause water to rise. Reconnoitre downstream, close to the trees where the creek branches. Use a stick, or hand-chain your group together for crossing. During low water, this creek is no problem.

After crossing the creek, head southeast across the stone wash for 2.5 kilometres (1.6 miles). The trail on the opposite side of the wash is found close to the pine trees and cottonwoods. The trail does not pass close to Slims River at this point.

The trail then breaks into the open and along the sand dunes past a 9.3-kilometre sign where it joins the Bullion Creek path. After the sign, cross some open mud flats which may be wet, depending on weather. Creek-crossing shoes are recommended for this section. Always walk on the flats where there is vegetation. There is quick-mud or glacial goop beside the river and it is dangerous. There are also sinkholes that are not visible on the surface. After the mud flats, climb the sandy hill toward the 12-kilometre sign. The sign is located near the river but the trail goes over the sandy hill, which has fresh water at the bottom.

From kilometre 12 to 15.4, more marsh and alluvial fans must be crossed. A definite pattern to the landscape is noticeable: marsh, alluvial fan, marsh, etcetera. The trail passes closer to the river at this point. Since the river grade is a mere 3 metres (10 feet) per mile, the hike up the valley is not steep, just wet in places.

There are horsetail plants growing in the swamps. The natives used these plants as sandpaper to smooth canoes and wooden objects.

At the 17.8-kilometre sign, located in the centre of a fan, follow the trail going toward the sides of the hills, not along the water's edge. Stay high. Parks Canada has laid a marked trail through this section of the route.

Finding the 20.3-kilometre sign is important. There is a tiny lake tucked beside the hill close to the sign. The trail goes to a sandy beach on the lake. Do not go around the point at the river's edge. The trail goes into the bush and over the bluff ahead. The trail is narrow and continues over two more hills before arriving at the primitive campsite at kilometre 22.5.

A few years ago, a hiker tried to walk at the river's edge around the bluff at the 20.3-kilometre post. She walked into quick-mud and was unable to get out. Luckily for her, three wardens were close by who, after about one and a half hours of struggle, managed to pull the hiker out. It was a long time to be stuck in cold muddy water.

Kaskawulsh Glacier, the most accessible valley glacier in the park, is two to three days from the trailhead.

The primitive campsite is wonderful. Camping on the hill away from cooking fires is recommended, but it can be windy. If camping on the hill, do not cook there. Winds from the Kaskawulsh Glacier are strong and increase during the day. The winds average 7 kilometres (4.3 miles) per hour in the morning and by midday they average 27.5 kilometres per hour. If it is windy or there are too many people at the campsite, you may want to camp along Canada Creek.

Camping near the outhouse and stream is popular because the area is sheltered from the wind. The prevailing winds in the park are from the southwest but generally they funnel up the valley in the daytime when the slopes are being heated by the sun. Then, the winds reverse in the night when the earth cools. Because this valley is dominated by the glacier, the winds, which spread dry glacial goop over everything, can be extreme.

Climbing Observation Mountain is worth every agonizing step of the four- to six-hour climb. At least carrying a heavy pack is not necessary, but rain protection and snacks are a good idea. Vibram-soled boots are needed for the steep terrain. Besides carrying a substantial lunch, you must carry water, as there is none after leaving Columbia

Creek and before the snow at the top. Cameras and extra film are a must. I recommend that you do this climb on a clear day as your destination has one of the most spectacular views in the park. However, this is a difficult day trip and should not be underestimated. If weather is bad, it makes the trip even more challenging and, worst of all, it threatens the reward of seeing the glacier at the end.

Some hikers have climbed the face of Observation Mountain for the challenge, but I see no need for extra pain when the rewards are equal in the end.

It takes about one hour to walk across the desert plains of the Canada Creek washout to Canada Creek Bridge. Walk southwest, up the valley until the fan narrows and you are beside cliffs on the north side of the creek. There is a cairn indicating where the path goes over the hill and enters the woods. The path leads to the top of the suspension bridge.

A sign says the bridge is closed. The official reason is that the far end of the bridge stops about 1.5 metres (5 feet) above the ground, making descent difficult. However, it is easy to get off before the end of the bridge. The unofficial reason for closing the bridge is that it was built without an engineer present on the site, so government officials do not want to be responsible in the event of a collapse. If you choose not to cross the bridge, Canada Creek will have to be crossed early in the morning; it is definitely too high and swift to cross at midday.

Camping on the west side of Canada Creek is recommended if the primitive campsite is crowded. There is a flat meadow at the junction of Canada and Columbia Creeks less than 1 kilometre (0.6 miles) from the bridge. Past the junction, Canada Creek has excellent examples of melt water erosion, creating spectacular canyons.

Continue up Canada Creek veering to the left and then up Columbia Creek. Crossing Columbia Creek is not necessary. A tributary creek from Observation Mountain has cairns at the entrance. Do not take this route to Observation Mountain, as it is steep and the earth is not stable. Continue along Columbia Creek to the next rock outcropping a hundred metres or so ahead, and ascend along these ridges. There is vegetation to walk upon when you're on the steep slopes. Continue along this slope until the vegetation gets lower and a trail becomes visible.

The trail leads to a ridge, crosses a mud saddle and then goes to another steep ridge and into the alpine meadows of Observation Mountain. The climb to the meadow takes anywhere from three to five hours from the campsite at kilometre 22.5. There are cairns to follow for most of the route.

Once in the meadows and on a gentler slope, continue to climb. There are many false summits during this last hour. Veer to the right if you wish to see the glacier quickly, and to the left if you wish to get to the real summit of Observation Mountain.

There is a second possibility of viewing the glacier if you continue along Columbia Creek, following tributary creeks to the left until you're at the plateau beside Observation Mountain [UTM (44-24) Slims R]. The views are not as spectacular as they are from the summit of the mountain, but the climb is far easier. According to Mark Ritchie, during high water part of this route must be followed as described for Observation Mountain. Once you're a little way up the mountain, drop to the right into the meadow and continue toward the glacier.

Glaciation occurs when snow accumulates, compacts, crystallizes and moves. Valley glaciers like the Kaskawulsh are being squeezed like toothpaste by the weight of snow in the icefields beyond. The movement causes erosion and deposits of earth and rock, altering the landscape. Kluane's glacial landforms originated between 29,000 and 12,500 years ago, with minor advances of the glacier occurring as recently as 2,800 years ago. The Kaskawulsh Glacier is 65 kilometres (40 miles) long and 3 to 7 kilometres (2 to 4 miles) wide, and looks like a painted highway. The glacier is up to half a mile thick at its centre and about 15 metres (50 feet) high at its toe. The roaring sounds heard from the glacier are caused by friction, as the centre ice moves more quickly than the bottom ice.

The natives thought glaciers to be supernatural. They would not fry meat near the ice as they believed this caused the glacier to creak, groan, and move down the valley. Therefore they ate only boiled meat when near the glaciers.

Bad weather and strong winds move in quickly in this area so always be aware of climatic changes. Do not camp on the top of Observation Mountain because of the delicate vegetation, lack of water, and high winds.

BULLION CREEK

Time: *4 to 6 hours*
Distance: *15.6 kilometres (9.7 miles) return trip*
Difficulty: *Easy to moderate*
Change in elevation: *150 metres (492 feet)*
Maximum elevation: *945 metres (3,100 feet)*
Topographical maps: *Congdon Creek 115 G/2, Slims River 115 B/15*
Equipment needed: *Creek-crossing shoes and hiking boots are needed. Maps are for interest's sake only.*

The route: This is an easy and historically interesting route. However, continuing much past the cabins is not recommended because of a high-walled canyon before Metalline Creek. The canyon is one of the park's best examples of melt water erosion.

0.0 km   Warden's cabin
5.8 km   Bullion Creek
8.0 km   Cabins

Trail access: Drive north from the Sheep Mountain Information Centre to the first access road on the left. Continue down this road to a small parking area.

The trail: Bullion Creek is a historical route because it was the scene of a small gold rush that occurred in Kluane after the discovery of gold near Burwash Landing. In September of 1903, Frank Altemose, Fred Ater, Morley Bones, and Joseph Smith went to Whitehorse with 43 ounces of gold, which they said came from Bullion Creek in Kluane Country.

By October, Bones and Ater staked a discovery claim on Sheep Creek. Within a short time, Bullion and Sheep were staked from top to bottom and more claims appeared on Vulcan, Metalline, Multi-metal, and Canada Creeks. A total of 2,000 claims were staked in the area.

Instantly, tent camps and small cabins spotted the banks of the creeks. Because there is a fair amount of timber in the Bullion Creek area, cabins and a hotel were built at Bullion City near the mouth of Sheep Creek. Those with claims on creeks without trees stayed in three-man canvas tents. However, few people made much money in the ensuing months. So when Burwash Creek was rumoured to be yielding nuggets instead of dust, miners moved on.

After the initial rush, the Breeze and Bullion Hydraulic Company invested over $300,000 in equipment. The company sluiced the sides of the creek, but made less than $1,000 in returns. Today, two cabins still stand on the creek, along with the remains of sluice boxes on the hillsides. The mouth of the creek, where the hydraulics were at work, is a mess.

The word "bullion" means ingots of gold or silver ready for the mint. Sluices are troughs in which ore is washed and tailings are the refuse left after washing ore is complete.

After parking, follow the road through the gate and past the Sheep Creek Trail. Turn right at Bullion Creek, about 5.8 kilometres (3.6 miles) from the parking area. Climbing the bluff at the junction is rec-

John Harris and Vivien Lougheed rest along the trail with a cup of tea after a long day of hiking. Photo by Joanne Armstrong

ommended in order to get a glimpse of the Slims River Valley and Kaskawulsh Glacier. Ten minutes up Bullion Creek there is an old campsite beside the remains of a bridge that once crossed Bullion Creek.

Old tailings from the mining days are visible shortly after the bridge. Erosion can still be seen on one side of the creek, where the mining company did hydraulic sluicing. A tributary creek, about one hour up Bullion and before the cabins, has a water pipe still in the ground. If the water levels are high, the cabins are as far as you should go.

The area around the cabins is a history book about the mining days. One cabin has a calendar from the 1960s that suggests how recent occupation has been. The cabin is still habitable, but I recommend using a tent rather than the building. If you do stay, be sure to leave it in better condition than when you arrived. This includes sweeping it out, hanging things up, and bringing in wood for the next person.

Blue plates on display at the Haines Junction Visitor Centre were found in this cabin, still on the table as if someone was expecting visitors. The plates are of the highest quality French Limoges china. The hand-hewn sawhorse beside the cabin is a photographer's delight. There is also a plunger-type washing machine in the attached shed to the side of the cabin. Please do not remove any artifacts.

There is a road behind the cabin that goes to the creek. Across from the cabin and up on the hillside are the remains of a flume that is still in fairly good condition in places.

 ### SHEEP-BULLION PLATEAU TO SHEEP OR CONGDON CREEKS

Time: *8 to 10 hours*
Distance: *24 kilometres (15 miles) return trip*
Difficulty: *Easy to moderate*
Change in elevation: *937 metres (3,074 feet)*
Maximum elevation: *1,737 metres (5,699 feet)*
Topographical maps: *Congdon Creek 115 G/2, Slims River 115 B/15*
Equipment needed: *Running shoes are sufficient and a map is*

needed only for interest's sake. Rain gear and some water should be carried. If you're returning by Congdon or Fisher Creeks, leather boots and overnight gear are essential.

The route: This is a moderately easy hike, but water must be carried as there are few streams with clear water. The trail is a mining road that is in excellent condition. The plateau has some of the rarest plants in the Yukon, and the plateau may eventually become a Zone 1 protected area, to be visited only with a park guide. You can return by the same route you took going in, or by going down Congdon Creek, or by circling back to Fisher Creek.

0.0 km	Warden's cabin; trailhead
2.8 km	Road to plateau
6.4 km	Weather monitoring station
9.3 km	Clear creek
12.0 km	Start of plateau

Trail access: From the Sheep Mountain Information Centre, drive north to the first access road on your left. Continue along this well-maintained road to the parking area situated beside a warden's cabin.

The trail: From the warden's cabin, continue along the road to the 2.8-kilometre signpost, which points north to the plateau. There are remains of a cabin on the right-hand side of the trail, just past the corner. Proceed uphill to the 6.4-kilometre sign, where a weather monitoring station can be seen in the bush. Views are excellent from here on. There is a clear creek half an hour up the hill and then water is not available again until Sheep Creek, past the 12.0-kilometre sign.

The top of the plateau starts at the 9.3-kilometre sign. The road goes around the hill for 3 kilometres (1.9 miles), ending at the 12-kilometre sign. At this sign you may cross the meadow to the left and follow the trail to Sheep Creek, or stay on the original road leading to Fisher Creek.

The plateau is noted for its rare species of sage, *Artemisia rupestris*, which is found only here and in Siberia. Sage was used by aboriginals as a smudge to repel mosquitoes. It was also used in sweat lodges because of its pungent odour. Some species contain traces of codeine.

If following the trail across the meadow to Sheep Creek, you may find mining artifacts such as pails and remains of sluice boxes that have been well preserved by the climate. Sheep and Fisher Creeks were staked from one end to the other soon after a man named Bones discovered gold. Altogether, there were more than 2,000 claims in this area.

The ridge of mountains ahead and to the west (left) is appropriately named Red Castle Ridge. The castle changes moods with different lighting and is worth photographing.

If planning a day hike to the plateau, it is advisable to return by the way you came, rather than along Sheep Creek or Fisher Creek where creek-walking is slow. The time would better be spent exploring the plateau.

To reach Congdon Creek, follow Sheep Creek and continue past Red Castle Ridge to a small lake at the top of the pass and the headwaters of Congdon. A second route to Congdon is by way of Fisher Creek. See the Fisher Creek description for this option. Returning to the Slims River Road by way of Fisher Creek adds about twelve hours to the hike.

SHEEP CREEK TO CONGDON CREEK

Time: *2 to 4 hours to the headwaters; 4 to 6 hours to the junction*
Distance: *10 kilometres (6.2 miles) one way*
Difficulty: *Easy*
Change in elevation: *215 metres (705 feet)*
Maximum elevation: *1,737 metres (5,700 feet)*
Topographical maps: *Congdon Creek 115 G/2*
Equipment needed: *Overnight gear, a map and compass, and rain gear is needed for this hike. A stove is recommended if you're staying at the lakes on the pass, and creek-crossing shoes may be needed to descend Congdon Creek.*

The route: This is an easy alpine hike that gives spectacular views, but the walk down Congdon Creek can require many creek-crossings.

Photographic possibilities and wildlife are abundant.

0.0 km	Sheep-Bullion Plateau
1.0 km	Sheep Creek
5.2 km	Small lake at pass [UTM (24-72) Congdon Cr]
9.4 km	Right On Mountain
10.0 km	Junction of creeks [UTM (22-74) Congdon Cr]

The trail: After leaving Sheep-Bullion Plateau, follow the road to Sheep Creek. Proceed up Sheep Creek until it closes into a mud canyon. Climb the hills on the west (left), towards Red Castle Ridge, and continue. Red Castle Ridge's red oxidized rock is believed to have developed during a warming trend between 8,700 and 2,700 years ago. Drop back to the creek bed when the walking becomes clear. The pass is near.

Looking south, the view includes Vulcan Mountain in the distance and the mining road coming from Sheep-Bullion Plateau in the foreground.

West (left) of Sheep Creek, near the pass, are two small lakes. This is a pleasant campsite if you are not planning to have a fire. Place tents on thick vegetation and spread out if there is more than one tent in your group. Even if you're careful, camping at Congdon Creek is better for the environment. Congdon is only another hour of easy walking with spectacular scenery.

The headwaters of Congdon are actually many creeks flowing into one. There is a park boundary sign on the side of the hill. The south side of Congdon Creek is within the park boundary and the north side is within the sanctuary. The gravel wash at the headwaters is an excellent place for a base camp from which to explore. The large mountain on the northwest (left) when coming from Sheep Creek is Right On Mountain, and the creek to the north (left) when looking down Congdon Creek leads to Dickson Creek Pass.

Those going over the pass to Dickson Creek should read the Dickson Creek Trail description.

Artifacts left on Fisher Creek by miners during the Kluane goldrush.

C16 FISHER CREEK

Time: *2-3 days return trip*
Distance: *9 kilometres (5.6 miles)to Sheep Creek, one way*
Difficulty: *Moderate to difficult*
Change in elevation: *550 metres (1,800 feet) to Sheep Creek; 945 metres (3,100 feet) to the pass*
Maximum elevation: *1,920 metres (6,300 feet) at the pass*
Topographical maps: *Congdon Creek 115 G/2*
Equipment needed: *Leather boots, creek-crossing shoes, overnight gear and raincoat are needed.*

The route: This is an interesting creek with many possible exploratory excursions. You can go to 48 Pup Creek and exit near the Bayshore Motel, go to Sheep Creek and exit by Sheep-Bullion Plateau, or go to Congdon Creek by two routes. There are the remains of three cabins along a 5-kilometre (3-mile) stretch of Fisher Creek, but there are also many canyons requiring creek-crossings or climbing to the slopes. If walking on the hillside, the ups and downs of the gullies take as long as creek-crossings along Fisher Creek. The average walking speed on this route is about 0.5 kilometres (0.3 miles) per hour.

0.0 km	Parking area on Slims River West.
3.8 km	Fork on Sheep Mountain Trail
4.8 km	Canvas cabin
6.1 km	48 Pup Creek; cabin
7.9 km	Log cabin
9.0 km	Sheep Creek
13.1 km	Lake above Fisher Creek
14.5 km	Pass to Congdon Creek [UTM (72-27) Congdon Cr]
15.7 km	Sheep Creek (9.0 km) to lake on pass [UTM (24-72) Congdon Cr] beside Red Castle Ridge

The trail: Follow the Sheep Mountain Trail to the fork at the 3.8-kilometre sign. You may continue along Sheep Mountain trail to 48 Pup (although you may not find this definition in the dictionary, the word "pup" in this context means a small creek), and follow the creek to Fisher. You will miss about four creek-crossings in a canyon area but you will also miss the canvas cabin. If you're not going to 48 Pup, follow the left-hand fork down to Fisher Creek. There is a park signpost at the bottom of the hill. Across from the post are eroding hillsides that were hosed down for mining a hundred years ago.

A canvas-covered cabin is across and down the creek, just around the bend. It takes about three hours to get to the cabin from the parking area beside the warden's cabin. The canvas cabin has two plank beds and a leaky roof, but the area is excellent for tenting. Do not attempt to cross the creek beside the park signpost during high water, as it is steep and swift. Go downstream before crossing.

Going upstream, there is a canyon just past the park signpost so cross where it appears safe or climb the bank. If walking along the hillside, the gullies are steep and frequent. However, if you are staying on the creek, there are a minimum of four crossings between the signpost and 48 Pup. The Kaskawulsh Glacier can be glimpsed from the hillsides.

The first sluicing area will be visible within two hours of walking along the creek. There are remains of a cabin at the confluence of 48 Pup and Fisher Creek. It was a beautiful spot to build a cabin.

Just past the third sluicing area are the remains of a log cabin with a caved-in roof. It is an excellent place to camp. Sheep Creek is beside the flat-topped mountain to the north (ahead), with vegetation on top and a grey-coloured scree slope on one side. To the east (right-hand side of Fisher) is a tall black obelisk – a distinctive landmark.

The back end of the flat-topped mountain has a lake [UTM (71-25) Congdon Cr] tucked into a horseshoe-shaped hill where camping is possible and views are far better than on the creeks. However, a stove is needed if you're camping there.

There is a wolverine that lives in the area of Sheep and Fisher

Vivien stands under the "Hanging Teat," an easy two hour walk from the highway.
Photo by Joanne Armstrong

Creeks. If you see cat-like, rounded-toe prints, suspect the wolverine. This magnificent animal, with glistening fur and beady eyes, is Kluane's most elusive creature. When he sits on the side of a hill, he is invisible unless he moves. The wolverine has never been known to attack a human, but I wouldn't push him. The name "wolverine" means "glutton."

Going to Congdon along Fisher Creek, the effort expended getting onto the side of the hills is a fair trade for the incredible views. Proceed up Fisher Creek until you're near the top of the valley. To get to the lake [UTM (71-25) Congdon Cr], approach from the north. Walk up Fisher Creek until you're beyond the second hump of the flat-topped mountain, cross over, and walk back down the mountain above the lake. The views from the headwaters of Fisher or from the little lake are of Red Castle Ridge, an extraordinary landmark. One advantage to staying at the lake is the protection it offers from the winds. The glacier winds are strongest during the day, when the temperatures of the land and ice are at their greatest difference. Winds increase proportionally with elevation so if there is a light wind of about 4 kilometres (2.5 miles) per hour on the creek, the winds on top of a mountain or pass will be more than double in velocity. The lake is tucked into a land fold, so it is partially protected.

To reach Congdon Creek from the little lake, ascend the hills to the north of Fisher Creek and walk up the valley, keeping to the right. The many steep gullies on this hillside make walking slow, but there is an obvious pass ahead [UTM (74-23) Congdon Cr] that leads to a tributary of Congdon and meets it at the Sias Cabin. It is an easy downhill walk from the pass to the creek with interesting rock formations along the way. There are numerous campsites along the tributary creek and one at the Sias Cabin.

If you're going up Sheep Creek from Fisher Creek, there is a road beside the razor-ridged scree slope that follows the creek and winds toward Red Castle Ridge. Numerous park markers and campsites can be found along Sheep Creek. At the 12-kilometre signpost, continue toward the creek below Red Castle Ridge. This leads to an alpine lake on the pass and to the way down to the headwaters of Congdon Creek.

Another option is to follow the road around Sheep-Bullion Plateau back to Slims River Valley.

WILLISCROFT CANYON

Time: *2 to 3 hours return*
Distance: *5 kilometres (3.1 miles) return*
Difficulty: *Easy*
Change in elevation: *305 metres (1,000 feet)*
Maximum elevation: *1,130 metres (3,800 feet)*
Topographical maps: *Congdon Creek 115 G/2 (for interest's sake only)*
Equipment needed: *Boots are recommended, but runners will do.*

The route: The walk requires boulder-hopping, but the canyon walls are spectacular and the waterfall is delightful. This is a great two-hour, after-supper hike.

Trail access: Drive or walk along the highway 4.3 kilometres (2.7 miles) from the Bayshore Motel and turn left at Williscroft Creek. Park off the highway, beside the bulldozed area running along the creek. There are park signs indicating Williscroft Creek.

The trail: Follow the bulldozed road to the canyons about fifteen minutes up the creek. As the walls become higher, more coloured rocks emerge. Continue to the waterfall with the hanging boulder resembling a woman's breast. At one time there was a much larger waterfall in the canyon, but an earthquake rearranged the landscape and left this configuration instead.

Porcupines, or stickle swines, are often seen in the park. They often hum when they walk, but they are skittish and scurry off into the bush if approached.

Wild strawberry, common throughout the park in early summer, is rich in Vitamin C. The dried leaves make a tasty tea.

CONGDON CREEK

Time: *8 to 10 hours, or overnight*
Distance: *25 kilometres (15.5 miles) return trip*
Difficulty: *Easy to moderate*
Change in elevation: *670 metres (2,198 feet)*
Maximum elevation: *1,525 metres (5,003 feet)*
Topographical maps: *Congdon Creek 115 G/2*
Equipment needed: *Overnight gear and creek-crossing shoes are needed if you're going to the headwaters. If you're hiking one of the circle routes, a map and compass are also required.*

The route: Hiking to the headwaters of Congdon Creek is easy and interesting. There are also many options for circle routes using Congdon as a starting (or ending) point. Besides exiting down Sheep Creek, you may take Fisher, Dickson, or Nines Creeks. Each route requires two or three days and all have spectacular scenery. This is a favourite area for ewes and lambs in the spring; the critical lambing period is around mid-May. At this time bad weather often kills the young. There are between three and four hundred sheep in the park.

0.0 km	Congdon Creek access road
3.0 km	Parking area; campsite
5.0 km	Beginning of canyon
7.0 km	End of canyon
9.5 km	Sias Cabin [UTM (77-25) Congdon Cr]
9.6 km	Tributary to Fisher Creek
10.5 km	Pass to Nines Creek
12.5 km	Right On Mountain

Trail access: Drive 17.1 kilometres (9.7 miles) north along the Alaska Highway from the Sheep Mountain Information Centre. There is a sign indicating the Congdon Creek government campground. The access road is on the left-hand side of the highway about 200 metres (124 feet) before the campground entrance. There is a park boundary sign at the entrance to the access road. Most vehicles can drive the 3 kilometres (1.9 miles) to the end of the flat access road. On the south side of the parking area, at the end of the access road, is a horse trail that leads to a campsite.

The trail: Gold was first found on this creek in 1904, and some say there is still gold there today. In the winter of 1905, the Bullion Hydraulic Company moved a 75-ton sawmill, by sleigh, from Whitehorse to the mouth of Congdon Creek. Then they moved the mill to Bullion Creek, but the season ended before flume and pressure nozzles could be used. It did not take long, however, for the gold rush to peter out thus making the sawmill a non-viable operation. It disappeared by the end of 1906.

The creek was named after Commissioner F. T. Congdon, a lawyer who defended gold hustlers like A. N. Treadgold, an Englishman who owned and lost half of the Klondike within three years of his arrival.

From the campsite beside the parking area, a horse trail follows the creek. The trail goes for about 1.5 kilometres (0.9 miles), ending back

Wes Harris cleans the grounds around the Sias Cabin on Congdon Creek.

on the creek. Do not touch any artifacts you may spot along the trail. Prospectors Altemose, Ater, Bones, and Smith found a little gold on this creek in 1904. From the looks of the boulders, I think mining would be difficult here.

Once you're on the creek bed, continue to the small canyon area, which is neither claustrophobic nor difficult to walk around. I found walking on the south side of the creek was generally easier, but there are about a dozen creek-crossings along Congdon before you arrive at the canyon. A large alluvial fan with a small washout on the opposite side must be crossed before you arrive at an area that is so disarranged it looks like a bomb has been dropped. The Sias Cabin is on the north side of the creek, about another ten minutes from the bomb site. Reaching the Sias Cabin takes about three hours from the parking area at the bottom of Congdon.

The cabin was built by Josie and Frank Sias from Kluane Lake. It is in good shape so if you stay there, be sure to leave it cleaner than when you arrived. The tributary creek about 100 metres (328 feet) up and across from the cabin leads to the pass above Fisher Creek. The tributary creek is wide, and is decorated with ragged peaks and splendidly designed cliff walls. The creek is easy walking and there are many campsites with water and wood along the way. However, do not camp under any cliff faces, as the rock is loose.

To reach Fisher Creek, follow the tributary to a junction near the top of the valley. Follow the right-hand fork around the hill. The one on the left gives good views, but goes nowhere except straight up. Once the pass is visible, cross between the two lower hills on the left [UTM (73-26) Congdon Cr] and then veer farther to the left along the first arm down to Fisher. Once on the pass, you may continue in a south-westerly (right) direction around the mountain to the lake on the pass between Sheep and Congdon Creeks, or you may follow Fisher down the valley to Sheep Mountain. Fisher Creek is difficult walking, but the artifacts are spectacular. Returning to the Slims River by way of Sheep-Bullion Plateau, with a mining road to follow for easier walking, is also recommended.

Continuing from the Sias Cabin along Congdon Creek, past the valley leading to Fisher Creek, the next landmark is the creek on the northwest (right) side going to Nines Creek. It is difficult to spot and taking the wrong draw makes for unpleasant bushwhacking. I recommend starting this route from the Nines side. However, to locate the creek that leads to Nines, pass the point of the pyramid-shaped mountain on the south-side of Congdon. The point is about half an hour or 1 kilometre (0.6 miles) from the Sias Cabin. There are spruce trees coming from the draw all the way to the banks of Congdon Creek. A grassy knoll sits above the bank in front of serrated teeth made of black and brown rock. Just inside the trees are some mining boxes. If you see them, take the next draw, which has serrated rocks, starting near the top of the pass flowing down to Congdon Creek. There are also sandy cutbanks near the shore.

Going to Nines Creek requires a little bushwhacking up the draw through the spruce trees. Once out of the trees, stay on the east (right) side of the creek and continue over the pass. The crossing to Nines should not take more than three hours. There are campsites with water on both sides of the pass. The pass sits directly across from the pyramid mountain. Once partway up the draw, do not take the valley leading toward the far left, as it goes to an unpassable wall. See the section on Nines Creek South on p. 154 if exploring this area.

If you're proceeding to the headwaters of Congdon instead of going to Nines, the creek becomes a bit steeper and requires some bushwhacking. The mountain to the west (in front) is Right On Mountain and camping at the base is recommended. If time permits, there are many side valleys off Congdon that could and should be explored. The scenery is both inviting and delightful.

From the headwaters of Congdon, you may either return the way you came, go southeast to Slims River Valley by way of Sheep Creek, or go northwest to Dickson Creek.

The walk to Dickson Pass is worth the effort even if you're not planning to exit down Dickson and the Duke. To get to Dickson Pass, see the Dickson Creek trail description.

To hike to Sheep Creek from the headwaters of Congdon Creek, take the creek flowing from the south (left) when facing Right On Mountain. The creek goes to a pass with a lake and ends on Sheep-Bullion Plateau. From there, you may exit by Sheep Creek to Slims River, by Fisher Creek to Slims River, or by Fisher Creek and back to Congdon Creek. See the individual trail descriptions.

C19 DICKSON CREEK

Time: *6-8 hours from headwaters of Congdon Creek.*
Distance: *12.5 kilometres (7.8 miles) to the next exit point*
Difficulty: *Moderate to difficult*
Change in elevation: *640 metres (2,100 feet)*
Maximum elevation: *2,073 metres (6,800 feet)*
Topographical maps: *Congdon Creek 115G/2*
Equipment needed: *Leather boots, overnight gear, a map, and orienteering knowledge are required. Due to bear activity a food canister and pepper spray are recommended. Read the entire section on bears.*

The route: To cross from Congdon to Dickson Creek is not difficult and the rewards at the pass are superb. There are numerous camping sites along Dickson Creek, but no wood until near the Duke River. Be aware of bears at all times.

0.0 km	Gravel washout at the headwaters of Congdon Creek
1.7 km	Fork of creek
4.3 km	Congdon-Dickson Pass [UTM (20-75) Congdon Cr]
5.5 km	Headwaters of Dickson Creek
11.1 km	Tree line
13. km	Duke River

The trail: Cross the gravel outwash at the top end of Congdon Creek (see Congdon route, p. 146) and follow the creek flowing into Congdon from the northwest (on the right) when facing Right on Mountain. The creek to the left comes from Sheep-Bullion Plateau. Walk up the valley toward the triangular moraine with a creek flowing on each side. Walking on the side of the hill is easier than on the creek bed, but it is not environmentally friendly. Walk up the valley, past two creeks flowing from the west (left). The second creek has a waterfall that is often ice-laden, even in midsummer. Pass on the left of the steep, grey-shale arm where the creek splits.

Near an iron-streaked tributary creek, choose the next section of the route. I recommend climbing the centre arm or pyramid-shaped mound lying between two small depressions. There are spots of vegetation on the arm. Once on the mound, climb toward the vegetated triangular patch on the brown scree slope above. When the scree slope becomes too steep, drop to the creek on the south (left) and ascend the opposite side. Proceed along the ridge while veering to the north (right). Once on the pass, cross to the creek below the greenish-tinged gravel pile. From the upper side of this creek, continue walking in a northwesterly direction (right). The Duke River may be seen far below.

While on the pass, look for holes created by volcanic gases. There is also basalt, a fine-grained, black volcanic rock believed to be between 9 and 15 million years old. The greenish-tinged gravel pile described above is probably basalt.

I was hanging from a cliff on the side of Right On Mountain, trying to find an easy route over to Dickson, while my partner John Harris scouted this area. He found the route, but never got a chance to hike down Dickson because a male grizzly decided he wanted to cross over to Dickson by way of the same pass. Since John never argues with grizzlies, he scurried out of the area.

If hiking to Bock's Creek, follow Dickson Creek for 5 or 6 kilometres (3 or 4 miles). Stay on the side of the hill above the Duke River until you reach the pass leading toward Bock's Brook [UTM (81-10) Congdon Cr]. Exiting by way of Copper Joe's Creek is also possible. See related creek descriptions.

There is a three-legged bear living on the far side of the Duke River which is about sixteen years old. The wardens suspect the bear was in an accident and lost her leg. She has been seen with males, but she has not produced offspring. Many young bears lose their lives due to accidents, like falling off cliffs, so the surviving three-legged bear is quite a phenomenon. If you see any odd animal behaviour, observe it, record it, and report it.

C20 NINES CREEK (North)

Time: *2 to 3 days round trip*
Distance: *33.2 kilometres (20.6 miles) return trip*
Difficulty: *Easy to moderate*
Change in elevation: *960 metres (3,150 feet)*
Maximum elevation: *1,800 metres (5,906 feet)*
Topographical maps: *Congdon Creek 115 G/2*
Equipment needed: *Leather boots, creek-crossing shoes, and overnight gear will be needed for this hike. A map is required if you'll be exiting by a different route.*

The route: Nines North is a pleasant walk that can be made into a circle by exiting down Bock's Brook or by going up Nines South and crossing to Congdon. The upper end of the Nines North valley was once used by natives to hunt for sheep. I have seen as many as seventy-five sheep grazing together at the end of the valley. In 1995, an earthquake dislodged one of the hanging glaciers and sent it rumbling into the valley. This was reported to the park office by a helicopter pilot. I haven't been up there to locate and view the results.

0.0 km	Access road
3.5 km	Parking area
4.7 km	Horse trail
6.8 km	Fork in creek
13.3 km	Bock's Pass [UTM (17-84) Congdon Cr]
16.6 km	End of valley

Trail access: Follow the Alaska Highway north for 25.7 kilometres (16 miles) from the Sheep Mountain Information Centre and 10.1 kilometres (6.3 miles) past the Congdon Creek government campsite. Take the first road to the left before crossing Nines Creek. Follow the access road 3.5 kilometres (2.2 miles) and park.

The trail: Follow the access road and creek for about one hour to cliffs that create a canyon on the northwest side of the creek. There is a horse trail on the south (left) side of the creek. The trail passes above the cliffs and a small waterfall. The trail is blazed and ends at a washout (notice if returning this way) where the creek widens. The water in the creek through the canyon area is very swift and crossing would not be possible.

Continue along the creek to the fork. Nines South is to the left and Nines North is to the right. Both valleys are inviting. See below for the Nines South description.

Camping at the fork is recommended because the scenery is spectacular. There is also wood available.

Continue to the right, following the creek bed for another two hours or about 4.5 kilometres (2.8 miles). Near the entrance to Bock's Pass, there are some poles and pieces of tin left from a hunting camp. Bock's Pass is the little pass to the north (right). Nines Creek continues to the southwest (left). Along the way to Bock's Pass summit there are decent camping areas. Other spots can be found along Nines Creek, but if you are not camping below the pass at the hunting camp, it is best to go to the end of Nines Valley another two hours away.

Crossing Bock's Pass presents no problems. The pass ascends 30 metres (100 feet) before dropping to Bock's Brook. There is a lake at the top of the pass that provides clear water for drinking. The top of the pass can be gooey so walk on the side of the hill.

Once over the pass, veer to the right and down to Bock's Valley. Going left up Bock's Brook will lead to Bock's Lake; going right returns you to the highway.

Continuing up Nines, the boulders become larger once you pass the Bock's Pass turnoff. A large triangular mound with grass on top comes into view with icefields just behind. Stay to the right of the mound, following the creek to the end of the valley. A great hanging glacier covers one wall. This may be the place where one of the glaciers became dislodged during a moderate earthquake in 1995. I suggest camping away from any rocks that could be shaken down.

The meadow at the end of Nines Valley is recommended for camping. The spot is exquisitely decorated with wild flowers and grazing sheep.

If you're camping in the meadow, climb the ridge to the west for a view of the Duke River Valley. Follow the first gully on the west (right) that comes off the ridge at the lower end of the valley. The slope is steep and the rock is loose. If there has been a lot of rain, the scree will be even looser. Do not climb with heavy packs or the intention of crossing.

 NINES CREEK (South)

Time: *2 to 3 days*
Distance: *13.7 km (8.5 miles) to lake*
Difficulty: *Moderate to difficult*
Change in elevation: *945 metres (3,100 feet)*
Maximum elevation: *1,951 metres (6,400 feet)*
Topographical maps: *Congdon Creek 115 G/2*
Equipment needed: *Overnight gear and a stove are needed if you're going to the lake. Maps are for interest's sake only.*

The route: Hiking to the lake requires a steep climb at the end of the day. Therefore, I recommend staying near the pass that goes to Congdon Creek and doing a day hike to the lake. The mountain walls beyond the lake are unique, like French castles with turrets. Exiting by way of Congdon Creek makes a pleasant loop. Within a short time of leaving your car, this hike reveals spectacular views.

0.0 km   Access Road
3.5 km   Parking area
4.7 km   Horse trail
6.8 km   Fork in creek [UTM (22-82) Congdon]
11.2 km   Congdon Creek Pass [UTM (23-78) Congdon]
13.7 km   Alpine lake [UTM (20-78) Congdon]

The trail: Follow the Nines Creek (North) Trail to the fork in the creek that is identifiable by the red-tipped wall of rock. Follow the left-hand fork. The creek bed is wide and provides easy walking. About half an hour up the south fork is a canyon. Scurrying over the hills on the north (right) side will be necessary during high water. After the canyon, the creek opens and curves to the northwest (right). There will be some easy creek-crossings within the next three hours of walking.

There is a high standing rock in the center of the creek, shortly after a curve. The next landmark is a lone, black-tipped, triangular-shaped mountain, trimmed at the base with vegetation. When it is about a quarter of a kilometre ahead, look for a creek coming from the east (left). This is the creek dribbling from the green slopes above that leads to Congdon Pass. There are flat spots to camp on either side of Nines Creek and lots of murky water even in dry periods.

To reach the lake, continue along Nines Creek around the corner and start up the green lumps, staying slightly to the left where the slope is the gentlest. There may be many sheep grazing on the slopes. If you're carrying a heavy pack, it will take two to three hours of gentle climbing to reach the top of the hills overlooking the lake. If going to the lake for a day trip, the walk takes about one and a half hours one way from the Congdon Pass turnoff.

The lake rests in a bowl surrounded by green meadows, against a background of rugged peaks. One wall of mountains look like a French chateau with hundreds of turrets. Only the French or the Kluane mountain gods could create such a sight.

To cross Congdon Pass, hike up the slope beside the creek, thus avoiding the willows. Drop to the creek bed once you're beyond the willows. It is an easy 150-metre (500-feet) incline to the pass. The pass is narrow on the Nines side, but opens near the top. There are campsites on the pass near clear drinking water.

To descend to Congdon Creek during low water, stick to the south (right) and drop to the first tributary creek. During high water descend on the north (left) and stay high until you're past the green knoll. Then take the gentle slope that leads to the tributary creek. After joining the tributary, there will be some minor bushwhacking before reaching Congdon.

C22 BOCK'S BROOK

Time: *3 to 4 days to Duke River and back by the same route; 4 to 5 days returning by Dickson and Congdon Creeks*
Distance: *15.7 kilometres (9.8 miles) to Duke River; 27.2 kilometres (16.9 miles) to Dickson-Congdon Pass*
Difficulty: *Moderate to difficult*
Change in elevation: *1,402 metres (4,600 feet) to pass*
Maximum elevation: *2,316 metres (7,600 feet) to pass; 1,844 metres (6,050 feet) to lake*
Topographical maps: *Congdon Creek 115 G/2, Bighorn Creek 115 G/3*
Equipment needed: *Leather boots, creek-crossing shoes, and overnight gear is needed if you're going to the lake or beyond. A stove is essential as there is no wood for most of this trip but water is available all along the route. Bears are present. Read the entire section on bears.*

The route: Bock's Lake is an emerald tucked into the toes of three rock glaciers. It is one of my favourite spots in the park. The Duke River is reached by crossing one of the rock glaciers around the lake and then descending a steep pass. Exits by the Duke River and Copper Joe's Creek, by Dickson and Congdon Creeks, or by Nines Creek all make excellent circle routes. Regardless of which exit route is chosen, seeing Bock's Lake is a must. The cover is a photo of Bock's Brook taken close to the first rock glacier.

    0.0 km   Bock's Brook turnoff
    3.0 km   Parking area
    5.4 km   Pass to Nines Creek [UTM (17-85) Congdon Cr]
    9.1 km   Bock's Lake [UTM [UTM (13-85) Congdon Cr]
   11.3 km   Duke-Bock's Pass [UTM (12-84) Congdon Cr]
   15.7 km   Duke River
   19.8 km   Dickson Creek via alpine pass
             [UTM (11-81) Congdon Cr]
   27.2 km   Congdon-Dickson Pass [UTM (20-75) Congdon Cr]

Trail access: Drive on the Alaska Highway 31.5 kilometres (19.6 m) north from Sheep Mountain Information Centre to Bock's Brook. Turn left onto the access road on the south side of the creek. Drive 3 kilometres (1.9 miles) and park.

The trail: Cross the creek at the parking area and start walking up the north side. The walk is easy and campsites are plentiful. Bock's Brook is murky, but there are many tributaries with clear water all the way to the lake – with the first one being about one and a half hours from the start of the route.

You will pass one washout and two small creeks before arriving at the pass leading to Nines Creek. The draw to the pass has a huge washout in front of a marble mountain with a low hill directly in front of it [UTM (17-86 (Congdon Cr] and just before the end of a pine tree grove on the right. The turnoff to the pass is about two hours from the car. There are two creeks coming from the Nines Creek Pass, but the first creek (at the washout) is easier to ascend than the second one (beside the marble mountain). However, once you're up the 100 metres (328 feet), the rest is easy regardless of which creek you choose.

Continuing up Bock's Brook, there are numerous campsites with clear creeks along the way. The next creek coming from the north (right) leads to Cluet Creek, but I have not explored the route. The views near the headwaters of Cluet are okay.

Bock's Brook turns slightly to the south (left), revealing a peak with a yellow-white face beside a sand-coloured rock glacier. This is the one featured on the cover. There is vegetation on the rock glacier. Follow the creek passing the rock glacier on the north (right) side. There is a steep staircase section beside the rock glacier that must be ascended with caution. The boulders are huge and you may have to hoist your pack up ahead of you in spots. The staircase takes about an hour to ascend.

Once up the stairs, follow the creek until the valley opens into an alpine meadow. Continue up, veering to the left. There may be claim stakes in the vicinity as this part of the hike is situated in Kluane Game Sanctuary, where mining is still permitted. As you approach the lake, a rock in the shape of a chesterfield will come into view. This distinctive

"Hello, two pizzas with pineapple to Bock's Brook, please."

(They didn't deliver)
John Harris

rock is at the top of the pass overlooking Bock's Lake. Camping is possible by the lake, but not recommended because the vegetation is delicate. It is better to camp closer to Bock's Brook on the other side of Chesterfield Rock.

There are many signs of sheep in the area. If you're staying at Bock's Lake, it is a four- to five-hour day hike up the rock glacier to the Duke-Bock's Pass and back. Another interesting day hike is to follow the right-hand side of the lake and ascend the creek on that side. There are some small icefields at the top of the valley. From Chesterfield Rock, Kluane Lake and the Ruby Range are visible. Regardless of where you explore, this area offers enough spectacular possibilities to last a summer.

To go to Duke-Bock's Pass and the Duke River with heavy packs takes about four to five hours one way from the lake. Descend to the lake and scurry around the east side (left) of it. Follow the creek beside the rock glacier due south and directly across from Chesterfield Rock. Walk along the creek until the side of the rock glacier looks gentle enough to ascend. Continue to the pass, walking up the centre of the rock glacier. There is a lake just below the pass where a hanging glacier deposits its melt water. There are flat spots protected from the wind at this lake. It takes about half an hour to reach the pass from the lake.

The pass is windy but spectacular, with the Duke River flowing below and the icefields glistening beyond. The descent is steep. If going to Dickson Creek, stand on the pass looking toward the Duke River. There is an obvious pass before the tree line, on the opposite side of the valley; this is the route that you should take. Once off the pass, cross the valley and head for the second pass. If going to Copper Joe's Creek, go to the Duke River and then walk downstream.

To descend from Duke-Bock's Pass, walk toward the rock wall on the east (left). The second draw before the wall is best. Traverse back and forth across the talus and scree, using the solid rocks for support. The slope is steep but manageable. Once you're on plant-covered ground, head downstream to the Duke, and over to the pass you saw earlier if you're going to Dickson Creek.

Routes and Trails

North
SECTION

Trail Legend

N1   Copper Joe's Creek to Cache Lake
N2   Granite Creek Cabin
N3   Granite Creek Headwaters
N4   Donjek Glacier "A"
N5   Donjek Glacier "B"
N6   Amphitheatre Mountain

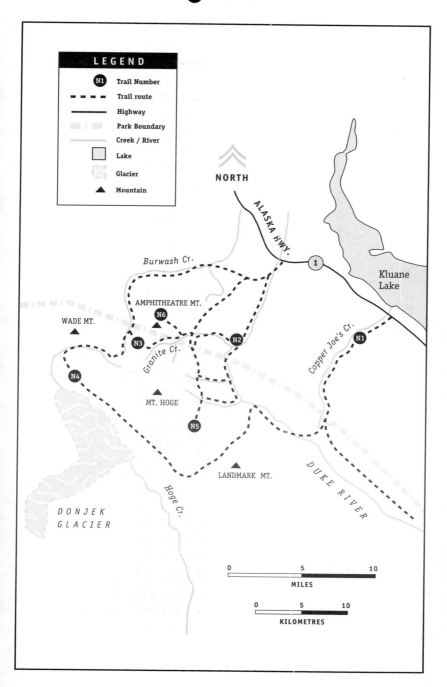

LEGEND

N1	Trail Number
- - -	Trail route
———	Highway
	Park Boundary
	Creek / River
	Lake
	Glacier
▲	Mountain

NORTH

ALASKA HWY.

Burwash Cr.

AMPHITHEATRE MT.

WADE MT.

Granite Cr.

Copper Joe's Cr.

Kluane Lake

1

N6

N3

N2

N1

N4

MT. HOGE

N5

LANDMARK MT.

DUKE RIVER

Hoge Cr.

DONJEK GLACIER

0	5	10
MILES

0	5	10
KILOMETRES

COPPER JOE'S CREEK TO CACHE LAKE

Time: *2 to 3 days*
Distance: *27 kilometres (16.8 miles) return*
Difficulty: *Easy*
Change in elevation: *570 metres (1,870 feet)*
Maximum elevation: *1,372 metres (4,500 feet)*
Topographical maps: *Bighorn Creek 115 G/3, Duke River 115 G/6, Burwash Landing 115 G/7*
Equipment needed: *Creek-crossing shoes are recommended. Runners are sufficient if you're going to the lake, but boots are necessary if you'll be exiting by another route. Rain gear, overnight gear, and a stove are required. Maps are for interest's sake if you're going to the lake, but necessary if you're going farther.*

The route: This is an easy overnighter with inviting views, and it's a good place to make further plans for another trip to the interior of the park. The lake is pretty and peaceful. It is possible to exit from Copper Joe's by way of a horse trail along the Duke River, by Bock's Brook, or by Congdon-Dickson Pass. These are much longer hikes than the one to Cache Lake. See the individual trail descriptions.

Copper Joe's Creek was once called Halfbreed Creek, but the name was recently changed. Ta Sun Tu Den, or "Copper Joe" in English, was the oldest of five brothers and the chief of the Copper Indian Tribe. He was also the grandfather of Josie Sias of Kluane Lake. Copper Joe left the White River area as a young man to live at Fort Selkirk, where he became a doctor. He was famous for his abilities as a healer, a weather forecaster, and an accurate predictor of coming events.

4.5 km	Parking area; turn-around
9.0 km	Canyon; creek fork
11.3 km	Park boundary sign
13.7 km	Cache Lake (8.5 miles)

Trail access: Drive north from Destruction Bay for 9.7 kilometres (6.3 miles) to the Copper Joe's Creek road sign. On the south side of the creek, turn left onto a solid creek-bed road. It looks like a bulldozer has made the creek in this section. Drive for 4.7 kilometres (3 miles) and park.

The trail: Follow the creek up the valley. The road is accessible for a few kilometres and often crosses the creek. Use creek-crossing shoes for these sections, as the water is cold.

The bulldozed road disappears and an old mining road appears. It runs up a hill and through a small canyon, with the creek flowing below. Shortly after the canyon, the road becomes scanty, and often nonexistent. Do not follow the east (left-hand) fork of the creek. Cache Lake is straight ahead and up the valley. Continue for about an hour. A park boundary sign will be your next landmark. Cache Lake is now close.

Past Cache Lake, continue along the road to the pass where the Duke River, Grizzly Creek, and possibly some weary hikers from the Donjek Trail will be seen. In the distance is Atlas Pass, from where the Donjek hikers will have come. There are many sun-bleached moose horns in this area. Looking toward the Duke, you can see landslide deposits that are believed to have been pushed there by moving ice.

To reach the Duke River, continue over the pass along the old road to the river. It is very easy and takes less than an hour to reach. Trail descriptions of Dickson Creek, Bock's Brook, or the Duke River section of the Donjek Glacier "B" hike all give directions for exiting Copper Joe's Creek.

GRANITE CREEK CABIN

Time: *1 to 2 days*
Distance: *7.6 kilometres (4.7 miles) one way*
Difficulty: *Easy*
Change in elevation: *152 metres (500 feet)*
Maximum elevation: *1,067 metres (3,500 feet)*
Topographical maps: *Duke River 115 G/6*
Equipment needed: *Runners are sufficient, but there may be lots of water on the road. Overnight gear is needed if you'll be staying at the cabin, as the building is not inhabitable. A map is needed for interest's sake only.*

The route: This is a pleasant walk along a road lending views to the south up Ptarmigan Creek, west up the Duke River, and north up Granite Creek as far as Amphitheatre Mountain. The trail can be walked early in the season, and with young children. Without packs, it takes about three hours to walk to the cabin. There are two small creeks flowing across the road and a larger creek just before the cabin where water can be obtained.

0.0 km	Parking area on Duke River
4.0 km	Clear creek
6.5 km	Fork in road
7.0 km	Descent to cabin
7.8 km	Creek
7.9 km	Cabin

Trail access: From Burwash Landing, drive 9 kilometres (5.6 miles) north along the Alaska Highway. Cross the bridge over the Duke River and turn left onto the first side road. Take the first right-hand fork turning away from the river and drive along a solid gravel road for 4.7 kilometres (2.9 miles). There is an outfitter's camp at the junction. The road continues another kilometre along the Duke River, where you may park near the remains of a log cabin. The other fork leads to an old mining campsite and is used by hikers on the Donjek route.

The trail: Walk another two hundred yards beside the Duke River to the end of the road. Cross a creek and follow the bulldozed road up the hill. Across the Duke River is Squirrel Creek, where the bulldozers are doing a mating ritual on the mountain side to the wild call of destruction. There is a road and cabin on Squirrel Creek.

A clear creek appears about thirty minutes along the road. Within an hour from the car is a clearing where Ptarmigan Creek, the Duke River, and Granite Creek valleys come into view. Within two hours from the car is the second clear creek. Camping is possible near this creek, but a fire isn't – the ground here is mossy and could catch fire.

Growing along the trail are *Bessaya alpina*, commonly called self-heal, which belongs to the figwort family. The root is cooked as a vegetable by the Inuit and the leaves are used for tea in Russia.

Continue to a fork in the road and walk to the left, toward the Duke River. There is a small creek that must be crossed but it is not difficult. The road will become visible again while descending the hill. You will see a post that reads "Yukon Placer Claim #P11683" just before the next creek crossing. This creek can be cold and swift during the high run-off season. Once you're over the creek, the cabin is 30 metres (100 feet) along the left-hand fork. The right-hand fork crosses a meadow and leads to the road that goes up and, finally, to Granite Creek.

The aspen and other vegetation growing along the Duke River flats below the cabin are most commonly found on the Great Plains.

The cabin is unlivable, but the outhouse is inviting. There are carved log chairs and a fire pit beside the cabin. Dry tent spots are at a premium, but firewood is plentiful. Return to your vehicle by the same route. Walking along the Duke River back to the parking area requires some bushwhacking.

 GRANITE CREEK HEADWATERS

Time: *2 to 3 days return*
Distance: *13.7 kilometres (8.5 miles) one way*
Difficulty: *Moderate*
Change in elevation: *793 metres (2,600 feet)*

Maximum elevation: *1,676 metres (5,500 feet)*
Topographical maps: *Duke River 115 G/6*
Equipment needed: *Overnight gear and leather boots are required. Maps are necessary if you'll be returning by a different route. Firewood is available along Granite Creek.*

The route: For a few hours, the trail follows a mining road above the Duke River. It passes the cabin described in the previous hike and continues for two hours up Granite Creek before it disappears. Some bushwhacking is required to descend onto Granite Creek. Exploring the upper end of Granite is spectacular and the choice of exits is extensive. You may exit by crossing behind Amphitheatre Mountain over to Burwash Creek, cross Burwash Uplands to a road, or walk south toward Expectation Mountain and follow the Duke River back to Granite Creek. Your final choice is to exit by the way you came. Read all options before deciding.

0.0 km	Parking area
7.6 km	Granite Creek Cabin
10.6 km	End of the road
13.5 km	Expectation Mountain turnoff
15.5 km	Headwaters of Granite Creek

Trail access: Follow the route to Granite Creek Cabin. From the cabin, walk across the boggy meadow and follow the road up the hill.

The trail: Carry water when you leave the cabin, as there is none on the hill until you return to Granite Creek. Five minutes up the hill, there is a clearing on the right. Go over to the ridge and look upstream. The well-named mountain at the end of the valley is Amphitheatre. Within an hour, the road starts to disappear. Continue along the side of the hill at the same elevation and the road will reappear.

Looking south, the Duke River canyon is visible from the hill. By the second lookout point, the Burwash Glacier comes into view to the north. The road ends at a bulldozed landing about two hours from the cabin but there is a game trail straight ahead through the willows [UTM (93-97) Duke R]. Follow it to the first creek bed that has a spruce-treed slope on the side. Descend by way of the creek bed to Granite Creek. There are many steep clay banks on Granite Creek, so if you're not taking the recommended creek bed, stay in the poplar groves to descend. Either way, make lots of noise – wildlife is abundant in this area.

There is a canyon on Granite Creek that is difficult to pass during high water. Shortly past the canyon the creek opens. On the right-hand side when walking up the creek, there is a stand of pines with many bleached stumps standing and fallen between the green ones. This is where the road ends. It can be followed up the hill for a bit, but does not connect with the other section.

Shortly after the bleached stumps, still on the north (right) side of Granite, is a creek with a small gravel washout. This is a good place to camp, but clear water is not available. There is a tarp frame made from poplar trunks that can be used as a hanging rack.

Across and a hundred metres or so up Granite is another tributary creek. It is before Badlands Creek, the next large washout along the north (right) side of Granite. The arm to the west of the tributary creek is the route that leads to Expectation Mountain and the Duke River. There is a lake about forty-five minutes up the arm that has possible camping when the weather is good. Otherwise the winds will make staying there uncomfortable. Continue past the lake, staying near the left side of the mountain but don't drop into the valley with the rock glacier because the terrain is unstable. Once near the top, you may continue to Expectation Mountain following the Donjek Glacier "B" route.

If you're not going to Expectation Mountain but are staying on Granite Creek, there is a gravel washout area just past the tributary creek and below the arm where camping is comfortable. Inside the spruce grove is a lone pine tree that may need a bit of pampering. If you find it, help keep it alive – I planted it on Canada Day, 1995.

The next landmark along Granite Creek on the north shore is a hunting camp with five-gallon, Klim-brand powdered milk cans strewn around. Last sold in the 1950s, the milk cans were flattened and used as cabin roofing during the mining days.

Beside Badlands Creek is a spruce grove with sheltered, flat spots for tenting. The water from Badlands is clear, unlike the water in Granite.

Joanne Armstrong hikes early in May along Granite Creek. The higher passes are not free of snow this early in the year.

The hill east of Badlands Creek, between the hunting camp and Badlands, is the one to take if you're exiting by way of Burwash Uplands. Across from Badlands Creek on the south side of Granite are the Lion's Paw Hoodoos, an easily spotted landmark. Just beyond the hoodoos, on the north side of Granite, is a wall of small hoodoos. Granite Creek then narrows for a hundred meters before opening up at the curve.

Once around the curve, climb the hill on the northwest (right) side of the creek, and start across the plateau. It is a spectacular walk. Hugging the hill on the left after leaving Granite Creek is recommended; follow the valley around, always veering slightly away from Amphitheatre Mountain. Soon tributary creeks will flow into a depression that will lead to Burwash Creek headwaters. It will take two to three hours to cross the plateau. Camping is good on the plateau, but a stove is needed. The warden's cabin is downstream from the confluence of Burwash Creek and the one you are on.

There are numerous sheep and eagles on the plateau and on the upper end of Granite Creek. If you're going out by way of Burwash Creek, follow the Donjek Glacier "A" route in the opposite direction.

N4 DONJEK GLACIER "A"

Time: *6 to 8 days return*
Distance: *93.8 kilometres (58.3 miles)*
Difficulty: *Very difficult; for experienced back-country travellers only*
Change in elevation: *1,158 metres (3,800 feet)*
Maximum elevation: *2,073 metres (6,800 feet)*
Topographical maps: *Bighorn Creek 115 G/7, Duke River 115 G/6, Steele Creek 115 G/5, Burwash Landing 115 G/7, Donjek Glacier 115 G/4*
Equipment needed: *Leather hiking boots, rain gear, and warm overnight gear are all mandatory. Orienteering skills are also necessary. A piece of rope, 30 metres (100 feet) long, is required to lower packs down one section of Hoge Pass. Stoves are essential for alpine areas. A pick-up vehicle would be handy if you're returning by Copper Joe's or Dickson-Congdon Pass, but I recommend returning along the Duke River.*

The route: This is a difficult hike: the passes are steep and one pass requires lowering packs with a rope; the trail is confusing, so orienteering skills are essential; and if bad weather prevails, visibility will be reduced making orienteering difficult. However, the trip is spectacular and is one of the most popular routes in the park. This trail should be walked in one direction only, due to the difficulty of the two passes. Although this trail describes the route to Copper Joe's Creek, I recommend coming out by way of the Duke River, thus completing a full circle back to your vehicle. The Duke River Canyons take about one and a half hours to pass, and ascending the hill to the Granite Creek road takes about forty-five minutes. Since this is a long hike in highly populated bear territory, *read the entire section on bears.*

0.0 km	Mining camp; parking area [UTM (98-03) Duke R]
7.5 km	Small Lake at Burwash Uplands; campsite [UTM (93-01) Duke R]
24.0 km	Burwash Creek
27.2 km	Burwash Creek warden's cabin; campsite [UTM (83-98) Duke R]
34.2 km	Hoge Pass
40.3 km	Donjek River; campsite
44.7 km	Toe of Donjek Glacier
55.7 km	End of glacier's toe
62.1 km	Bighorn Creek; campsite
69.0 km	Atlas Pass
75.8 km	Duke River; campsite
82.1 km	Copper Joe's Creek
84.0 km	Cache Lake; campsite
93.8 km	Car (we hope)

Trail access: Drive north along the Alaska Highway for 9 kilometres (5.6 miles) from Burwash Landing to the Duke River (the river looks friendly here). Turn left onto the mining road just past the bridge. Take the first right-hand fork away from the Duke River. Drive to the second fork 4.7 kilometres (2.9 miles) up the road. Turn right again at an outfitter's camp. The hill is steep; during wet weather, leaving your vehicle at the bottom is advisable. If you are driving up the hill, park at the abandoned mining camp.

The trail: Follow the mining road past the abandoned camp at the top of the hill. Within half an hour, beautiful tundra backed by icefields will come into sight. Continue along the road, up the hill, through the tundra, and past two lakes. Burwash Upland, an obvious hump on the tundra to the south (left), will be in view for two or three hours. Other than muskeg water, there are no creeks from which to get drinking water. This is prime caribou habitat and you will find the animals more curious than frightened.

Pass a number of small lakes on the tundra before coming to a clear-water creek that the road passes through (not over). Continue around Burwash Upland along the mining road to its end, and then head south (left) across the tundra towards a low saddle on Amphitheatre Mountain. Once you're over the saddle, drop down to Burwash Creek. It takes about four to five hours to cross the tundra because it is uphill and spongy, with tufa mounds or frost hummocks making it difficult to walk (some call the hummocks "Canuck heads"). The heads have weak necks, which makes the terrain more difficult. Walking with a backpack on a trampoline for a few hours each day would be good practice for tundra walking.

Looking back from the tundra before dropping into Burwash Creek, Tatamagouche Creek is visible. Natives found copper along these creeks, and as far south as Dalton Creek and Kathleen Lake. They used the metal for axeheads, arrowheads, knives, and cooking utensils. The creek was first staked in 1905 by H. B. Mining and Imperial Oil Ltd., who were looking for copper. Imperial Oil also tried drilling for diamonds, but in 1971 their lack of success stopped the exploration.

Once you reach Burwash Creek, walk along the creek bed to the warden's cabin at the base of a rock outcrop. While you walk, Amphitheatre Mountain and Burwash Glacier will dominate your views. At the curve in the creek are two wooden tripods marking the park boundary. The warden's cabin will be visible from the boundary line.

Camping beside the cliff below the cabin is excellent. There are flat tenting spots and clear water that has been filtered while running through the rocks.

Burwash Creek was first staked in 1904 by the famous four: Altemose, Ater, Bones, and Smith. They caused a small stampede to the Tatamagouche area, and as far as the Donjek River.

The warden's cabin is a miniature museum. On the porch of the cabin are sheep, caribou, and moose horns, petrified wood, and a wonderful rock collection. If you find any other artifacts in the area, please deposit them at the cabin. Do not remove any items from the porch. The cabin is locked unless a warden is in residence.

Continue up Burwash Creek to the forks. Take the right-hand fork as the left one goes to the plateau and Granite Creek. There is a road on the side of the hill, visible from a creek. Follow the road. It peters out to a trail – often obstructed by boulders that must be circumnavigated. Nothing is difficult, however, and this is easier than following the creek bed below.

Hoge Pass takes one and a half to two hours to reach from the warden's cabin. When you're near the top, do not go directly ahead and over the inviting grassy pass. Instead, veer to the left and up the gravel mound known as Cow Paddy Hill (the rocks on the top suggest this name). Continue along the gravel ridge in a southerly direction to the lowest gravel pass on the right. It is a steep descent to the creek bed. The views of the icefields from Cow Paddy Hill are the nicest in the north end of the park. Far below is Spring Creek running from the icefields into the Donjek River. The alluvial fan at the mouth of Spring Creek is one of the most perfect examples in the park.

Hoge Mountain is a Zone 1 protection area, which permits only

Vivien crosses the taiga at Burwash Uplands. Photo by John Harris

minimal or no public use. Be certain to leave no markings on this mountain, especially in the vegetated areas.

The creek to the right beyond Spring Creek is Steel Creek, which carries the melt waters of the Steel Glacier. Although most glaciers are retreating today, some surge occasionally. Whether retreating or surging, glacial movements are usually constipated. In 1967, Steel Glacier advanced 12 metres (40 feet) in one day. No one knows what caused the gush, but Steel Glacier is now referred to as the Galloping Glacier.

Cross the pass and start down the scree slope on the left. At first it is easy, but it soon becomes steep. At an impassable canyon, where the drop becomes too steep, cross the scree slope to the south for about 22 metres (75 feet). The crossing is dangerous, but once you're over, descent is possible. It is advisable to lower packs with a rope and descend without a pack. You will need 30 metres (100 feet) of rope for this. Stop partway down, at the patchy green slope dubbed Golf Hole Number 9, and refuel. This stress uses a lot of energy.

The right-hand gully from the pass is steep and rocky, but passable. It eventually joins the left-hand branch before joining Hoge Creek. This route was recommended by E. J. Hofer.

There are several gullies on Hoge Creek; all are steep with loose scree. Be careful. Hoge often runs high, so creek-crossings will be frequent.

After passing Golf Hole Number 9, the descent to Hoge Creek is easy. Follow Hoge toward the Donjek. Hoge Creek is muddy and does not clear during the night; however, there is one clear tributary creek flowing into it. If you're camping along Hoge Creek, watch for the tributary on the north (right) side. This is the only comfortable campsite other than at the horse camp just before the Donjek.

The horse camp before the Donjek is on the east (left) side of Hoge Creek. It will take about two hours to reach from the pass. The site is recognizable by the many trails and flat spots just inside the bush from the creek bed. The trees in the grove are balsam poplar and spruce, and give protection from wind. Since this is an outfitter's horse camp, it could be occupied, in which case camping on the Donjek would be the next possibility.

You may wish to bushwhack in a diagonal direction from the horse camp to the glacier, instead of following Hoge Creek to the Donjek

River and then walking up the Donjek. There is a steep cutbank (and you may feel you have had enough steep climbing for one day) above the Donjek but follow it along the edge to a slope that offers an easy descent to the Donjek flats.

Forested peat lands are found in this area. The peat thickens by about 7.5 centimetres (3 inches) every hundred years. Do not make a fire on the peat.

At the confluence of Hoge Creek and the Donjek River are coluvial deposits, which are usually angular rocks mixed with sand, silt, and clay. The polygons, circular rocks with sharp-edged sides, are indicative of surface ice wedges from a glacier. The wedges carve the rocks. Huge ice wedges with deep crevasses between them can be seen on the Donjek Glacier.

The Donjek Glacier has larger crevasses close to its toe than any other accessible glacier in the park. This is the reason for its constant creaking and banging. It also gives you a clear idea why crossing a glacier is a dangerous sport, and should only be attempted by experienced climbers.

Follow the river's edge to the toe of the glacier. The spectacular Donjek Falls are downstream from the toe. I have never gone there, so I do not know how difficult the trip is. Nonetheless, I suggest a day hike. When miners were working the area, there was a cable ferry across the Donjek River; I would love to see it resurrected, which would make some of the areas across the river accessible to hikers.

After enjoying some glacial ice cubes in your tea, walk up a dry creek bed and back onto the hill – because the Donjek River soon runs into the cliff. Once you're on the hill, walk away from the river in a diagonal direction for fifteen or twenty minutes, until you come to a horse trail. It is difficult to find but worth the effort. Walking along the horsetrail beats bushwhacking. Follow the horse trail to Bighorn Creek. Carry water, as streams crossing the horse trail appear only once every hour.

The walk through the meadow and subalpine shrubs is pleasant, with great views of the glacier due to the elevated vantage point. About 1 kilometre (0.6 miles) past a murky glacial stream that cuts across the horse trail, there is a clear creek, open flat meadows, and an excellent place to camp. The boxcar crashing and gunshot bangs of the Donjek Glacier will entertain you all night.

The horse trail often becomes undetectable, but stay on it as much as possible as the trail is shorter than walking along the Donjek shoreline to Bighorn Creek. During high water, stay on the hills past Expectation Mountain because Bighorn Creek can be wide and fast, running against the cliff edges. During low water, follow Bighorn Creek as far as possible, unless you wish to climb Expectation Mountain for better views of the glacier. I did this hike during high water, so I could not walk up Bighorn. I spent a few torturous hours bushwhacking above Bighorn and then sliding down a shale slope to Chert Creek.

If you're not going to the summit of Expectation Mountain, descend the hill by crossing in a northeasterly direction, coming down to Chert Creek [UTM (91-82) Bighhorn Cr]. Drop to the creek a half kilometre before its confluence with Bighorn because the banks farther up become too steep. While on the hill, look toward the glacier. The warden's Donjek cabin at Bighorn Lake, between the eskers and the river, is a comforting sight. If time permits, this is an interesting area to

Sheep horns may be found anywhere in Central and North Kluane.

explore. Some hikers fly into Bighorn Lake and hike out, thus avoiding Hoge Pass. Bighorn Lake is one of three landing sites in the park.

One year, a boulder came off the side of the mountain along Bighorn Creek and hit a hiker, breaking his leg and seriously tearing his leg muscle. One of his co-hikers stayed with him, while a second companion walked back to Destruction Bay twelve hours away to get help. This is a good example why hikers should never hike alone. Your chances of seeing another person within a reasonable time limit are slim.

Once you're above the mouth of Bighorn Creek (where it enters into the Donjek River), veer to the west (left). Chert Creek is below.

The Tutchone Indians came to Chert Creek to find obsidian, a rare non-chrystallized glass-like rock that was used to make sharp cutting tools. Obsidian is found only where recent volcanic activity has taken place, and tends to crystallize into a finely grained rock, and eventually decomposes if it takes on moisture. Therefore, no obsidian is very old.

For a good view of the glacier, follow Chert Creek to the north side of Expectation Mountain before ascending to the summit. The climb is 457 metres (1,500 feet) in less than two kilometres so it is steep but well worth the view.

About 1 kilometre up Chert Creek is a camping spot with excellent kitchen facilities: the campsite is 30 metres (100 feet) back from the creek. The water can be muddy, but there is firewood, flat ground for tenting, shelter from the wind, and downed logs to sit on.

Continue up Chert Creek to the major forks. Before the fork, you may have to do some climbing to get around cliff edges, but walking is easy during low water. Before reaching the fork, you will see some bright orange stones, which are coloured by minerals coming from a tributary spring. The water tastes like iron. Do not follow this creek, but go on to the next fork. At the next fork, turn north (left) as the east (right) fork leads to Landmark Mountain.

Continue up the creek to the alpines and get your bearings by identifying Landmark Mountain. It is appropriately named.

The area from Bighorn Creek to Atlas Pass can be confusing. Once you're off Expectation Mountain or Chert Creek and in the alpines, Landmark Mountain and Landmark Glacier will be toward the east (right). From this alpine meadow you may continue north over a pass to Black Valley [UTM (91-87) Bighorn]. Follow the sloped scree valley north past a rock that looks like the petrified backpacker. To continue along this route, see the description for Donjek Glacier "B."

If going to Atlas Pass, cross the alpines towards Landmark Glacier. There are two valleys: one from the glacier in the distance and a closer one that leads to Atlas Pass.

Continue up the creek to the end of the valley. Fill water bottles as Atlas Pass is a dry place. There is a hill with rock formations that make the mountain look like a medieval fortress. The pass is the slight depression to the south (right) of this wall. While still on the creek, veer to the right until at the pass. Once you've reached the top, take a deep breath and head for the left side of the valley. The eastern side of the pass is not a pass at all, just a steep slope. Cross the scree and descend along the arm. Go slowly, as you get only one chance at this crossing.

While standing on the pass, you will see a creek on either side. Choose the ridge between the creeks. Cross the intimidating steep scree slope. Once above the left-hand ridge, descend to the final saddle (don't go over the last hump). From this saddle, descend to the creek on the left when facing the Duke River. Once you're off the saddle, the rest of the walk is a piece of cake. There are flat spots and fresh water along the creek for camping.

Atlas Creek meets the Duke River at a rock wall on the north east side of the Duke. Choose your route to Copper Joe's Creek while you're still high on Atlas Creek. At the end of the wall on the Duke is a prominently pointed peak to the east (right). Walk past that mountain and up the east side of it. There is an excellent draw to follow. If you walk to Grizzly Creek, you have passed the entrance to Copper Joe's.

Do not cross the Duke River at the wall, as it will braid and become shallower about 4.5 kilometres (2.8 miles) up the river. There is a horse trail along the south side of the Duke that you can follow for most of the distance. However, even at the braided spot the river can be a difficult crossing. In high water, it may be impossible. Water levels are considerably lower in the morning.

In the event that water levels are too high, follow the Duke River downstream out to the road. There is a horse trail to Granite Creek, past two tributary creeks and through the Duke River canyons that take only one or two hours to cross. Follow the directions for Donjek

Glacier "B" to take the horse trail to Granite Creek Cabin, and then back to your car at the mining camp.

Another alternative to crossing the Duke is to follow the river to Grizzly Creek, a large tributary to the Duke. Cross Grizzly Creek first, thereby eliminating a lot of water. After crossing Grizzly, try crossing the Duke. The river is wide in this section. Once you're across, return down the river to the draw that leads to Cache Lake and Copper Joe's Creek.

After crossing the Duke, look for a small trail that goes up the draw you chose while you were still on Atlas Creek. Partway up the hill is an old mining road leading to Cache Lake. Follow the road to the summit and look back. Atlas Pass is in the distance – this shows how far you've come, and it makes an impressive photo to show friends once you're home. Follow the road to Cache Lake, Cache Creek, and then Copper Joe's Creek. It takes four to five hours to walk from the lake to the highway. See the description for Copper Joe's Creek.

N5 DONJEK GLACIER "B"

Time: *3 to 4 days to Black Valley Pass, return; 5 to 6 days to Expectation Mountain, return; 6 to 8 days to the toe of Donjek Glacier, return*

Distance: *103 kilometres (64 miles) to the Donjek Glacier*

Difficulty: *Very difficult*

Change in elevation: *1,463 metres (4,800 feet)*

Maximum elevation: *2,347 metres (7,700 feet)*

Topographical maps: *Duke River 115 G/6, Bighorn Creek 115 G/3*

Equipment needed: *All overnight gear, leather boots, stove, and topographical maps are needed. This hike is recommended for experience back-country travellers only, because of the length of the trip and the steepness of the one pass.*

The route: This route, with four possible alternatives, may be walked in part or in whole in either direction. My instructions introduce the various alternative hikes, so you might avoid confusion by marking your route on your contour map before you start hiking. The most scenic route follows the Duke River to Archway Creek or Black Valley Creek, over the pass to Expectation Mountain, and back out again by way of Grizzly Pass and Burwash Uplands. Although it's easier to exit by way of Burwash Uplands, hiking in the opposite direction is also recommended. The nicest part of all the routes is that there is no bushwhacking, and getting lost is almost impossible due to the distinctive landmarks. The downside is that the pass at the top of Black Valley Creek is steep and difficult. With a large pack it becomes very difficult. If going only to the top of Black Valley Pass, which can be reached with a day pack from Black Valley Creek instead of going all the way to the toe of the glacier, this hike reveals views of the Donjek Glacier and cuts off 50 kilometres of trail. If you're going only to Expectation Mountain, it cuts off 28.2 kilometres (17.5 miles) of the least scenic section of the trail. Whichever route you decide on, it will be a long one. Read the entire route description before deciding, and also read the entire section on bears.

0.0 km	Parking area
7.6 km	Granite Creek Cabin
10.0 km	Granite Creek and Duke River
18.4 km	Black Valley Creek and Duke River [UTM (94-89) Bighorn Cr]
26.0 km	Black Valley Pass [UTM (91-86) Bighorn Cr]
32.4 km	Expectation Mountain summit
34.6 km	Chert Creek
37.1 km	Bighorn Creek
46.5 km	Toe of Donjek Glacier [UTM (83-83) Bighorn Cr]
74.6 km	Black Valley Pass
86.7 km	Granite Creek [UTM (89-97) Duke R]
94.6 km	Road beside Burwash Uplands [UTM (93-01) Duke R]
102.5 km	Parking area

Trail access: Drive north along the Alaska Highway for 9 kilometres (5.6 miles) from Burwash Landing to the Duke River (the river looks friendly here). Turn left onto the mining road just past the bridge. Take the first right-hand fork away from the Duke River. Drive to the second fork 4.7 kilometres (2.9 miles) up the road. Turn right again at an outfitter's camp. The hill is steep; during wet weather, it's advisable to leave your vehicle at the bottom. If you're going up the hill, park at the abandoned mining camp.

The trail: From the junction of the mining road and the outfitter's camp on the Duke River, follow the trail description to Granite Creek Cabin.

There are two possibilities for getting to the Duke River Horse Trail. First, drop to the river behind the cabin and walk along the gravel riverbed to Granite Creek. This requires some scurrying past areas where the river flows against the bank. The recommended route is to cross the meadow at the cabin and follow the road up the hill. Once near the top of the hill, continue for about 1 kilometre (0.6 miles). Descend through the bush in a diagonal direction, heading up Granite Creek. Do not go directly down the hill because the Duke River bends to the west before it meets Granite Creek. There are many gullies on the bend between the cabin and the confluence of the Duke River and Granite Creek. Once you're on Granite Creek, look for signs of a camp near the confluence of the creek and the Duke River. The horse trail around the Duke River canyons is directly across the creek from the camp.

Cross Granite Creek and find the trail. There is a post at the entrance. Once on the trail you will find that it disappears occasionally, but stay close to the edge of the hill and finding it again should not be difficult. The bush is moderately thick and there are many animal trails to follow. Do not walk too close to the edge, however, as there are some cornice ridges that could give way. It takes two to three hours to pass the canyons. The horse trail follows the river all the way to Atlas Creek. If you return by this route, it will take about one hour to climb from Granite Creek up to the road again.

Once you're past the canyons, the walk along the Duke is pleasant. The first gravel washout is an unnamed creek [UTM (95-92) Duke R] that can be taken into the alpines. For convenience, I have named this creek Archway Creek. It flows from the depression separating Corner

*Vivien at Archway
Creek on the way to
the Donjek Glacier.*
Photo by John Harris

Mountain (not an official name) from the next one. There is a flat plateau behind the rock face on the south end of Corner Mountain. The walk up the creek is steep and gets quite rocky near the upper section. At the forks of the creek, take the north or right-hand side staying close to the grey granite crags. Near the top of the creek there is a huge slab of rock that has fallen and formed an archway. Just past the archway is a spiked peak that looks like a middle finger sticking up. Ascend the hill on the south (left), just past the finger.

Do not go all the way to the top of Archway Creek unless you are returning to Granite Creek. In that case, continue up the creek to the grassy slopes at the top and then head north (right) over Grizzly Pass and down to Granite Creek. The pass is called Grizzly Pass for a reason, so be very cautious. There are flat spots and clear water for camping along this creek past the archway, but there is no wood so a stove is necessary.

If you're going to the Donjek, climb the hill on the south (left) side of Archway Creek. At the top of the hill, you will see the Duke River, the large gravel river to the east (left), and Black Valley (not the official name) straight ahead. Black Valley has numerous scree slopes and black rock glaciers dotted with hanging glaciers. If the sun is not shining, it looks foreboding. Camping is possible in Black Valley, but there is no vegetation or wood.

To reach Black Valley, follow the first creek on the west (right) that flows south. Drop into this creek early, as the banks get steep farther down. This creek flows into Black Valley Creek. Unless you can get all the way over Black Valley Pass – another five hours of steep climbing – I advise you to camp on the grassy flat spots at the confluence of the two creeks. If you're making a day hike to the pass, this spot makes an excellent base camp.

At the curve of Black Valley Creek are the remains of a glacier hidden under the rock. If you're hiking down that creek, you must walk along the hillsides for about 1 kilometre (0.6 miles). Do not attempt to walk on the glacier, as there are sinkholes and crevasses. Although this glacier is small, it is still about 61 metres (200 feet) thick in places and falling into a crevasse could be disastrous.

To get to Black Valley Pass, continue up the valley and cross over to the east (left) side after about 1 kilometre (0.6 miles). Be careful not to cross too soon as you will end on the rock-covered ice.

If you do not take Archway Creek, continue up the Duke River to the next gravel washout that flows into a rock wall on the elbow of the Duke River. This is Black Valley Creek [UTM (89-96) Bighorn Cr]. Although it is wide and an easy creek to follow, Black Valley Creek may require some creek-crossings during high water. There are numerous campsites along this creek.

Follow Black Valley Creek, staying on the south (left) side until you see a small washout coming from the side of the hill. It looks like a bulldozed road for about 15 metres (50 feet). It comes before the curve of the creek, where the routes from Archway and Black Valley Creeks meet. It is also before the toe of the glacier. The glacier is not recognizable when you're walking upstream, so watch for the washout and be certain to avoid the glacier. Proceed up the washout to the side of the hill and circumnavigate the hill, dropping back to the valley floor well past the curve.

Stay in the valley floor and follow the creeks on the north (right) side of the valley. Once you are at snow level, it is easier to walk on the snow than along a creek. Continue to cross the most logical pass ahead. A scree amphitheatre with mounds of black and brown rock will appear. Go to the next obvious pass, constantly veering slightly to the right where another amphitheatre and more rock mounds will appear. There is water all the way to the pass. If you are carrying big packs, it may be necessary to camp in one of the amphitheatres. These can be windy and cold or very hot, depending on the weather.

There is one 15-metre (50-foot) section of steep creek-climbing, after which you will arrive at the last amphitheatre. Once you are there, go to the dubious pass on the right, beside the one with the hanging glacier. The pass on the left looks about the same, but it isn't the one to take. This last section is steep but only the last fifteen feet require scrambling. It is advisable to walk on the snow. Once at the top, the Donjek Glacier in the distance is accented by the icefields behind. It is a spectacular view.

Continuing to Expectation Mountain is easy from Black Valley Pass. Follow the ridge along the pass to the west (right) and drop into the valley when it looks good. If you stay on the creek in the valley, there is nothing to think about. It is easy downhill walking; there are no canyons and there are great views. Continue south until Chert Creek [UTM (82-92) Bighorn Cr] flowing into Bighorn Creek appears. Start veering to the east (right) about 1 kilometre (0.6 miles) before reaching Chert Creek, and ascend Expectation Mountain from its north side. This is Expectation Pass [UTM (88-82) Bighorn Cr].

If you are going to the toe of the Donjek Glacier, follow that section (written for those going in the opposite direction) of the route description for Donjek Glacier "A" on p. 172.

The options for returning are to cross back over Black Valley Pass, or to cross Atlas Pass and drop back to the Duke River, or to ascend Hoge Pass (Donjek Glacier "A" route) and return by Burwash Creek. Read the descriptions of all possible routes before you decide.

Black Valley Pass with the Donjek Glacier in the distance.
Photo by Elsebeth Vingborg

To return by way of Black Valley Pass, follow the same route by which you came. Once at the curve of Black Valley Creek, the first option is to follow the creek downstream to the Duke River and then up the Duke back to Granite Creek Cabin. This is very easy.

If you are going to Archway Creek, continue to the north end of the valley and take the creek on the west (left) as far as it goes. Cross to the alpines on the east (right) where the banks are not too steep to climb. Proceed over the alpines to Archway Creek. Hiking down this creek and exiting by way of the Duke River is an excellent route.

If you're going to Grizzly Pass, walk north, following Archway Creek to the grassy slopes. Climb to the pass, being careful to watch for bears. I have never been able to cross this pass because it has always been occupied. If there are bears on the pass, exit by way of Archway Creek.

Once you're over Grizzly Pass, follow the arm directly above the little lake visible below and slightly to the right but do not fall into the valley directly to the east (right). It is much too steep to descend, especially when there is a gentle alpine slope on which to walk. Looking north across Granite Creek is another pass [UTM (89-98) Duke R] with a lake. This is the recommended route if you're exiting by way of

Burwash Uplands. Exiting by walking down Granite Creek to the Duke River is another option. The distinctive mountain to the west is Amphitheatre Mountain.

Camping at the lake below Grizzly Pass is not very pleasant, especially if the weather is foul. I suggest dropping to Granite Creek, where there are excellent campsites in wooded gravel washes beside the creek.

To continue to Burwash Uplands, cross Granite Creek and climb the creek just east (right) of Badlands Creek. Once you are partway up, leave the creek bed and veer to the east (right). Bushwhacking is unavoidable here. The ascent to this pass takes less than an hour with big packs. Once at the pass, turn and look from where you came. It is impressive with Burwash Glacier on one side, Grizzly Pass in the centre, and the craggy mountain to the east. Camping at the lake on the pass is okay, but it can be windy and cold. There is no wood for a fire and the ground is spongy.

Walk past the lakes in a northeasterly (right) direction across the tundra. The hump ahead is Burwash Uplands. Pass on the lower east end and continue across the tundra to the whitish line visible on the horizon. The line is the mining road that will take you back to your vehicle.

Once you are on the road, the walk is downhill and water is available in the tundra ponds. I do not suggest drinking the water without boiling it first. The road is wide and clear all the way to the mining camp; the parking area is farther down the road on the Duke River. The walk from Burwash Uplands to the parking area takes three to four hours.

 ## AMPHITHEATRE MOUNTAIN

Time: *3 to 4 days*
Distance: *41.7 kilometres (27.2 miles) round trip*
Difficulty: *Moderate*
Change in elevation: *700 metres (2,300 feet)*
Maximum elevation: *1,768 metres (5,800 feet)*
Topographical maps: *Duke River 115 G/6*

Equipment needed: *Leather boots and a map are required. Overnight gear and rain gear should be adequate.*

The route: This trail follows a road, goes up a creek, across an alpine plateau, over a pass on the tundra, and back to your vehicle. It is scenic and, because there is less precipitation in the north end of the park, this trail usually offers dry conditions – even if it does not always offer sun. However, the tundra is boggy for most of the year, so your feet could get wet. This trail may be walked in either direction.

0.0 km	Parking area
7.5 km	Small lake at Burwash Uplands
24.0 km	Burwash Creek
26.0 km	Amphitheatre turnoff
30.0 km	Burwash Plateau
37.0 km	Pass
40.0 km	Road; larger lake
43.7 km	Parking area

Trail access: Drive north along the Alaska Highway for 9 kilometres (5.6 miles) from Burwash Landing to the Duke River. Turn left onto the mining road just past the bridge. Take the first right-hand fork away from the river. Drive to the second fork 4.7 kilometres (4.3 miles) further and park. During dry weather, driving up the hill to the old mining camp is possible. It saves about 5 kilometres (3.1 miles) of walking. During wet weather, the road may be muddy and the hill may not be driveable.

The trail: Follow the Donjek Glacier "A" trail (p. 172) to the warden's cabin on Burwash Creek.

The turnoff for the Amphitheatre Mountain is just before the cabin, which is a comfortable place to camp. There is clear water and flat spots on gravel where the impact will be minimal. The cabin itself is interesting to explore, with its miniature museum on the porch.

Cross Burwash Creek from the cabin and follow the creek to its headwaters. It flows beside Amphitheatre Mountain. The walk is not steep. Continue over the pass to the plateau. Once in the open, Amphitheatre Mountain displays turrets and wind-carved rocks with obvious sedimentation lines. This is a rare example of sedimentary rock in the park.

There are many clear creeks flowing onto the plateau. Cross the plateau in a southeasterly (right) direction, staying low and heading toward Granite Creek below. Granite is the main gravel washout going down the valley. Do not go too far east on the plateau before dropping to Granite Creek, as there are steep clay banks that are not possible to descend.

Continue down Granite to Badlands Creek, the large gravel fan flowing from Amphitheatre Mountain (north). This is an excellent place to camp as the trees offer shelter, the water from Badlands is clear, and there is some driftwood for a fire.

Just below Badlands Creek is an old horse camp where you can pitch a tent, but camping at Badlands Creek will cause less ecological damage. Continue down Granite to the next creek bed coming from the north (left) and ascend it, staying on the right-hand side until the creek becomes too steep. Bushwhack up the hill on the right-hand side of the creek and continue up, veering to the east (right). There is a steep gully on the west (left) side of the creek. Once you are out of the brush, the pass becomes obvious.

There are two lakes on the pass. The second lake has a place to camp, but it is somewhat boggy and there is no wood. From the pass, walk northeast (right) toward Burwash Uplands. Aim for the lower east end of the hill. You may come across claim stakes on the hill. Crossing the tundra from the pass to the road takes two to three hours. Near the uplands are some old marking posts leaning into the wind. Park posts have changed in recent times.

Another option, recommended by Mark Ritchie of Haines Junction, is to continue past the lakes on the pass in a northerly direction, passing the front of Amphitheatre Mountain and dropping down into Cooper Creek before hitting the mining road again. As a side trip, you may follow Cooper Creek to its headwaters, turning west before the hill becomes steep. There is an arm on the west side of Amphitheatre that can be climbed, which will lead you to the top. Wade Mountain and the Donjek Range are visible from this section of the trail. There is another mining operation at the confluence of Cooper and Burwash Creeks. This extension provides an extra day of hiking. The trail can be walked in either direction.

If you are not going to Cooper Creek but are continuing toward Burwash Uplands, cross the hump of the uplands, and look for the white line along the horizon. It is the road going back to the parking area. You should hit the road near a little tundra lake. Continue to the east, down the road to your vehicle, which is about one or two hours away.

The tundra has a large variety of flowers to enjoy. There are also numerous caribou in the area. Like the sheep at the end of Nines Creek, caribou sightings will be so numerous that they will become ho-hum.

Appendix A

EATING WELL ON THE TRAIL

Not only must food be sufficient to keep your body in top shape but it should also taste good. If you are hiking for more than a single overnighter, planning the menu involves considerations of weight – so I pack dehydrated foods, all of which I make myself. Below are a few sample meals, but I urge you to be creative and try some of your own favourites.

Dehydrating Food: Commercial dehydrators are easily obtained from most department stores. Heat is controlled accurately in the better-quality commercial dehydrators, and a fan seems to work better than the natural air circulation used in some homemade dehydrators.

Homemade dehydrators are inexpensive and easy to make. The trays can be any size, but about 30 centimetres (12 inches) square is sufficient. Nail window screening into wooden frames. Make the stand so that the stacked trays slide in and out easily. The bottom of the stand should be open and a top cover should slide back and forth to control ventilation. Place an electric frying pan in the bottom centre of the stand (*i.e.,* below all the trays). This will provide sufficient heat to dry most foods, including things like spaghetti sauce or sweet-and-sour hamburger.

Another possible heat source is a small electric heating coil with a fan attached. If you are a handy person, these can be rigged in a short time. Place the heater/fan at the back of your hand-constructed frame and plug it in. If you have a fan, the sliding lid described above is not necessary because the fan circulates the air.

Generally, food must be chopped, sliced, or mashed to make it small enough to dehydrate. For liquids (e.g., sauces and yogurt) place a plastic sandwich wrap on the tray and spread a thin layer of sauce over top. It takes about twelve hours to dehydrate foods like spaghetti sauce. Turn the food sitting on the plastic wrap once, so it dehydrates on both sides. Measure the amount of hydrated food put on each tray and then measure the dehydrated food. The difference equals the amount of water you must add when rehydrating these foods in the bush. Mark this amount on the plastic bags when packaging the food. If you do not measure, add enough water to cover the dehydrated food plus about another inch. If the sauce is too thick, add more water. If it is too thin, be assured that you probably needed the extra liquid anyway.

Since meals seem to lose some flavour after being dehydrated, add a bit more spice, sugar, or vinegar than you normally would. After cooking these meals, thicken the sauces and dehydrate. Place some plastic sandwich wrap on the tray and spread the food over top. Once the top is dried, flip the meal over, pull off the sandwich wrap and finish dehydrating. Package in the portions you need and label the bags. This is important because all meals look the same (like dog food) two weeks later. Nothing bugs me more when I am tired and cranky than to have my taste buds lined up for spaghetti that turns out to be stew.

Another method used for drying some foods such as strawberry slices, vegetable slices, and mushrooms is the same as that used by people for centuries: the sun. Place the thinly sliced foods on a tray and place it in the sun. Turn the food every few hours until it is dry.

Fruit

Overripe fruits dehydrate beautifully because they have a high sugar content. Bananas are especially good for this, and their high potassium content makes them good for muscle movement. Avoid unripened dehydrated bananas, as they taste like sawdust.

Dried strawberries are also a good idea. They keep their tartness, which is a treat when you're thirsty. They make an excellent dessert if you add a touch of sugar and boil them for a few minutes. As a power snack however, they do not have much bulk and I don't find them very satisfying. Pineapple, on the other hand, is a must and apples are delicious. I also like dried pears because they keep their flavour so well. I have tried some exotic fruits like papaya and honeydew melon, and they also keep their flavour. Peaches should be dehydrated with their skins on. Because they do not provide much bulk, fruits like peaches and strawberries should be considered a dessert to be hydrated with sugar, rather than eaten as snacks.

Fruit leathers, made from mashed fresh fruits, are also light weight and nutritious. Rhubarb stewed with raspberries makes an especially good fruit leather. When dry, cut the leather into bite-sized chunks, separate each chunk with plastic, and seal in bags. Yogurt also makes a good leather, and fulfills your calcium requirements. Home preserves can also be drained, pureed in a blender or food processor, and then dehydrated – a nutritious, sweet, and inexpensive trail snack.

Main courses

Stew, spaghetti and sweet and sour hamburger, cooked according to your favourite recipes, are excellent when dehydrated, as long as the meat is fat-free. Fat does not dehydrate because it contains no water. Instead, it becomes rancid, and rancid fat is unpalatable – and a great way to attract bears! Chicken is easy to dehydrate and is tasty with a creamy white sauce, but it remains crunchy after it is rehydrated.

Examples of meals I have tried are stew served with instant mashed potatoes, spaghetti and meat sauce, sweet-and-sour with rice, curried hamburger with rice, and ratatouille with couscous. I have carried chili con carne, Swiss steak made with hamburger and lots of onions, and barbecued beef with mashed potatoes. Macaroni and cheese is another great meal on the trail. A tin of corned beef adds the needed flavour. The beef is salty, filling, and even has a bit of nutrition!

Appendix B

EQUIPMENT

My thanks to Rik Shedden of Vancouver, B.C., for reading a draft of this section and offering many helpful suggestions. Rik, who has many years' experience in the sports retail business, has also done extensive backpacking in southern Australia, Africa and Nepal. Recently, he discovered and fell in love with Kluane. At the time of his research, he was working for Coast Mountain in Vancouver, a branch outlet of Coast Mountain in Whitehorse. I respect Rik's vast knowledge and am grateful to him for his input.

Shoes: This is the most important item for any type of hiking trip. If you're just going off the road and onto a short trail for twenty minutes, running shoes will usually suffice. If the terrain is difficult or wet, runners are dangerously slippery and an accident would be inevitable – so boots are recommended. Any footwear less sturdy than runners is unthinkable. Any trip longer than a day hike or more difficult than a dry, level trail, requires boots.

The perfect all-round hiking boot does not exist. Light breathable boots are good for day hikes but a solid, all-leather boot is needed for back-country trips in Kluane. Leather boots prevent your feet from being cut on the rocks.

When looking for a boot, eliminate the ones that feel soft in your hand. Flex them, checking for rigidity in the sole and lateral support. Look for a pair that come well above the ankle; generally the taller a boot, the more support it will give. Make certain the tongue and gussets are all leather, otherwise waterproofing becomes difficult. Ask for boots with a full shank to give the needed support. Good grip on the sole of the boot helps your footing in slippery places. Also, when travelling with a heavy pack in hot weather, leather boots help keep the bottoms of your feet from burning.

When fitting boots bring along your own socks. Use your largest foot and size your boots accordingly. Keep in mind that after a few hours of backpacking, feet swell so a little extra room in a boot is good. It is critical that the length of your boot is sufficient. You should be able to splay and wiggle your toes comfortably.

After you purchase boots, take them home and wear them in the house for a few hours. If there are pressure points or any heel rubbing, you may still return the boots. If you have chosen leather boots, rub a silicone snow or water sealer on them and then sit the boots near a warm draft or in the sun so the sealant soaks into the leather. Avoid waxes as they corrode the stitching. Some leathers are impregnated with silicone so treatment only at the end of the season is needed.

Sport sandals are an excellent second shoe to carry. They provide foot protection for creek-crossings (thus keeping boots dry), they double at the end of the day as a slipper, and they are not heavy to carry. The velcro attachments come with bonzo rings so the velcro, which loses 30% of its stick power when wet, will stay fastened while crossing a creek. Short neoprene canoe booties are excellent for warmth during creek-crossings and they easily fit inside sport sandals.

It is important to remember to clip your toenails. This will prevent "black-toe syndrome," which is painful and ugly. When hiking downhill with a heavy pack, your feet are pushed to the front of the boot which causes bruising of the toes if the toenails are too long. Also, tighten the laces on your boots before descending steep hills. This helps keep your foot where it belongs instead of slipping forward.

Socks: I recommend wearing a wicking liner-sock to keep your feet dry and a hiking sock over the top to provide padding and warmth. Capilene socks wick better than polypropylene and capilene does not retain body odours.

For an over sock, choose a "hiking" sock that is padded in the sole and heel and lighter on the top. Natural fibres like cotton and wool

Boots drying at the campfire while supper rehydrates and hikers enjoy a glass of wine.

absorb and retain moisture while synthetics do not. The higher the wool content, the warmer the sock.

Gaiters: These are highly recommended. They help keep stones out of your boots and protect your legs from mud and scratches. Gaiters with velcro up the front and a leather strap that fits under the boot are the most convenient; those without a full opening have to be put on before boots.

Backpack: There are numerous styles of packs with different convenience gadgets or materials from which to choose.

For longer trips, the external frame packs are not as popular as the internal frames because the internal frames seem to produce fewer rub spots. Unless you can afford an expensive external frame pack, like the Kelty, I would suggest staying away from them. I like the type of pack that has many pockets in order to keep things organized.

Wearing a well-fitted pack allows about 80% of the weight to be transferred to the hips and large rump muscles. The hip belt should fit snugly leaving the shoulder straps for stability with the pressure at the front of the shoulder, not the top. A strap across the sternum helps keep the pack from jiggling when trying to make precarious moves over logs and rocks.

Do not purchase a pack that is too big for your frame. A pack should have some torso length adjustment capabilities. A 70-litre pack for men and a 60-litre pack for women are the average sizes needed for longer trips. Carry your heaviest objects in the middle of the pack close to your back to minimize offsetting your centre of balance.

When attaching tents, bags or bear canisters to your pack, pile them above or to the sides rather than behind. This helps maintain your centre of balance.

I advocate proportional weight distribution. In other words, bigger people should carry more weight than smaller people. When adjusting for weight distribution, use the formula, weight of pack over weight of body is equal to unknown weight of pack over weight of second body. For example: $45/150 = X/100$. Cross multiply and "X" becomes 30. This means that if a 150-pound (68-kilogram) man is carrying 45 pounds (20 kilograms), then a hundred pound man carrying the same weight would have a stress level equal to carrying 67.5 pounds (31 kilograms). $(45/100 = x/150)$. Therefore, the 100-pound (45-kilogram) man should carry 30 pounds (13.6 kilograms) when the heavier man is carrying 45 pounds (20 kilograms). This will make the stress levels equal. Of course the formula must be adjusted to compensate for disabilities like weak knees or old age.

If purchasing a new pack, be certain that the construction is sturdy, the belts and straps are well padded and the material is of good quality.

As for colour, I like a bright (usually red or yellow) coloured pack because it looks nicer in photos. Bright colours are also easier to spot should you become lost.

Pack fly: Pack flies are nice to have and they do help keep gear dry. Whether using one or not, keep your clothes and sleeping bag protected with heavy-duty plastic bags. I also recommend purchasing the orange or yellow bags in the event that you become lost or injured. Bright coloured garbage bags are easy to spot from a helicopter.

Tents: Your tent must be waterproof. There is little value in a tent that lets in all the elements. After choosing a good quality material (which translates into a mid- to high-end brand name), you must decide on size and weight.

Free-standing tents do not need to be secured to the ground so in Kluane, where the terrain is often rocky, they are your best bet. However, make certain when using a free-standing tent that something is put inside as an anchor because the winds in Kluane will whip an unanchored tent away quickly.

If looking for a good three-season tent, make sure it is well ventilated with mesh side panels to prevent condensation from accumulating. Also, a functional vestibule for boot storage is recommended. Do not put your pack in the vestibule as it will more than likely have odours on it.

Tents with aluminum poles are lighter than those with fibreglass poles. Tents with pole clips (like the Moss) are easier and quicker to set up than those with pole sleeves.

Single-wall tents are very light but expensive. Four-season tents are designed for winter season or mountaineering use and are heavy for backpacking.

All tents should have a waterproof floor and fly. In the morning, be certain that the tent is dried completely before packing it, even if this means standing around a fire acting like a human clothesline. Packing a damp tent can produce mould which will ruin the tent's fabric.

If your tent does not have taped seams, be certain to use seam seal or seam grip on all the seams so that moisture will not come in the fine holes caused by the sewing of the seam. The best of tents need this precaution.

Some people like to carry a bivouac sack instead of a tent. This keeps the weight down but at the cost of comfort. A bivy sack slips over a sleeping bag and has a small tent-like area for the person's head. These sacks weigh around a pound. A bivy sack is recommended for day hikes in the event of sudden bad weather or an accident.

Sleeping bags: A good night's sleep is necessary if you are going to enjoy your days in the wilderness. A good three-season sleeping bag will keep you warm in the event that an unexpected snow storm should arise (which is possible at any time in Kluane) or if you have become wet and need to warm up.

Down bags require extra care and, if they do become wet, they are useless. However, down is comfortable to sleep in and you will never be too hot or too cold as long as the bag is dry. They are also the lightest in weight and the most compact of all bags. However, down bags are

Joanne McLean puts on warm clothing to prevent hypothermia when a storm moves in.

expensive and becoming difficult to purchase because manufacturers are not making them.

If choosing a down bag, remember that the higher the loft, the lighter the bag. High loft (700 fill) means that less down is needed to fill a bag and achieve the same temperature rating as low loft (550 fill). High loft results in a compact bag with greater longevity.

If your adventuring often takes you in close contact with water then synthetic fill would be more appropriate. A synthetic bag keeps its loft when wet, thus keeping you warm in potentially life-threatening situations. Your two basic choices are polarguard or liteloft. Polarguard uses a hollow single fibre construction, reducing its overall weight but not its bulk. It is warm with a high loft but it takes up a huge amount of space. Lifeloft or primaloft uses short fibres matted in a lattice work providing greater warmth with less loft. In the -10ºC category they are light and compact. Synthetic bags dry quicker than down bags.

Sleeping bag stuff sacks should be lined with a plastic bag. Because of the seams and draw cord system, no stuff sack is water-tight.

Mattress: A mattress certainly helps at the end of a long day when the body is tired. I recommend carrying a good one. The blue Airolite foams are made from a closed-cell foam and are hard to sleep on but they keep the cold from coming up beneath you. There are also closed-cell foams called Ridge Rests which are lighter and more comfortable than Airolites, but bulky when rolled up.

Therm-a-Rests are great. Undo the valve and the mattress blows itself up. Therm-a-Rests add warmth and padding for your hips and shoulders. With care, Therm-a-Rests last for years and are easy to repair so the high price is well worth the comfort.

Therm-a-Rests come in two lengths, the full body length and the shorter three-quarter body length. Choosing a three-quarter length mattress means saving on weight but skimping on insulation for your feet. A full length mattress keeps your bag off the tent floor which may tend to get damp. Get the mattress with a non-slip surface so your bag does not slide.

Some Therm-a-Rests are up to 50mm (2 inches) thick but again they are much heavier. A full length, 50mm Therm-a-Rest weighs 1,135 grams (2.5 pounds).

Stoves: Kluane Park is a low-impact camping area so a stove is essential. The alpines, where much of your hiking will be done, have little wood. The alpine trees that are available take up to seven hundred years to grow and the wood supply would deplete rapidly if hikers used alpine wood for cooking. Besides, a fire pit would leave a scar on the earth.

A hiking book written in the early 1970s stated that it would be approximately 300 years before wood shortages would be noticeable in our forests. In heavily populated areas such as Jasper and Banff National Parks, wood shortages are a great problem only twenty years after that prediction was made. I suggest leaving the wood in the event that hypothermia sets in on a hiker.

Finally, the Yukon, even Kluane, is a dry area. The fire hazard is often high, which results in the prohibition of campfires.

There are three basic types of stoves with many variations to each type. There are stoves that burn white gas, butane canister stoves, multi-fuel stoves or methyl hydrate (alcohol) stoves.

Methyl hydrate stoves like the Sigg model use alcohol and are the simplest, safest stoves of all. No priming is needed and they burn clean. However, the BTUs (measure of heat) produced by burning alcohol are the lowest of all fuels.

Butane canister stoves have canisters that will last about three hours of cooking time but must be packed out of the bush. This is added weight. There is also no indication as to how much fuel is left in the containers. Butane stoves do not put out as many BTUs as white gas or kerosene stoves. The water in Kluane is often glaciated and the weather cold and windy, resulting in longer cooking time.

White gas stoves are excellent because they put out a lot of heat and fuel is easy to obtain, but you must carry the liquid fuel. Weight again. There are many variations to the white gas stove. One thing to consider is that the base of the stove be big enough so as not to make the pot tipsy when cooking.

Multi-fuel stoves may burn kerosene or white gas and have a performance rating similar to the white gas ones. The advantages of kerosene over white gas are that it may be more available in foreign countries, it produces more BTUs and it is not as volatile. However, kerosene is not as readily available in Canada and it does not burn as clean.

Stoves that must be primed may have a pump that requires frequent oiling and maintenance. Some self-priming stoves do cause problems when temperatures are below freezing because they do not build up enough pressure to light the stove.

White gas should be carried in aluminum bottles which are specially made so they do not leak or puncture easily. One litre of white gas lasts about four hours. The newer white gas stoves are becoming noticeably energy efficient, which makes the overall weight of fuel much less.

Fuel containers: These can be purchased in lightweight aluminum with excellent, safe screw tops. They also come in different colours for easy identification. Whisperlite stoves fit Sigg aluminum containers but Sigg containers are not guaranteed for use under pressure. Use only the recommended containers for your stove. Plastic bottles may have contaminants in them and should not be used to pack gas.

Pots: Aluminum pots are light in weight, durable, and quick-heating. They retain soot which should be left as it conducts heat. Some people prefer the stainless steel pots because it is believed that too much aluminum in the diet contributes to Alzheimer's disease.

Swiss army knife: These handy gadgets are of the utmost value. They come with many attachments including tweezers to remove rose thorns, magnifying glasses to start a fire when your waterproof matches get lost, toothpicks to replace the dental floss you forgot to put into the comfort kit and corkscrews to drool over when the mirage of a bottle of wine appears. The only warning I have is that there is a cheap "Made in China" model that just does not compare to the real Swiss model. I advise you to pay the extra money and get something that will last (as long as you don't loose it).

Another piece of equipment used by many is the Leatherman multi-tool. Although heavy, it has as a serrated blade and saw that safely locks into place.

Bear-resistant food canisters: These are mandatory on some trails in Kluane and the park will provide them. Occasionally however, the park runs out. In that case you would not be allowed on the trails requiring the canisters. The cylindrical canisters are made of hard plastic so that a bear cannot get a grip on the container with his teeth or his claws. The containers come in two sizes, 8″ x 12″ (20 cm x 31 cm) or 8″ x 18″ (20 cm x 46 cm) and the smaller one weighs about three quarters of a pound (1.8 kilos). The small container holds 9.6 litres or about 38 cups (4.2 kg) of granola. I had a terrifying bear encounter one year (see end of Lowell Glacier Overland, p. 78) and ever since have carried my own canister when hiking.

Studies have shown the canisters are useful in decreasing the aggressiveness of bears towards people. If a bear does not get the reward of food when he approaches humans, he will not bother them. And a fed bear is a dead bear. We want to keep the bear population high in Kluane so please use the canisters.

The cost of purchasing a canister is less than $100 Canadian. If you purchase one, there would be no problem of going on a hike, even if the park ran out and they were mandatory for that trail. Also, if you purchase your own, there is the advantage of using it in areas where they are not mandatory.

We sprayed our canister with fluorescent paint, making it easier to find in the event that a bear swats it into the bush. The parks have put coloured handles on them for the same reason.

The canisters are available from Garcia Machine, 14097 Ave. 272, Visalia, Cal. 93277, Phone: (209) 732-3785

Bear spray: Pepper or mace sprays are a must in Kluane. If a bear comes close, the spray will give you five minutes to find safety. Some bears will give up after one spray. If hiking with a number of people, the combined force of spray power will drive off even the most persistent bear.

Some spray containers come with holsters that can be attached to your waist and worn comfortably at all times. This is the only piece of equipment I ever take into my tent at night. Although not a guarantee that it will prevent a bear attack, it is one more measure to make your experience safer.

Brian Bakker, a foreman of Kluane's trail crew, had a terrible encounter with an older and experienced male grizzly. Since then Brian will not go to the bathroom in town without his spray attached to his waist. During his encounter, he played dead for almost an hour while the bear circled him, breathing foul breath down Brian's neck. When the bear went into the bush for a minute, Brian jumped up and started to leave. The bear saw Brian move and charged. Brian, now able to get his canister, sprayed the bear and "it stopped him like a wall." Brian got away.

Some researchers on the other hand, claim that if a wild animal is intent on attacking, even sprays will not deter it. You must not develop a false sense of security when carrying a spray. It is to be used only after everything else has failed and an attack is imminent. Basic rules should never be ignored because you have a spray.

Binoculars: Although not essential, binoculars are handy. They enable you to observe, from a distance, the wild animals and birds that are in Kluane. The binoculars are also good for locating landmarks while reconnoitring or for checking a meadow for bears before entering.

Dishes: I like to carry a tin cup on the outside of my pack, attached to the front harness with a shower-curtain hook or a spring-loaded carabiner. The tin makes a bit of noise which helps warn bears that someone is in their territory and it is handy if stopping at a stream to have a quick cup of water. Tin does not break or burn; you can even use a tin cup for cooking or reheating coffee. Plastic is a bit lighter but it melts.

For utensils, I usually take a metal spoon and a Swiss army knife. I know a fork is more elegant when eating spaghetti, but the spoon sort of matches the old sock I use for a napkin. I also take a tin bowl for my meals. The bowl has a lip around the rim for holding safely when it is hot. Some people eat out of the pots to lessen weight but I like to use the pots for more than one course so I use a bowl.

First aid kit: This need not be elaborate but some precautions should be taken in the event of accidents or even normal body wear and tear. I take only small quantities of medicines and often use labelled film containers for pills.

Antibiotic powder: Cicatrin powder is a prescription drug and is good for any oozing (wet) skin disorder. Neosporin is also available in powder form which will work just as well. The powder does not deteriorate as rapidly as a liquid antibiotic.

Antihistamine cream: This prevents itching and thus it keeps you from scratching the many mosquito bites you will get.

Antihistamine tablets: Useful in the event of allergies, an unexpected cold or a reaction to a sting. Wasps abound in Kluane during the month of August, especially during a dry summer. Natives say this indicates a cold winter. One wasp sting leads to another because a pheromone is released that attracts other wasps.

Analgesics: A few in a film container, well labelled, will be sufficient. However, for the active ingredient ASA found in Aspirin, chew on willow leaves. They taste awful, but they have ASA in them.

Band-aids: I find those with elastic material on the outside are the best. A few butterfly band-aids are recommended in the event of a deep cut.

Burn ointment: This is a must. Get a cream recommended by your druggist. Burns can occur from the fire, the stove or the sun.

Disinfectant: Chlorine tablets enable you to make bleach water if necessary. A topical disinfectant such as rubbing alcohol or detol is recommended for cleaning a cut or infected blister. Film containers leak so use a plastic container with a screw-top lid for liquids.

Laxative and a plugger-upper: If stomach problems occur three days from the road, it could be an unpleasant slide back. Giardiasis is a fact of life, even in Kluane (see p. 31). Flagel, Tineba or Modium may keep these problems under control. Tineba causes side effects more uncomfortable than the runs, so it should be your last choice. If you're constipated, drinking lots of water will usually do the trick.

Linament: I have gone steady with Ben Gay for years. Without him or his non-smelling equivalent, my body would go on strike. And, as my buddy Joanne never ceases to remind me, "No self-respecting bear would ever touch anyone who has that stuff on!"

Moleskin: This should be the first item put into the kit. Never break a blister to relieve the pressure. Blisters are nature's band-aids. If the blister does break an infection is possible so use cicatrin as a precaution.

Polysporin: This is an excellent non-prescription antibiotic and comes in cream, liquid or powdered form.

Tensor bandage: One tensor is necessary in the event of a sprain or a shin splint. It can also double as a sling in the event of an arm injury.

Comfort kit: A comfort kit is what I call my bag of personal belongings. There must be some privacy and personal space even on a hiking trip and if you feel justified in carrying something personal or frivolous, then this is the place for it. I once met a fellow who thought it would be a blast to put a plastic blow-up doll on a mountain and photograph the reaction of other hikers. The following items are more serious suggestions for a comfort kit.

Soap: Always biodegradable and never used in the rivers, lakes or creeks.

Toothpaste and brush: The toothpaste can be carried in a film container or your dentist may give you sample tubes.

Hair comb or brush: I like to look good for ten minutes every day so a comb is necessary.

Chap stick: Lips become chapped and sore from the sun, the wind, and heavy breathing (when hiking).

Skin cream: Skin becomes dry and chapped from silty water.

Razor: I would hate to be eaten by a bear with hair on my legs! Men occasionally want to shave although a beard provides protection from mosquitos.

Mirror: A good compass with mirror will double as a dressing table mirror.

Towel and lufa scrub: The chamois sports towels are lightweight and soft. Lufa helps keep sore feet and sun-burned faces in good condition.

Other personal stuff: Contact lens cleaner, extra glasses or anything that you may need to make the hike better. My partner never goes without a book – just in case he gets lost and must wait for a rescue. I have a friend who carries more candy than the corner store because she feels she needs the security of extra energy, but she does not carry a pepper spray.

Camera: There are many lightweight 35mm cameras on the market today. They do an excellent job. Those with a 35-80mm zoom lens make for a good range. This provides a large format for scenery plus it does a nice job of catching friends falling in the river or any other memorable data you may wish to record. It will not take good flower, bird or animal pictures. If you are an avid photographer and have a particular subject or style in mind, you know what you must carry.

Candle, fire starter, matches: The heat from a small candle can be enough to keep you alive under some circumstances. Fire starter that is manufactured for lighting barbecues is an excellent and lightweight assurance that you will not be caught without heat. However, in a pinch, spruce pitch can be used to start a fire. Wooden matches, not paper ones, are the only type to take. If placed in a plastic screw-cap bottle along with a piece of fire starter you will not have any trouble getting heat. Since some matches will ignite only with special material, put some of the striker material from the side of the box in which the matches came, into the lid of your match container. Lighters are dangerous because they must be held upside down in order to light the fire or stove. The lighter could ignite causing a serious burn. "Strike anywhere" matches are the best but they are harder to find.

Survival blanket: This is lightweight and can fit into a first aid kit.

Repellent: This is essential when travelling in the North because the bugs there are alive and well. Repellents with more than 20% DEET are toxic. The repellents with 95% DEET are supposed to be diluted before use and even then they are for dipping clothes into, not for placing directly on skin. Citronella smells beautiful but is not all that effective. Light coloured clothing is said to help keep bugs away, especially if the clothes help keep you free from sweat. Choose places where there is a breeze for camping or rest stops as the bugs do not like wind.

Toilet paper: Use a biodegradable, bleach-free paper.

Rope: Rope is useful in Kluane. It may be used to lower packs down steep inclines or as a harness for creek-crossings. A rope is needed to hang food bags or to dry clothes. If your boot laces break, a piece of rope will replace the lace.

Clothes: Warm clothing is essential in Kluane. Layering is of course the best way to stay warm. To keep your skin dry, wear a wicking material next to your body. Start with a polypropylene or capilene top, a t-shirt, a long-sleeved wool shirt, a warm fleece jacket or wool sweater, and finally a windbreaker.

Rain gear is essential. Rubber will make you wet on the inside from sweat; poor quality rain gear will make you wet on the inside from rain. My experience with Gore-Tex, although most people dealing in sports gear disagree, is that it is not good enough to keep you dry in the extremely heavy rains common in the south end of Kluane. Some people hike with an umbrella, though it is useless in heavy bush.

Long underwear is necessary in the cold and shorts are needed for warmer weather. Rather than carrying long pants, some people have two pairs of longjohns, and wear shorts overtop the second pair when the weather is colder. Shorts and pants should have zippered pockets. Never wear jeans. They are heavy, take a long time to dry and actually, when wet, pull body heat out of your body. Fleece, wool, cotton, or some of the new light, wind-resistant materials are excellent.

I wear a cotton neck scarf for warmth. It doubles as a head band, a wash cloth, a hanky, a tea towel, and a bandage. Finally it adds colour and fashion for photos. A toque is necessary. It may also be used while you are sleeping in colder weather. Waterproof mitts may keep your hands warm during cold, windy days.

Whatever you choose, always be prepared for wind, snow and sub-zero temperatures. If you can stay warm and dry under those conditions, you will have a great hike with lots of stories to tell.

Appendix C

SERVICES NEAR KLUANE

Haines Junction (Mile 1016, Alaska Highway): Dakwakada, or High Cache, was the original Indian name for Haines Junction. Today, the village is Kluane's main metropolis with a year-round population of 800, and is the crossroads for those going north to Alaska or south to Haines, on the Alaskan coast. Incorporated as a municipality in 1984, Haines Junction has more services available every year. They include motels, restaurants, the best bakery in the Yukon, a library, a liquor store, a bank (open two days a week), a general store, a swimming pool (opens in May), and the Kluane Park Visitor Information Centre, where registration for any overnight camping in the park is mandatory.

The O'Hara Bus Company was the first company to offer a charter between Whitehorse and Fairbanks, passing through Haines Junction. Later, the White Pass Bus Company competed for the tourist trade. As an added attraction, they offered a meal at Haines Junction's first restaurant, located in a large canvas tent.

In June, 1944, Dr. A. Leahey, a specialist in field husbandry with the Department of Agriculture, explored the area around Haines Junction and chose mile 1019 along the highway as the site for an experimental farm. The first building, a dove-tailed log cabin, was erected in the same year. When the experimental farm was closed in 1970, the buildings were either dismantled or sold. One of the original buildings has been moved to the Cabins B&B across from Kathleen Lake where it was repaired and preserved. It is now used as a rental unit.

The quonset-hut church, still used today was constructed by Father

Morsat in 1950 for families running the experimental farm. After the church was built, a rectory was added and Father Morsat lived there until he retired to Edmonton.

Services

Paddle/Wheel Rentals and Tours: Located in the log building next to the bakery, this is the most photographed house in the Yukon. The business occupies a small portion of the building. Besides carrying a wide range of books about the north, the shop sells outdoor supplies such as topographical maps, bear bells, bear sprays, and water filters. For hikers, they also offer pick up and delivery service to the trailheads. The proprietors, Val Drummond and her son Lee, can also book Tatshenshini River rafting tours and glacial flights.

Equipment rentals are also available from Paddle/Wheel Rentals and Tours. They offer canoes and mountain bikes and some outdoor equipment like tents and dry bags. If a guide is wanted for mountain bike riding, or hiking in the area, that too may be booked at the shop. To reserve equipment or guiding services write to the shop at P.O. Box 2079, Haines Junction, Yukon, Y0B 1L0, or call (403) 634-2683. Val Drummond and her son Lee have explored the area for years and will be able to guide cyclers or hikers into remote (secret) places that others may not know about.

Kluane Park Adventure Centre: Located next to the Mountain View Restaurant on the Alaska Highway approach from Whitehorse, the centre is a specialized travel agency. There you may purchase maps for hiking in Kluane, plus the maps needed for excursions outside the park. There is a shuttle service for pick-up and delivery to hiking trails. They offer rafting down the Tatshenshini River – a one-day trip that should be on everyone's itinerary. Depending on water levels, the trip starts at Bear Flats or the Blanchard River and runs to Dalton Post. The centre will also book and co-ordinate plane rides over the icefields, or heli-hiking trips. They will also book B&B's, excursions with llamas, cycle tours, fishing tours, and canoe rentals. If you wish to book ahead, write them at P.O. Box 5344, Whitehorse, Yukon, Y1A 4Z2. During the winter, you may phone (403) 633-5470 or fax (403) 633-3820. After June 1, phone (403) 634-2313.

Kluane Park Information Centre: All overnight hikes must be registered at the information centre. At the time of writing, the fee for overnight camping is $5 per person per night or $50 for a season's pass. Food canisters are available at no cost. You need leave only your credit card or driver's licence in exchange for the canister. De-registering is also necessary, and those failing to do so could be charged with the cost of an expensive search.

From the middle of June until the first weekend in September, Parks Canada offers short guided hikes where you may hear some interesting facts and stories about the area. These hikes are offered in different locations and at different times. Check with the information centre for the current schedule. If a walk is not to your liking, you may wish to take in one of the evening campfire talks. The talks are presented at the government campgrounds, along with tea and coffee – so bring your own mug. You'll find the schedule for the talks in the same pamphlet as the guided hikes. There is a small fee for both these services.

The information centre also offers an international award-winning audio-visual slide show, which is worth taking the time to see. The presentation captures the natural beauty of the park, and some of its human history – including Tutchone Indian legends and European influences. There is a small fee to see the show, which runs continuously throughout the day.

If you should require further information, you may telephone the Kluane Park Information Centre at (403) 634-7207, from 8:30 a.m. to 9:00 p.m.

Libby Dulac Studio: Libby is an artist with exceptional talent and has long been known for her interpretations of the Kluane area. She is most famous, however, for designing the twenty-five cent coin commemorating Canada's 125th birthday. Her studio is located on Rainbow Street, which runs through the centre of the Alsek cul-de-sac.

The Canadian Imperial Bank of Commerce: This branch, at the back of Madley's store, is only open two days a week. They will cash cheques drawn on Imperial Bank accounts, if your home branch approves and if you have acceptable picture identification. They also give cash advances on your bank credit card.

Liquor store: This is open Tuesdays to Saturdays from 11 a.m. to 1 p.m. and 2 p.m. to 6 p.m. It is next door to the library and just south of Madley's General Store, in the James Smith RV Building.

Medical services: The local health unit has trained medical staff and an ambulance service. Telephone: (403) 634-2213.

Post office: The local post office is located in Madley's General Store.

Sifton Air: Their fixed-wing flights, similar to heli-tours, leave from the airport which is just off the Alaska Highway on the approach to Haines Junction. These flights require a minimum of three people. I recommend fixed-wing flights rather than helicopter flights during windy weather. These tours can be arranged through Kluane Park Adventure Centre.

Trans North Helicopters: Offering heli-tours over the Kaskawulsh Glacier, over Vulcan Mountain, or over both of the above plus the Stairway Glaciers between Pinnacle Peak and the Kaskawulsh Glacier, this company is sensitive to the needs of hikers and animals. The air routes follow areas not frequented by hikers, and the pilots are always aware of the paths animals are using and stay away from them. When I took one of the tours, the pilot, Doug Hladun, did not know I was checking him out so I did not get any preferential service. In my opinion, he gave a first-class tour, exhibiting extreme sensitivity to those below while flying over some of the most spectacular country I have ever seen in my life. The helicopter holds a pilot and four passengers; the trip will be most cost-efficient if you give the pilot time to co-ordinate a full group.

Food

Madley's General Store: Since its recent expansion, this store has almost anything you could want to eat, including fresh meat, fruit, and vegetables. They also have a hardware section, which carries camp fuel and fire starter. While Madley's does sell umbrellas for those who wish to reinforce their rain gear, any high-quality hiking equipment should be purchased or replaced at Coast Mountain in Whitehorse.

Mountain View Hotel and Restaurant: In my opinion, this licensed restaurant serves the best fried chicken in the Yukon. All meals are ample and well-presented. Some are gourmet.

Raven Hotel and Restaurant: Named after the official bird of the Yukon, this is the classiest establishment in Haines Junction. The hotel rooms are spacious, exquisitely decorated and very comfortable. The restaurant offers only high-quality gourmet meals, prepared by a professional European chef. The hotel is located close to the Information centre. I highly recommend at least one dinner, if not a weekend room, for a special treat while you are in the area.

Tasty Freeze: On the highway, this is reputed to have the best breakfasts in town.

Village Bakery: Directly across from the Kluane Park Visitor Information Centre, this is the most popular place in town for sandwiches, coffee, and baked goods. The cinnamon buns, reputed to be the best in the Yukon, are great before, during, and after a hike. If you tell the staff that you're a hiker and want a gooey bun, they will be accommodating. Because of its popularity with both the rubber-tire crowd and the hiking crowd, the food is always fresh. (In fact, I have seen them run out of cinnamon buns by midday.) Enjoy your coffee or a meal at one of the picnic tables on the sundeck. There is also a large bulletin board on the deck for leaving messages.

Accommodation

Gateway Motel: This centrally located motel is one of the less expensive in Haines Junction. The rooms can be hot in the evenings, but the laundromat is a big draw.

Kluane RV Kampground: The campground, located behind and across the highway from the information centre, has fully serviced sites for motor homes, and many secluded tent spaces nestled in the trees. The tent spaces have soft ground on which to pitch a tent, fire pits, and picnic tables. There are also coin-operated showers with copious amounts of hot water, a laundromat, pay phones, fax service, and a store on the grounds.

Laughing Moose B&B: Centrally located at 120 Alsek Crescent, this facility does not allow smoking or pets indoors. For reservations, contact the Kluane Park Adventure Centre or write to P.O. Box 5432, Haines Junction, Yukon, Y0B 1L0.Telephone: (403) 634-2335.

Pine Lake Campsite: There is a government fee for staying at this site, which is six kilometres before Haines Junction on the Alaska Highway when coming from Whitehorse. There are excellent tent sites close to the lake and wood is available for the fire pits, but there are no showers or flush toilets.

Stardust Motel: On the highway across from the graveyard, this is probably the next best Haines Junction motel to stay in after the Gateway. The Stardust also has a laundromat.

Valhalla R&R: Besides being a comfortable place to stay in Haines Junction, the Valhalla offers interpretive and photographic tours and fishing charters. For reservations, write to P.O. Box 2010, Haines Junction, Yukon, Y0B 1L0. Telephone: (403) 634-2135.

Entertainment

Entertainment is ongoing in this busy community, and event schedules are posted at the town hall across from Madley's store, the Kluane Park Adventure Centre, and the Village Bakery bulletin board.

June: The main tourist attraction is the Alsek Music Festival, which features mostly Northern Canadian bands – though bands have come from as far away as the Faroe Islands in Denmark. The festival includes a weekend of music, dancing, and children's events.

The music festival is followed by the bike relay race from Kluane to Chilkat, 240 kilometres (149 miles) south along the Haines Highway. The event has become an international race, with over 500 contestants comprising teams of two, four, or eight people.

July: Mid-month, Canada Parks Day is marked by talks and guided interpretive hikes, offered by Parks Canada. The Pine Lake Regatta has events for everyone, but the big attraction is the snowmobile races on the lake without snow.

August: The month is wrapped up with the Miner's Ball, held at the Kluane Wilderness Village north of Burwash Landing. Highlights of the ball include moose-turd spitting and burl-toss competitions.

Ongoing: The Village Bakery has weekly entertainment on the deck. Proprietors Boyd and Liz Campbell hold a music jamboree every Monday evening, where everyone, especially visitors, is encouraged to contribute to the entertainment by singing, playing an instrument, or reciting poetry.

Alaska Highway: You may want to visit some of the following sights and services along the Alaska Highway. They are listed from the south end of the park and going in a northerly direction.

Million Dollar Campsite: This is 79 kilometres (48 miles) south of

Haines Junction, or 5.4 kilometres (3.4 miles) south of the Dalton Post turnoff and then about 2 kilometres (1.2 miles) in from the highway. It has a covered cook-shed, well water, wood, and fire pits. None of the eight available tent sites are on gravel, and the campsite is seldom full. There is a short hiking trail to the waterfalls where the Takhanne River, forcing its way through bedrock, has created a spectacular canyon.

Klukshu Indian Village: The village is situated 3.4 kilometres (2.1 miles) south of the St. Elias Lake turnoff. Located on the Klukshu River, ("L'ukshu" means "coho place" in Tlingit), this is an Indian village where visitors are welcome. The village has a craft shop, barbecue pit, fish traps, traditional houses, and smoke houses. There are interpretive signs around the village that explain traditional lifestyles. The museum houses many artifacts, but of special interest is a trail marker with a carved face. A locally-made gopher blanket is also on display. Baked and barbecued salmon are available in season.

On the river there is a trap about 2.5 metres (8.2 feet) long, 1 metre (3.3 feet) wide and half a meter (1.6 feet) high. Made of spruce saplings tied with willow roots, the spruce poles are tied several centimetres apart so water can flow freely. The traps sit several centimetres into the water so that when fish are trapped, there is not enough water for them to flip out of the traps. The traps are secured to stakes driven into the stream.

Natives camp at the river at the beginning of salmon season, waiting for the run to begin. The first fish caught is cooked and served to everyone present.

Dezadeash Campsite: Located 2 kilometres (1.2 miles) north of the Mush Lake Road on a point jutting into Dezadeash Lake. Many of the twenty campsites face the lake. There is a cookhouse, fire pits, wood, outhouses, and government campground self-registration. The site is picturesque, but during windy or stormy weather it is better to camp at the sites off the lake.

Dezadeash Lake is remembered by natives as the site of a massacre in the 1800s. After insults had been exchanged between the Upper Tanana and Southern Tutchone tribes, revenge was sought. When the Tutchone were camped at the spring fishing camp on the northern end of the lake, the Tananas snuck up and massacred over a hundred of them. Of the three survivors, one was a girl who had been hidden by her mother under a pile of animal skins. Tutchone elders still recount the story with bitterness toward their enemy tribe. The name of the lake comes from the Tlingit word "Daas'ediyaash," but the Tutchone called the lake "Titl'at Man," meaning "head of lake."

Kathleen Lake Campsite: Located 26.4 kilometres (16.4 miles) south of Haines Junction. There are park signs along the road. The South Tutchone called Kathleen Lake "Mat'atana Man," which means "lake captured inside."

There are forty-one sites in the campground, but they are designed for motor homes. It is difficult to find a soft spot for a tent, but the sites do have fire pits and cut wood. The outhouses are well-maintained and there is fresh well water. The picnic shelter by the lake is large, bright, clean, and a great drawing card. There are two stoves in the shelter, so it is an excellent place to dry off or make meals during poor weather. Camp fire talks are held in the campground's amphitheatre. Check at the information centre for scheduled times and topics.

The Cabins B&B: This B&B is across the road from the Kathleen Lake campsite. It has five historical cabins, named Kluane, Dezadeash, Kathleen Lake, King's Throne, and Quill Creek, that sleep from two to six people each. All the cabins have kitchenettes with propane stoves. The proprietors supply well-water for cooking and drinking, and portable toilets for night use if visitors do not want to walk to the outhouses. This historical and ecologically-friendly establishment should be visited, even if you're not able to stay.

The main house is constructed from the logs of local trees, on a foundation of old bridge timbers. A breakfast of fruit salad, homemade granola and yogurt, and fresh baked goods is served in the sun room, which is glass on three sides and faces southwest to a forest dotted with wild flowers. The wrap-around porch is decorated with antiques and flower baskets. The house's electrical power is generated by wind and solar energy. The shower and sauna, in a separate building close to the house, use well-water heated by propane.

The property sits on a glacial esker left by the receding valley glaciers. The skiing/hiking trail behind the cabins was cleared in 1943 by the Haines Road construction camp. Artifacts left by the camp are being used by the proprietors, Wenda and Brent, as flower pots.

The Kluane Cabin was one of the first buildings constructed at the experimental farm where the warden's station is now located. Built in the early 50s from fire burnt logs, the cabin was moved to its present site by Brent and Wenda in 1980. The sun room/kitchen was added by Brent.

Dezadeash Cabin on the hill is protected by trees but has a mountain view from the front porch. Originally built by Chuck Egli and Mike Crawshay as a guest cabin, it was sold and moved several times before finding its current location. There are still three of the original windows in the cabin.

Quill Creek Cabin is my favourite. It was originally built about three miles down Quill Creek by Dick and Polly Mahoney, local dog mushers. The Mahoneys built the cabin by numbering the boards so they could easily dismantle and move it to a different location. However, the Mahoneys abandoned the cabin while it was still in its original location. When the lease ran out on Quill Creek and improvements had to be made to the decaying building, Brent moved it to its current location, made necessary repairs and added the porch.

After leaving the Yukon and relocating in the US, Polly Mahoney became involved, during the early 1990s, in moving abandoned dogs out of the Antarctic. The dogs were not native to the area, and the dog's do-do was causing ecological damage so they had to be destroyed or relocated. Polly helped relocate them to the Churchill area of Canada.

To make reservations at the Cabins, contact Kluane Park Adventure Centre, or write to P.O. Box 5334, Haines Junction, Yukon, Y0B lL0. Telephone: (403) 634-2626.

Kathleen Lake Lodge and Restaurant: Located a kilometre up the road from The Cabins B&B. The lodge, a family-run business, has clean cabins, friendly service, and good coffee. The meals are also tasty. If you're not staying at the lodge, it is possible to have a shower for $3 per person. The manicured yard has a fire pit and a playground for children.

Mackintosh Lodge: This is a family-run operation about 8.5 kilometres (6 miles) north of Haines Junction, at milepost 1022 and across from the road leading to the Alsek Trail. The motel has clean rooms that are comparable in price to any other along the highway. Camping, which is not in a treed area, is $5 per night and includes one shower per person. For those with young children who want a day hike on the

Alsek Trail, owners Barbara and Jerry Halushka offer a babysitting service. There are also toys to amuse children while parents enjoy a peaceful meal in the restaurant.

Of special interest to the visitor, the Halushkas have a sod-roofed log cabin that is chinked with moss, reminiscent of the native style built years ago. The cabin has a stove that warms piped creek water, which flows into a homemade hot tub.

Although, everything that comes out of Barbara's kitchen is excellent, her most famous dish is the buffalo burger, made with meat purchased from Hutterites in Grand Prairie, Alberta.

The Arctic Institute: Located just south of Sheep Mountain Information Centre, the Institute has weather monitoring stations on the Kaskawulsh Glacier and Kluane Lake, and another farther in on the icefields. At present, it is is affiliated with the University of Calgary.

For climbing information, contact Ted Williams at the Arctic Institute or make arrangements with the Kluane Park Adventure Centre.

Kluane Bed & Breakfast: Located 56 kilometres (35 miles) north of Haines Junction, this is my favourite resting spot along the highway. The immaculate A-frame cabins sleep up to six people. There are hot showers, and the breakfast is truly French cuisine – served in prospector-sized portions. You may also use the kitchen facilities for cooking, as long as you clean up after yourself.

Having lived in the area for so long and being naturally curious people, proprietors Josie and Frank Sias are a respected repository of local history. Josie's father was Louis Jacquot, who started the trading post at Burwash Landing. For a night's rest after a long hike, this haven of tranquillity is a must. For reservations, write to General Delivery, Destruction Bay, Yukon, Y0B 1H0. Telephone: Whitehorse Mobile Operator 2M3924.

Silver City Ghost Town: This was originally called Bullion Creek, then Silver City. In 1905 it became Kluane. The ghost town is located at the south end of Kluane Lake, next to Kluane B&B. During the gold rush, Silver City was the hub of the area with a trading post, roadhouse, doctor, and Royal Northwest Mounted Police station. The first post office opened in 1904. After many battles fought by post master C. A.

Munro trying to keep the office open, it was closed in 1910, reopened again in 1913, and closed permanently in 1921. The town was also used as a fox farm; some of the fox pens are still standing.

Silver City had a population of a hundred people in 1907. This dropped to seventeen by 1910, and only two people remained in 1912. The population increased slightly in 1913, but declined to zero by 1921. Today Silver City is a black-and-white photographer's delight.

Bayshore Motel: This is located at milepost 1064 on the Alaska Highway. It has recently been renovated and is tastefully decorated. The motel has a family suite that sleeps up to six people. The licensed cafe, run by Yukon Jim and Sheep Mountain Shirley, offers home-cooked meals, a salad bar, and excellent desserts. The cafe serves no fried foods. A glassed-in dining area overlooks the lake, but you might prefer to sit on the sundeck on warm days. The Bayshore offers a relaxed atmosphere and caters to those with time to enjoy their meals. Those staying at the Bayshore can have the pleasure of a hot tub, also situated beside the lake. Those not staying at the Bayshore must pay $10 for the use of the tub. Camping spots on the lake are also available.

Cottonwood Park: This campsite is just 5 kilometres (3 miles) past the Bayshore Motel, at mile 1067 on the Alaska Highway. It has numerous motor home and trailer sites on Kluane Lake, but there are also some quiet tent spots away from the centre. There is a shower room and a laundromat with unlimited hot water. Pizza is their specialty. It costs $12 a night to pitch a tent.

Congdon Creek Campground: Located 5 kilometres (3 miles) past Cottonwood Park. The sites numbered 40 to 80 are best for tenting at this excellent campground, as there are many flat spots on soft ground and among the trees which offer protection from the wind. There is a covered cooking shelter, well-water, and cut wood.

Destruction Bay: This village is 108 kilometres (67 miles) north of Haines Junction. The village served as a camp during the construction of the Alaska Highway. Some believe it got its name after a wind storm in 1942 decimated many boats in the bay. Natives believe it was so named because of the large amount of driftwood that was found on the floor of the bay, which indicates many past storms in the area.

The Talbot Arms Motel: This motel in Destruction Bay was rebuilt after a fire consumed the original building in 1980. It offers comfortable rooms, a campsite, and a service station (that fixes flat tires). There is also a restaurant, a liquor outlet, and a post office at the Talbot Arms.

Sahja Services: Located at mile 1083 along the highway, next to the Talbot Arms. The name comes from the Guichen Indians of the Northwest Territories, and means "welcome." The restaurant was given its name by its first owner, a Guichen woman who made it famous for lake trout and whitefish chowder. Tent sites are available on an open field without any services. The water comes from an artesian well and is delicious to drink. Campsites are $10 per night and include unlimited use of facilities, including showers. The owners also offer a communal tent where one can stay for $2 per night. Laundry may be washed and dried for $3 per load, soap is extra.

Burwash Landing: Located at milepost 1093 on the Alaska Highway, it was named after Major Lachlin Taylor Burwash, a mining recorder who was based at Silver City. The village was originally a native settlemen, but when Tagish Charlie started the gold rush on the nearby Fourth of July Creek in 1903, things changed. Louis Jacquot took the largest single claim, which consisted of 220 ounces of gold worth about $4,000. Unlike many miners, Louis used his money wisely. He and his brother Eugene built a trading post at the landing. They also built cabins for the native families who came from the Donjek and White River areas. After the rush, the Jacquots continued to live in the community, working as outfitters. Louis married a local woman, but sent his children to France to be educated. His daughter, Josie Sias, returned to Kluane after completing school. Like her father, she married, raised a family, and is still contributing to the community.

By 1904, the 2,000 to 3,000 men working in the Burwash area did not clear $20,000 between them. But in 1907 the Jacquot brothers discovered copper, which coincided with copper developments occurring around Whitehorse. Mining continued, though not with the same fervour.

Getting supplies was the most difficult hardship suffered by those living in the Burwash area before the highway was built. Bacon and beans were the main staple and occasionally a case of eggs would find its way to the settlements around Kluane. However, after travelling the 282 kilometres (175 miles) across rough roads to Burwash, the eggs were good for little more than scrambling. By 1905, a wagon run was developed between Whitehorse and Haines Junction, which continued on to Silver City and finally ended at the Chisane River in Alaska. By 1908, the road had improved so much that a wagon carrying loads of 680 kilograms (1,500 pounds) could reach Kluane in four days.

Father Morissett Eusebe, a local hero of Burwash (and the Yukon) was born in 1915 at St. Michel de Billichasse, Quebec. He came to the Yukon as a Catholic missionary in 1943, where he was known as Father Morsat (an easier rendition of his original name). When Father Morsat arrived at Burwash in the winter of 1944, the Jacquots lent him a cabin in which to stay. That year, Christmas mass was celebrated in the little cabin. When Father Morsat started teaching twelve local children the following January, the Jacquot's cabin was expanded to a schoolhouse. Today, the cabin houses the Burwash Museum.

Buck Dickson, for whom Dickson Creek is named, lived near Burwash at the mouth of the Kluane River at the same time as Father Morsat lived there.

Burwash Landing Resort: This was built in 1946 by Bob Porsild, who was hired by Eugene Jacquot to build the lodge. Porsild is also credited for building the lodge at Johnson's Crossing. The Jacquots used the lodge at Burwash for hunting parties. The lodge is still in operation today and is a wonderful place to spend a night after a tough hike. The restaurant overlooks the lake and the specialty of the house is lake trout, sold for a reasonable price. There is also a pub on the premises, with a pool table, video game, and an off-sale service.

Burwash Landing Museum of Natural History: The museum has a complete collection of stuffed animals found near or in Kluane. Displays found outside the museum show native life during the early days of European settlement. Behind the museum is a typical bear cache, like the ones built by miners during the gold rush years. The museum is open from mid-May to mid-September, from 9 a.m. to 9 p.m. There is an entry fee.

Dalan Campground: This is a privately owned site, one kilometre off the highway. Water is hauled in by truck. There is a recycling bin, picnic tables, firewood, and outhouses. The tent spots are on the ground, not on gravel, and are within walking distance of the lake. The cost is $10 per night.

Whitehorse: Whitehorse is the capital city of the Yukon. It is where forgotten supplies may be purchased, or broken equipment may be repaired. The town, with a population of about 22,000 permanent residences (*i.e.,* they stay all winter), is an interesting place to learn some of the territory's history. It is also a place to mend the body with food and fun after a gruelling hike in Kluane. Some of my all-time favourite cafes are in Whitehorse.

For places to stay and things to do, visit the Whitehorse Tourist Information Centre at 302 Steele Street. Telephone (403) 667-2915.

Recommended Reading

Hiking

Be an Expert with a Map and Compass, by Bjorn Kjellstrom. Collier Books, 1994. The practice exercises in this book will help anyone wanting to improve their orienteering skills.

Medicine for Mountaineering and Other Wilderness Activities, edited by James Wilkerson. The Mountaineers, Seattle, 1992.

Simple Food for the Pack: Sierra Club Guide to Delicious Natural Food for the Trail, by Claudia Axcell, Diana Cooke, and Vikki Kenmont. Sierra Club Books, San Francisco, 1986. This book has some excellent ideas for nutritious recipes that will give meals variation when on the trail.

The Essential Outdoor Gear Manual, by Annie Getchell. Ragged Mountain Press, Camden, Maine, 1995.

Wildlife

In addition to the huge population of grizzly bears, Kluane National Park is also home to the black bear, moose, caribou, goat, dall sheep, marmot, pika, mule deer, wolverine, coyote, wolf, lynx, fox, rabbit, porcupine, chipmunk, and the low bush grizzly commonly known as the Arctic ground squirrel. While your chances of seeing wild animals, especially sheep, caribou and grizzly are high, be sure not to disturb the animals.

Bear Attacks, by Steve Herrero. Hurtig Publishers, Edmonton.

There is a new edition of this book expected soon. However, any edition is recommended reading.

Hiking in Bear Country, by Keith Scott. Nimbus Publishing, Halifax.

Kluane: Pinnacle of the Yukon, edited by John Theberge. Doubleday Canada, Toronto. This book is now out of print, but most libraries carry a copy. It gives a good overview of the park, including wildlife.

Birds

There have been between 92 and 118 types of birds spotted in Kluane at one time or another. Identifying unknown birds can be fun.

Birds of North America: A Guide to Field Identification, by C. S. Robbins, B. Bruun, and H. S. Zim. Golden Press, New York, 1983.

Audobon Society Field Guide to North American Birds: Western Region. Knopf, New York, 1977.

Fish

Kluane has some interesting fish populations, especially around the Kathleen Lake area.

Freshwater Fishes of Canada, by W. B. Scott and E. J. Crossman. Environment Canada, 1973

Plants

The variety of flora in the park is as vast as the land itself. To date 745 species have been identified. There are spruce, birch, pine, alders, willows, and subalpine and alpine flowers. Some species of sage found on the Bullion Plateau can be found only there and in Siberia. Kluane also has some rare grasses and flowers of the tundra.

Plants of Northern British Columbia, edited by A. MacKinnon, J. Pojar, and R. Coupe. Lone Pine Publishing, Edmonton, 1992. Although this book covers northern B.C., it is also relevant to Kluane. Not only does it have excellent descriptions, but it also identifies some of the medicinal properties of plants.

Rocky Mountain Wild Flowers, by A. E. Porsild. National Historical Service, 1974. This can be ordered from the National Museum of Canada Marketing Services, catalogue number NM95-17-2

Vascular Plants of Continental Northwest Territories, by A. E. Porsild, 1980. Porsild studied the park's plant life for five years before publishing his guide.

Mountain Wild Flowers of the Pacific Northwest, by Ronald Taylor and George Douglas. Binford and Mort, Portland, 1975.

Native Trees of Canada, by R. C. Hosie. Canadian Forestry Service, Dept. of Environment, Ottawa, 1973.

Geology

Kluane park is a haven for geologists and those interested in the formation of the earth. The area is young in Earth terms; the St. Elias Mountains are less than 20 million years old, whereas the Rockies are between 600 to 200 million years old. As a result, the park features many new land formations like rock glaciers, hanging valleys, small hoodoos, and the remains of lakes a few feet above present-day valleys. Because of the moving Denali Fault on which Kluane sits, there is evidence that some of the bedrock in the area found its origins as far as the 20th parallel south and 320 kilometres (199 miles) east.

A Field Guide to Rocks and Minerals, 5th edition, by Frederick Pough. Houghton Mifflin, Boston, 1996.

Geography

From Trail to Highway, by Kwaday kwatan ts'an ek'an tan kwatsin. Champagne Aishihik Indian Band and Sha-tan Tours, 1988. This is an excellent summary of regional history and customs dating back to pre-Alaska Highway days. Many stories interspersed throughout the hiking book are taken from this book. If you read no other book about the area, read this one.

G l o s s a r y

GEOLOGICAL TERMS

Alluvial fan: gently sloping accumulation of rounded to subangular rock usually found at the mouth of creeks and rivers. There are many in Kluane.

Bog: shallow accumulation of peat with pools of water on the surface.

Cirque: steep-walled mountain basin shaped like half a bowl

Colluvium: gentle to steep slope of unsorted rubble.

Eskers: gravel ridges deposited by glaciers. Normally represent the remains of rivers that ran on top of the glaciers. These can be seen at the toe of the Kaskawulsh Glacier.

Floodplain: flat accumulation of gravel, with small surface irregularities. There is a good example of this on the Slims East Trail.

Forested peatland: accumulation of peat draped over a surface of moraine deposits and growing trees. In this area it takes about 100 years to produce 7.5 cm of peat.

Lake beaches: small ridges of sand and gravel generally paralleling present shorelines. Excellent examples on the Alsek Trail.

Landslide: moderately sloping earth with surface irregularities and accumulation of poorly sorted debris.

Outwash: extensive flat area of sand and gravel well above stream levels.

Rock glacier: coarse bouldery drift – front edge usually steep, upper surface flat – may have ice glacier beneath. Many of these in the park. They look like huge tongues hanging from passes.

Sand dunes: elongated dunes with blowouts. Found along the Alsek trail.

Tallus fan: moderate to steep sloping accumulation of coarse angular bedrock.

Thermokarst: water-filled sinkholes, usually found on north-facing slopes, caused when warmer weather melts the permafrost.

Till-covered slope: bedrock slopes mantled with a mix of stone, gravel, boulders, and clay.

Valley glacier: glacier going down valley from cirques. Kluane has the largest and most plentiful valley glaciers in the world.

I n d e x

Notes

N O T E S

NOTES